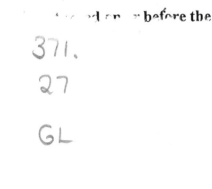

Studying and Learning *at* University

Studying and Learning *at* University

Vital Skills for Success in Your Degree

Alan Pritchard

Los Angeles • London • New Delhi • Singapore

© Alan Pritchard 2008

First published 2008

SAGE Publications Ltd
1 Oliver's Yard
55 City Road
London EC1Y 1SP

SAGE Publications Inc.
2455 Teller Road
Thousand Oaks, California 91320

SAGE Publications India Pvt Ltd
B 1/I 1 Mohan Cooperative Industrial Area
Mathura Road, Post Bag 7
New Delhi 110 044

SAGE Publications Asia-Pacific Pte Ltd
33 Pekin Street #02-01
Far East Square
Singapore 048763

Library of Congress Control Number: 2007931481

British Library Cataloguing in Publication data

A catalogue record for this book is available from the British Library

ISBN 978-1-4129-2962-2
ISBN 978-1-4129-2963-9 (pbk)

Typeset by C&M Digitals (P) Ltd., Chennai, India
Printed in Great Britain by The Cromwell Press Ltd, Trowbridge, Wiltshire
Printed on paper from sustainable resources

I would like to dedicate this book to the people who encouraged and allowed me to study and learn at university, and eventually to teach at that level. The list is long and includes Ruth and Alan, my Mum and Dad; Linda and Diane, my sisters; Jackie, Maria and Frances, the divine and delectable nuclear family; and Rog (Roger Bull, MSc) for the years of laughter, ideas, discussion, Speckled Hen, plumbing and other assorted repair work above and beyond the call of cousinhood.

Contents

Acknowledgements

My thanks must go to all of the students and my colleagues who have contributed, in many cases unknowingly, to this book. Thanks to Liz Coates and the ECS team for asking me to become involved in their course way back in the beginning. Also thanks for the support and encouragement given by Patrick Brindle at Sage and to the anonymous referees who commented on the drafts. Thank you.

Introduction

You are probably looking at this book because you feel that you might need something extra to help you with settling into your role of undergraduate. You may be feeling anxious about the demands that will be made of you and perhaps feeling that everybody else will know already what to do, how to behave, how to get down to work and to take part in everything else that might be expected of you. The point to bear in mind at times like this is that everybody is new. Even the slightly older students, even those who exude confidence, even those who seem to have inside knowledge, are all new to the same things that you are new to. Whether they choose to discuss their worries and weaknesses is a different matter. Most, probably all, new students are anxious about how they will approach their work. They are not sure, no matter how successful they might have been in previous settings, whether they will be able to manage in their new setting. You should rest assured that in the same way as some people are ill at ease in some social situations, but manage not to show it, there will be an overwhelming majority who are anxious in their new guise of university student.

This book cannot instantly resign your concerns to history, but it can provide many pointers, strategies and suggestions as well as a good deal of background, and even foreground, information that will help you devise a way of working which fits in with your new-found opportunities for socialising, which you really should capitalise on, in what can seem like a strange new world.

The title of this book implies that universities are places of study, and also of learning. Both of these activities should be active and not passive. All too often, in supposed learning situations the would-be learner is expected to remain passive and to internalise whatever is presented to them. This actually works for some; for others there is often only a partial absorption of what is presented. For the rest, the time spent as a passive member of an audience is not particularly beneficial.

Most university teaching includes lectures; lectures can be times of passive loss of interest. The learner must take steps to stay awake and be actively involved in the proceedings. It is because some university teaching is not as good as it could be that a book of this nature can help those new to the arena to become active and receptive learners able to take full advantage of the opportunity for study at a higher level.

The opening chapter of *Studying and Learning at University* briefly outlines the constructivist view of learning. This view suggests that learning takes place through engagement and activity, and that learning is indeed an active process. It does not take long to realise that the mainstay of much university course teaching is the lecture; what more passive way of learning could be invented without resorting to indoctrination during sleep? An old university joke describes a lecturer as someone who talks in your sleep, and for some this is not far from the truth. The purpose of this book is not to shake up the university teaching force – there are many members of that force who are not in need of a shake-up anyway – but to allow full participation in the process of studying and learning no matter in what higher education teaching context you find yourself.

The first chapter is recommended as essential reading as it gives an insight into the processes which underpin your learning, whether you realise it or not. It also provides thoughts about how best to proceed with the tasks faced by those new to higher level study, in a situation where, unlike most schools, the teachers are not always on hand to provide minute-by-minute support. Those teaching in universities have a range of pressing commitments and duties apart from teaching. The typical academic contract includes one-third for research, one-third for teaching (including preparation, marking and organisation) and one-third for administrative duties, such as unit, departmental and university committees, admissions, exam boards, and module and course co-ordination. This is why you will be left to work independently and why at times you may well feel isolated. Obviously to become an independent learner is an aim that you should be working towards, but the sudden change from school to university can come as a shock. Some universities give higher importance to research than others and it is sometimes the case that teaching in these universities is given a lower priority than one might expect. This can be seen as a necessary result of the financial implications of good and excellent performance in the regular national assessment of university research output, the Research Assessment Exercise (RAE), in which all universities are rated according to their output and excellence in research and from which follows a large proportion of their funding.

Another fairly widely accepted point is that lecturers are not necessarily good teachers (though it must be said that many are very good teachers); they are often appointed as a result of their research record, not their successful teaching. There are naturally a great many counter-examples to this and it is likely that you will be taught by some inspired teachers and you will benefit, in many cases, from a high level of professionalism and attention to detail. However it could be the case that some of your lecturers may not have had training or preparation for the teaching elements of their job. This is changing, however. The Higher Education Academy (HEA) takes a great interest in teaching and teaching standards in universities and provides prestigious accreditation to university teachers who meet the required standard of excellence in teaching. Many universities run internal programmes of training in university teaching, some of which lead to accreditation by the HEA, and many of which are mandatory for new members of staff.

Using this book

Chapter 1: The purpose of this chapter is to give you insight into the processes of learning and what we currently understand about it. It will also provide a consideration of how learning might be optimised. This chapter underpins much of what follows and there are references made to the content of Chapter 1 throughout the book.

Chapter 2: Since effective reading is a crucial element of study at university, this chapter is devoted to it. Even the seemingly most efficient, or the speediest, of readers do not always operate as efficiently as they might. This chapter suggests strategies for improving your reading and, importantly, coming to a better understanding of what you read.

Chapter 3: Having easy access to what you have read, or to the content of lectures, at a later date is another crucial element of your work. If you allow your note-taking to become a cumbersome or chaotic affair you will not benefit from looking back at your notes when the time comes to write an assignment, or to revise for exams. There is probably nothing worse than looking at what you imagined were meaningful and incredibly helpful notes, only to find that what you are looking at has no meaning for you at all. Writing too much is sometimes as bad as writing too little. This chapter looks at different approaches to keeping a record of your work, and relates it to learning through the process of engagement.

Chapter 4: In order to learn from the work and writing of others you need to have access to it. You could buy every book on your reading list, and a few more besides, but this is not at all realistic. In any case much of what you need to consult will be in the form of journal articles or reports. You need to be a skilled user of the library and its related services if you want to be efficient and economical with your, all too precious, time. This chapter introduces the multitude of advanced library facilities, beginning with classification systems, but going far beyond the simple numbering of books.

Chapter 5: The information that you need will be traceable via the medium of the internet in many cases. The library will give access to electronic versions of most academic journals, but there is a new world of high speed, well-targeted searching of wholly academic material in virtual work areas such as those provided by Google Scholar and similar dedicated academic sites. The dangers of falling into the trap of internet-mediated, cut and paste plagiarism, whether intentional or not, are considered, as are the consequences. There is more detail and advice about avoiding plagiarism in Chapter 7.

Chapter 6: Assessment arrangements are usually at the forefront of most student minds when they begin a new module; certainly more questions are asked in the first session about the assessment than any other topic. This chapter deals with the mainstay of ongoing assessment (as opposed to the traditional exam), the essay. How to plan, write and, most importantly, how to develop an argument in your writing, is covered. Dissertations too are considered in detail. The importance to the academic fraternity of clear and accurate referencing is also outlined.

Chapter 7: To balance the chapter devoted to essay writing this chapter considers the other types of assessment that you are likely to encounter. Report writing, which is more common in science-based subjects, is dealt with and the whole process of examinations is also covered.

Chapter 8: Increasingly, sometimes for purposes of assessment but at other times too, you will be asked to make a presentation. A well-planned and executed presentation can be a pleasure for both audience and presenter; the converse is also true – a badly planned and poorly delivered presentation can serve no purpose but to embarrass the presenter and bore the audience. This chapter looks at the basics of planning and of producing the sort of visual aids which seem to be mandatory in the world of technology – although just because PowerPoint can produce a virtual firework display with your words hidden amongst the stunning whistles and bells, does not mean that you should aim at impressing the audience with the excesses of electronic style over content.

Finally, there is a glossary of common university terms and jargon, including some mysterious acronyms and many other related terms.

Transferable skills and the qualities of a graduate

The notion of 'graduateness' is covered late in the book, and you might want to peruse Appendix 1 before you move on to using the rest of the book in earnest. We consider the nature of the features that a degree-level education should provide to a successful graduate. It has been said that the important elements of an education are those that remain after the factual content has been forgotten, and there is a lot in that idea. This not only refers to the skills of finding out and of reasoning, which of course a graduate education should provide, but to a whole range of other transferable skills which will serve well in a world of increasing complexity and technological advance. Above all, graduates should be skilled communicators across a range of different contexts and media. The aim of this book is to help in the process of dealing with the potential difficulties faced by those new to university study, and to help in achieving the status of well-rounded, knowledgeable and skilled graduate, ready to face the challenges of the next stage of study, of career, or of whatever you choose to do next.

1 How We Learn

For some lucky people approaches to learning come naturally and rest comfortably alongside everything that they do. For others it is not nearly so straightforward. Some learners have been encouraged to work in ways which, when considered in any depth, do not suit them at all. This encouragement may have come from teachers, friends, or perhaps parents, and was given sincerely, but it might just happen to be the wrong advice for the individual in question. It is very easy to assume that because one way of studying and learning works well for you, that it should be recommended, or even insisted upon for others. We will see that this is not the case. In this first chapter an overview of the background to learning is considered, in particular the differences between individuals are looked at and the great importance for learners of engagement and mental activity, terms which will be explained later.

After reading this chapter you might well want to reconsider some of your approaches to your studying and learning.

Many undergraduates have been interested, and sometimes amazed, to discover more about the process of learning. Despite obvious success in formal learning, evidenced by the passing of exams, and by arriving at university, new awareness of learning and explicit consideration of personal preferences and approaches have given a new impetus, in many cases, to tackling the study challenges of higher education.

It may be that you are aware of current thought and the received wisdom concerning learning. In this case you might like to look through the chapter quickly, or to return to consult it when reading later chapters which make reference to what is included here.

In many ways learning in higher education is not unlike learning in many other contexts, although clearly there are some differences, for example, between learning to ride a bike and learning to compare different schools of philosophical thought; the learning experienced in a formal setting for five-year-olds will necessarily be different to the formal setting of a university. If we set aside such differences for the present, and concentrate on what learning actually means, we will see that learning is something in which we participate almost all of the time. This relates to what is known as 'life long learning' and has also been called learning 'from the cradle to the grave'. Learning encompasses all human behaviour and all human endeavour. There have been great efforts made over the years to understand learning, both in humans and in other animals; some researchers have made interesting discoveries by relating what has been discovered about rats or even pigeons, for example, to human development. The links are not always obvious, but the behaviourist school of learning, especially when in its infancy relied heavily on animal experiments.

KEY PRINCIPLES

Behaviourism: a broadly based theory of learning which is based on the idea of training, reward (positive reinforcement) and punishment (negative reinforcement). Behaviourist learning leads to a situation in which the learner knows and is able to do certain things, but does not necessarily understand. Behaviourist learning is good for learning set routines and for being able to recall facts easily. Behaviourism is based on the work of B.F. Skinner for the most part, but its origins lie with Pavlov at the beginning of the twentieth century.

So, the purpose of this chapter is to introduce some of the basic principles involved in learning and some other related areas (learning styles for example) so that you are able to understand better the reasoning behind some of the strategies which are introduced later. Some of this chapter is theoretical and gives insight into the ways that learning is thought to take place – this is helpful if you are in need of explanations of some of the strategies which follow in the rest of the book. Some of the chapter is more practical, the question of physical location for working, for example. Both theoretical and practical considerations can play an important role in helping you to develop a personal and effective approach to studying at university.

It is possible to differentiate between formal and informal learning. Informal learning includes such things as learning to talk, learning the rules of a game by playing it, even learning not to try to touch a flame, and formal learning is something which takes place within the educational and training institutions of the world – schools, colleges, universities and training centres. Formal learning is planned and in most cases informal learning is not; informal learning is something that happens, often without any prior expectation and in a wide range of different situations – talking to a friend, watching television, walking along the street. Within the sphere of formal learning, especially at the higher levels, there are certain expectations that are made concerning the way that the learner will behave. It is expected that the learner will be motivated to learn, will attend taught sessions when required to do so, will 'work' at other times in order to make progress. For some it is the need to undertake work, or to study, which can present problems. In many cases a little understanding of the processes involved in learning and the ways that individuals respond to particular types of learning activity can help to overcome, or at least minimise, these problems.

There are distinct similarities between 'school learning' and 'university learning', and there are some differences. For both, the importance of understanding, rather than memorising, should be of prime importance. This means that learning should lead to more than the acquisition of knowledge. Knowledge without understanding is sometimes thought of as being of little use, although it is very useful in pub quizzes, and in some forms of examination. A 'good' education will lead to the amassing of knowledge, but it will also lead to an understanding of ideas and of connections between ideas, facts and skills. In some school contexts understanding is given a lower priority than it should have. Some teachers have even been guilty of saying something like: 'You don't need to understand it, just remember it.' Understanding can allow for the application of knowledge in different situations, and we will see that being able to make use of knowledge, concepts and skills in a range of different situations is one of the hallmarks of a well-educated person.

An important difference between school and higher education is often the amount of support and supervision which is given. At school a teacher will meet pupils relatively often, they will set and monitor homework on a regular basis and generally be on hand to marshal the learning which they hope is developing. In contrast a university tutor may not meet students very often, although this varies from place to place and even, sometimes, from tutor to tutor. Also, a university tutor is likely to deliver lectures, seminars and tutorials on a particular topic, and then assess the work done by a student in as little as one assignment or one exam paper. Obviously assessment procedures differ from place to place, subject to subject and, on an even smaller scale, from module to module. The point here is that as a new university undergraduate it is possible to feel very much alone and remote from your new teachers, and it is very likely that the new undergraduate will have to take on more responsibility for planning and completing work, far more so than when at school. It is this difference which, for some, creates a need for this sort of book.

Learning

Learning is defined in a range of ways, as we would expect with a concept that embraces a very wide spectrum of activity and expected outcomes. Looking at even a small part of the literature available we find that learning is defined as:

- The acquisition of knowledge.
- Knowledge gained through study.
- The gaining of knowledge of, or skill in, something through study, teaching, instruction or experience.
- The process of gaining knowledge.
- A process by which behaviour is changed, shaped or controlled.
- A change in behaviour as a result of experience or practice.
- The individual process of constructing understanding based on experience from a wide range of sources.

It is the last definition which should be of most interest here, although all of them will have resonances for learners in different situations, including universities.

Four from the list mention knowledge, two include the notion of behaviour and the idea of individual construction of understanding based on experience is mentioned only once. We will see later that the ideas relating to construction and to understanding are actually very important to all learners, not only those in universities.

Deep and surface learning

There is a distinction made between what has become known as deep and surface learning (Biggs and Moore, 1993). Deep learning, they say, is most likely to take place when the learner becomes very involved in the task(s) that they are undertaking. Surface learning comes about when the learner undertakes the minimum amount of work possible to meet the requirements of the task. They continue by saying that: 'The deep approach is ideally what … learning should involve' (1993: 313). They characterise three types of learner, defined by their attitudes, as a way of explaining the difference between deep and surface learning, and include a third category – the 'achieving' learner (Table 1.1).

A deep learner asked to read and consider the story, plot and implications of a play or story, would do just that. Not only would they know the story in detail, but also they would be able to consider the outlook of different characters, consider the ramifications

Table 1.1   Characterisation of three types of learner.

Deep learner	Surface learner	Achieving learner
'I want to learn'	'I want to have fun'	'I want top marks'
Real involvement with the topic	Minimal amount of work	Cost-effective use of time
In-depth engagement with topic	Scratches the surface of the topic	Finds out what will help achieve high marks

Source: Based on Biggs and Moore, 1993

of certain aspects of the story and be able to relate the story to a wider perspective. A surface learner when confronted with the same task would be able to relate the story, and name the characters and perhaps little else. An achieving learner would be interested in being able to answer questions in an exam, or being able to impress the tutor with their knowledge. A deep learner undertaking an assignment concerning the effect of a particular enzyme in varying conditions of alkalinity and acidity would not only complete that task, but would also find out about how the enzyme operates at different temperatures and would compare this with other similar enzymes, make links between the differing results and draw general conclusions about the ways in which enzymes fulfil their roles. A surface learner would simply explore the effect of pH on the enzyme in question and, again, the achieving learner would take time to find out what was required for the assessment for the work in order to achieve very good marks, and aim at that.

Learning theory: an overview

Knowing the detail of a range of psychological theories of learning is all well and good, but from a practical point of view, and in the context of this book, it is probably more worthwhile to restrict the overview to the most relevant theories and then to move forward with the practicalities of learning as they are likely to apply to individual learners in a higher education setting.

There are different schools of learning theory, but it is not intended to go into detail here; there are many good introductions to the theory of learning should you feel the need to explore further (Pritchard, 2005, for example). What we will do here is to outline what is meant by constructivist learning, as this has bearing upon certain approaches to learning activities which will be discussed and recommended later.

Constructivism

The area of constructivism, in the field of learning, comes under the broad heading of cognitive science. Cognitive science is an expansive area, and has its roots in the first half of the twentieth century at a time when academics from the disciplines of psychology, artificial intelligence, philosophy, linguistics, neuroscience and anthropology realised that they were all trying to solve problems concerning the mind and the brain.

KEY PRINCIPLES

Constructivism: this theory suggests that learning takes place when new information is built into and added on to an individual's current structure of knowledge, understanding and skills. We learn best when we actively construct our own understanding.

The reference in the definition of constructivism to knowledge, understanding and skills refers to what is commonly considered to be a description of the types of learning that we become involved with. No matter what the level of our learning, pre-school to postgraduate, when we learn we are dealing with knowledge, concepts, skills and, a fourth, attitudes (DES, 1985).

All of the above can be learned. Knowledge – facts – can be amassed and remembered; concepts, or ideas, can be internalised and understood; skills can be mastered, whether they are mental skills such as solving differential equations, or practical, physical skills, such as mixing paint on a palette and applying it to canvas; attitudes can be formed and shaped as a result of learning and understanding, for example an understanding of the potentially devastating effects of extreme climate change and the reasons for it, may lead to well-developed attitudes towards the conservation of energy and the planet at large.

KEY PRINCIPLES

Knowledge: something that you can know.

Concept: an idea or theory that you can understand.

Skill: an activity that you can undertake; this can be mental or physical.

Attitude: a stance that can be taken towards ideas or on an issue.

Wray and Lewis (1997) single out four aspects of constructivist learning theory which they consider to be of the greatest importance. They are:

- Learning is a process of interaction between what is known and what is to be learned.
- Learning is a social process.
- Learning is a situated process.
- Learning is a metacognitive process.

If we look briefly at each of these headings in turn we will come to recognise the underlying principles of constructivism and see the relevance of the theory to learning, not only across the whole learning spectrum, but to studying in universities in particular.

Learning is a process of interaction between what is known and what is to be learned   Constructivists believe that as individuals we have mental constructs or models of a vast number of items of knowledge and understanding. Each construct, sometimes referred to as a **schema**, is related to a topic – a fact, a concept, a skill or an attitude perhaps, and represents the individual's current state of knowledge and understanding in relation to the central theme of the schema. Schemas can be as large or small as necessary; they have a wide range of internal links and also links with numerous other schemas; they form the framework of our knowledge and understanding.

Figure 1.1 offers a greatly simplified representation of a schema; essentially it is not possible to draw something so multidimensional and complex as a schema. However, an idea of the complexity and vast number of the links involved is obvious. The words in the rectangular boxes are a small sample of other schemas to which links exist.

KEY PRINCIPLES

Schema: a notional mental framework for storing, remembering and understanding information. We construct our own schemas, constantly adding to and amending them as we experience more. Schemas contain links internally and to other schemas. Schemas are personal and can be idiosyncratic. Schemas are not necessarily accurate representations, but are always open to change.

The process of learning involves adding to and amending these mental structures. If a structure is to be added to, it is a sound principle to have the mental structure 'activated' or we could say, 'brought to the front of the mind'. It is a good idea to refresh the memory and rethink what is currently known and understood about a particular topic before pressing on with new learning. Many teachers understand this principle and before beginning a new topic they will revisit what has gone before, perhaps in an earlier module, or if the topic has not been taught before they will encourage the group to think about what they might already know about the topic. For each individual learning begins from what can be very different starting points when a new topic is introduced. This principle will hold good at all levels of learning and undergraduate learners as well as six-year-old learners will benefit from an initial revision and review of what is already 'known'. Before a lecture in a series it would be a good strategy to review briefly the content of the previous lecture and any additional reading that you might have undertaken. In doing this you will be activating schemas and preparing yourself for the next stage of learning in this particular topic.

The terms **assimilation** and **accommodation** relate to how we deal with new information and ideas. Assimilation is the gathering together and stockpiling of facts and ideas and skills; accommodation is the making of changes to existing structures when new conflicting information is encountered.

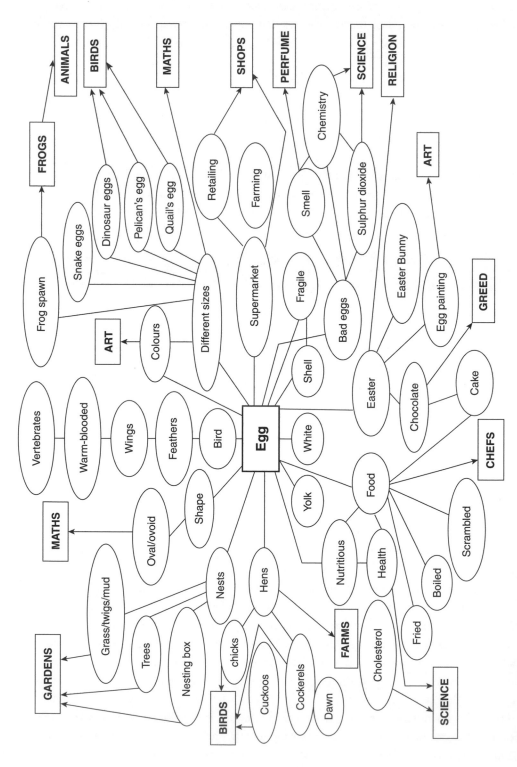

Figure 1.1   A simplified representation of a schema

KEY PRINCIPLES

Assimilation: the process of adding new data to a schema.

Accommodation: the process of amending a schema in order to accord with new or contradictory data.

Learning is a social process   The branch of constructivist learning theory known as 'social constructivism' stresses the importance of dialogue and of social interaction in the process of learning. That is to say, a good deal of understanding can arise from discussion with others. The discussion does not necessarily have to be with more knowledgeable others; even airing ideas with someone less knowledgeable can be valuable. At the time of the Ancient Greeks Plato defined learning as dialogue, meaning the dialogue between teacher and pupil, or group of pupils. In many universities this tradition continues, with tutors engaging students in detailed discussion in small tutorial groups.

We will see later that individuals have different learning preferences; some prefer to work alone, without social contact, while others thrive on it. For the vast majority of learners, social constructive learning is valuable. Simply chatting about the content of a session as you leave or move to wherever the coffee is to be found can be valuable, in that you are reviewing the subject matter, possibly questioning ideas and gaining alternative interpretations. It is not at all unusual for a part of a lecture to be almost incomprehensible before talking about it afterwards with someone who perceived it differently from you.

Learning is a situated process   All learning takes place in a context. This may refer to a physical setting, but more importantly, it may refer to a social or cultural setting, or to the position of the content of the learning in relation to the wider content area to which the specific learning belongs. For example, advanced geometry is set in the context of less advanced geometry which is in turn set in the far wider context of mathematics. There would be little point in attempting advanced geometric content unless the content to be covered had been located in the context of what precedes it in a hierarchy of learning. This may seem obvious, suggesting that firm foundations need to be in place before more advanced work might be attempted. From a socio-cultural perspective an example might be the attempted learning and deeper understanding of a particular Shakespeare play without having any knowledge or understanding of the prevailing social climate of the time and place where the action is set. (It is probably the case that some experts on Shakespeare would not agree completely with this statement, according to their view on interpreting his work, but as a general principle it holds good.) Students following modules in an English department where Dickens, or Austen, or some other writer dealing with a specific historical period, or even geographic location (China in the 1960s perhaps), might be disadvantaged in their studies if they were not aware of the mores, conventions and even, perhaps, the prevailing political conditions, of the setting in question. Learning which is set in a context outside of the experience of the learner is likely to be less effective learning than if the learning is set in a context that is familiar to the learner. This is perhaps an argument to support the importance of wider reading in advanced study.

If you consciously make connections between what you are experiencing as a learner and what you know and understand about its 'situation', you may well come to understand it better. If you have no immediate way of studying the situation you might find it helpful to undertake some basic research in order to help you to place the new material in its wider context, or situation.

Learning is a metacognitive process   Metacognition is concerned with thinking about thinking. We all have an enormous number of thought processes taking place, both consciously and unconsciously, all of the time. When we become aware of our thinking and our patterns of thought we are working metacognitively. To a certain extent metacognition can be seen as being about individuals learning about their own learning.

KEY PRINCIPLES

Metacognition: Metacognitive knowledge is the knowledge an individual has about their own cognition, which can be used to consider and to control their cognitive processes.

Brown (1987: 67) offers a simple view of metacognition when he says that it 'refers loosely to one's knowledge and control of [one's] own cognitive system'. To be aware of one's own *modus operandi* in terms of thinking and learning is to be metacognitively aware. Effective learners often use this awareness to good advantage in learning situations.

When attempting to understand new, possibly complex ideas it is worth considering precisely how you are approaching the task. Are you simply reading and re-reading a difficult passage? If this is the case you might like to try a different strategy, such as some of those introduced in a later chapter dealing with reading for academic purposes.

Mental activity

All of what has gone before in this chapter points, more or less, to what should be a very important element of learning. That is, mental activity. Mental activity should be at the centre of learning, and can be developed in a variety of ways. When dealing with new experiences, learning seems to proceed well if, and probably only if, there is mental activity on the part of the learner.

Perhaps the image of academics sitting in ivory towers thinking – or we could say 'engaging' with ideas – is an important one. Many academics would dislike the propagation of the

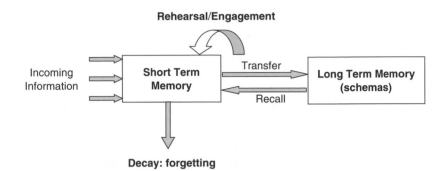

Figure 1.2   Simplified model of the process of storing information, showing the importance of engagement in the process of learning

ivory tower analogy, which is perhaps outdated in the twenty-first century when much academic work, although dependent on a high level of engagement, is firmly rooted in application and not so fully removed from the rigours of everyday life as the notion suggests.

Learning is not something others can undertake for you, it is something you must do for yourself. Adults, whether teachers, or trainers, or parents, cannot assume that if they exert thought and effort, directed towards teaching, that learning will be the inevitable result. Learning requires effort on the part of the learner. Without effort and mental activity it is very unlikely that learning will take place. Learning is an active, not a passive activity; learning is not something which is done to you. Teachers continually put into place situations in which learning is likely – reading tasks, discussion opportunities, assignments – but without the required effort and activity on the part of the would-be learner the outcome is not at all certain. Howe (1999) tells us that: 'Learning always necessitates mental activities being undertaken by the individual learner … Learning does not always have to be deliberate, but it does always require the engagement of mental processes. The mental activities of individual students form a particularly powerful source of influence on what is actually learned' (Howe, 1999: 23). We are being told that we need to exert effort into our learning, it will not happen just because we want it to. This mental activity is crucial in all learning. It is sometimes described as engagement. The idea that a learner engages with what is to be learned in a mentally active way can be seen to be at the heart of the learning process. Figure 1.2 gives a simplified model of how new information is rehearsed, or engaged with, and then transferred to long term memory where it will remain accessible. The more rehearsal and engagement that takes place, the more easily knowledge, concepts and skills are transferred to the long term memory store. Rehearsal and engagement are a result of purposeful mental activity.

Engagement

Everything about the constructivist approach to learning, in a simple and practical way, points towards the importance of learners getting close to the material content of what it is hoped they will learn, and then 'doing' something with it. By undertaking actions and activities, mental or physical, which centre on the facts, concepts or the skills in question, learners are in a position to move forward in their learning. This 'closeness' is possible in a wide range of different ways and is referred to as 'engagement'.

There is a five-stage model for learning, put forward by a group of Australian teachers and academics (Reid et al., 1989), which puts engagement at the start of the process of learning. The model takes a wholly constructivist approach, and the importance of the individual and of activity is stressed. As we have seen, from the constructivist point of view, learning is not a passive process, and so, with reference to what is known about effective learning, and with due attention paid to the notion of engagement, it is possible to map out approaches to learning which encompass the best and most effective of what is currently known about learning.

The five-stage model of Reid et al. below sets out a route which, if followed, is likely to provide the conditions required for learning to result.

- Engagement.
- Exploration.
- Transformation.
- Presentation.
- Reflection.

KEY PRINCIPLES

Engagement: getting close to the information by reading, thinking, re-reading, discussing, writing or otherwise recording. Any activity which supports the development of a better understanding of the material or topic.

Engagement is described as 'the time during which students acquire information and engage in an experience that provides the basis for, or content of, their ensuing learning' (p. 28). The next stage in the model – exploration, is closely related to the stage of engagement.

KEY PRINCIPLES

Exploration: the process of providing an overview of what is contained in the information under consideration. It may take many forms, including reading and writing, finding things out and answering questions, more manipulative activities, matching and comparing, drawing or compiling charts or diagrams, discussing and arguing, and many other diverse and related activities.

The exploration stage can be an open-ended process, where students follow their instincts.

KEY PRINCIPLES

Transformation: reproducing notes and other ideas from a text to be in a format which best suits the needs of the learner. The needs might be to do with understanding, answering a particular question or simply in order to make the ideas more readable. For example, ideas might be transformed into diagrams or vice versa.

Transformation is the stage in which information that has been fully explored might be re-configured into a form which allows for presentation (the next stage), but importantly, transformed into a format that suits the needs of the learner. From the point of view of the student certain questions will now be able to be answered. Transformation and the resultant presentation is not the end of the process.

KEY PRINCIPLES

Presentation: information can be set out in the way that suits particular needs. It could be in a format related to assessment, or to an oral or visual presentation. It could be as an end product, or simply in a different state in preparation for later use.

At some levels presentation will mean presenting something for others to see. It can also mean presenting various stages of your work and understanding of new ideas in ways designed to help you to understand them better.

KEY PRINCIPLES

Reflection: a time when ideas can be revisited and reviewed. All new ideas need time to become fully understood and assimilated. Reflection and review over a period of time can help greatly in this process.

This stage offers time to reflect upon what you have experienced, the process and the content, gives the opportunity for internalisation, and for a deeper level of understanding to be developed. Reflection can also take many forms: thinking, re-reading notes, re-writing notes, creating a chart or diagram, presenting ideas to others informally, or simply thinking about the ideas involved.

When looking through the five stages you may be able to relate to your own learning practices and identify which of the tasks that you complete are related to particular stages. It might be that you recognise that you do not work through these stages, even in a loose and informal way. In later chapters we will consider ways and means of generating deeper engagement with the content of learning.

Learning styles

Each of us has a particular approach to learning which suits us best. Technically this is referred to as a learning style. To the uninitiated it is simply a preferred way of working. In some cases, when a learner does not realise that there are different approaches to learning that might be chosen, or when they might have been encouraged always to work in one particular way, learning might prove difficult. Learning might well have been problematic over a long period. If a preferred style of learning can be recognised and steps taken towards making use of what has been recognised, it is possible that learning might proceed more smoothly and with consequent improved results. This section will help you to understand the different ways in which individuals prefer to approach learning, and in this way lead you to a better understanding of your own preferred style. In turn this may well have benefits for you as you begin to work in ways which are more suited to your preferences. This can be true because in a great many cases learners do not consider that there could be a different, more personal and more productive way of working, and persist with what they consider to be the only way of working.

There has been a great deal written about learning styles, and there are many definitions to consider. To look briefly at some of them will act as a useful starting point.

A learning style is:

- A particular way in which an individual learns.
- A mode of learning; an individual's preferred or best manner(s) in which to think, process information and demonstrate learning.
- An individual's preferred means of acquiring knowledge and skills.
- Habits, strategies, or regular mental behaviours concerning learning, particularly deliberate educational learning, that an individual displays.

We can see then that a learning style is a preferred way of learning and studying, for example, using diagrams instead of text, working in groups as opposed to working alone, or learning in a structured rather than a freer and unstructured manner. Learning preferences refer to an individual's preferred intellectual approach to learning, and have an important bearing on how learning proceeds for each individual.

The term 'learning preferences' has also been used to refer to the conditions, encompassing environmental, emotional, sociological and physical conditions, which an individual learner would choose, if they were in a position to make a choice (Dunn et al., 1989).

The area of scientific study known as Neuro-Linguistic Programming (NLP) provides one way of describing learning styles. There are many others, but for our purposes it will be sufficient to consider just one, relatively straightforward, approach to the topic. Over many years, and through many research projects, including close and detailed observation of the way we communicate, three particular learning styles – visual, auditory and kinaesthetic – have been identified. They are described as follows:

- **Visual learners**   If you are a visual learner you will prefer to learn by **seeing**. You will have good visual recall and prefer information to be presented visually, in the form of diagrams, graphs and maps for example. Video recordings and television programmes will suit you.
- **Auditory learners**   If you are an auditory learner you will prefer to learn by **listening, hearing and saying**. You will most likely have good auditory memory and benefit from discussion, lectures, interviewing and audio tapes for example. You will like sequence, repetition and summary.
- **Kinaesthetic learners**   If you are a kinaesthetic learner you will prefer to learn by **touching and doing**. You are probably good at recalling events and you associate feelings or physical experiences with memory. You enjoy physical activity, manipulating objects and other practical, first-hand experience. Kinaesthetic learners benefit from regular breaks in learning activities.

Whenever we read about learning style, especially for the first time, there is a tendency to apply what is read to our own situation and consider our own learning style. Below is a simple learning style assessment inventory which will give an indication of your preference for visual, auditory or kinaesthetic learning. This will only give an indication. If you are keen to find out more precisely, or to investigate other classification systems, a simple Internet search will lead you to online assessment inventories and detailed explanations of this area of interest in learning.

Learning Style Assessment Schedule

Choose (a), (b) or (c) from each question according to which choice most suits your preferences or behaviour.

1. when I use new equipment I prefer to:

   (a) read the instructions first
   (b) listen to an explanation from someone who has used it before
   (c) go ahead and have a go, I can work it out as I use it

2. When I need directions for travelling I prefer to:

   (a) use a map
   (b) ask for spoken directions
   (c) follow my intuition

3. If I am teaching someone something new I prefer to:

   (a) write things down for them
   (b) give them a verbal explanation
   (c) demonstrate first and then let them have a go

(Continued)

(Continued)

4. When I go shopping for clothes I prefer to:

   (a) imagine what they would look like on
   (b) talk to the shop staff
   (c) try them on in the changing room

5. When I am choosing a holiday I prefer to:

   (a) read the brochures
   (b) listen to the experiences of others
   (c) imagine what a particular place would be like

6. If I was buying a new car I would prefer to:

   (a) read reviews in car magazines
   (b) talk to friends
   (c) test-drive lots of different cars

7. When I am learning a new skill I prefer to:

   (a) watch what the teacher is doing
   (b) talk things through with the teacher
   (c) give it a try and work things out as I go

8. If I am choosing food from a menu I prefer to:

   (a) imagine what the food would look like
   (b) talk through the possibilities with someone
   (c) imagine what the food would taste like

9. When I concentrate I prefer to:

   (a) focus on the words or the pictures in front of me
   (b) discuss the problem and the possible solutions mentally
   (c) move around a lot, fiddle with pens, pencils and touch things

10. My first memory is of:

    (a) looking at something
    (b) being spoken to
    (c) doing something

11. When I am anxious I:

    (a) visualise worst-case scenarios
    (b) talk over in my head what worries me most
    (c) cannot sit still, I fidget and move around

12. I feel especially connected to other people according to:

    (a) how they look
    (b) what they say
    (c) how they make me feel

13. When I have to revise for an exam I prefer to:

    (a) write lots of revision notes and draw diagrams
    (b) talk over my notes, alone or with other people
    (c) imagine making the movement or creating the formula

14. If I am explaining to someone I prefer to:

    (a) show them what I mean
    (b) explain to them in different ways
    (c) encourage them to try, and talk to them as they do it

15. I find it easiest to remember:

    (a) faces
    (b) names
    (c) things I have done

16. When I meet an old friend I:

    (a) say 'It's great to see you!'
    (b) say 'It's great to hear from you!'
    (c) give them a hug or shake hands

17. I remember things best by:

    (a) writing them down
    (b) saying them aloud or repeating them in my head
    (c) doing and practising the activity or imagining doing it

18. If I had to complain about faulty equipment that I had bought I would:

    (a) write a letter
    (b) complain by telephone
    (c) take the item back to the shop

19. I often say:

    (a) I see what you mean
    (b) I hear what you are saying
    (c) I know how you feel

20. The first thing I notice about people is how they:

    (a) look and dress
    (b) sound and speak
    (c) stand and move

Count how many each of (a), (b) and (c) you have chosen:

(a)	(b)	(c)

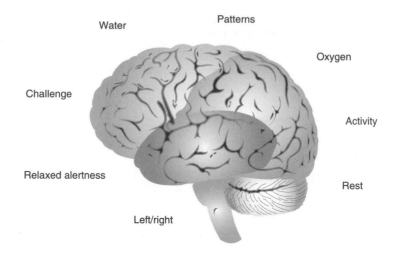

Figure 1.3   Some of the factors affecting effective brain function in learning situations

If you have chosen mostly (a) your learning style is more visual. If you have chosen mostly (b) your learning style is more auditory. If you have chosen mostly (c) your learning style is more kinaesthetic. Most of us have a blend of styles, not wholly in any of the three classifications. It is probably more unusual to have a style which is entirely in one, especially in this sort of assessment, which is not particularly thorough although it gives a reasonable indication.

It can be very helpful to have some understanding of your own preferred style of learning. If you are aware of ways of working that suit you best then you can arrange for these conditions to be in place. For example, it may be that discussion (a good social constructivist approach to learning) may be a part of your preferred style. If this is the case you would be well advised to arrange with others certain times when you can perhaps work together and discuss and argue about the topic of your work. Similarly, you might discover that you have a strong visual preference and that you might benefit from making more use of diagrams in your note-taking or revision.

Brain-based learning

During the past twenty years, or thereabouts, there has been an upsurge in both research and interest amongst educators in what has become known as 'brain-based learning'. Since this area of research is relatively new there is, understandably, some level of scepticism and disagreement concerning its real value.

Chipongian (2004) suggests that the term 'brain-based learning' sounds redundant, and in many ways she is right – where else could learning be based? However, much of the new research and writing can be translated into useful and practical ideas that may help individual learners.

Susan Greenfield, an eminent and well-known researcher of the brain, writing in *The Times Educational Supplement* (Greenfield, 2005), says that 'Brain research is poised, if it can rise to the challenge, to make the biggest contribution of all to how the brain learns through interaction with the environment. ... Now more than ever before educationalists and brain scientists need to work together.'

Based on work undertaken by neuroscientists which has been related to teaching and learning by psychologists and other interested parties, we have at our disposal a good deal of information about how the brain is likely to function to its full potential in learning situations.

This is not the place to provide an in-depth review of the work in question but we will consider some of the potentially more important aspects of what is a growing field of research and application.

We can list certain of the 'truths' of the brain-based movement and comment on them as appropriate. Some of the more radical and possibly questionable points made by some researchers will be omitted here.

1. The brain needs food, water and oxygen in order to function effectively.
2. The brain seems to need a certain amount of challenge, but closes down under conditions of negative stress.
3. The brain seems to thrive in conditions where activity is encouraged and patterns are allowed to develop.
4. Learning in broad contexts with connections to other areas of understanding seems to be beneficial.
5. Learning that takes place in a safe and stimulating environment, allowing for what are known as relaxed alertness, active processing and orchestrated immersion, is likely to lead to conditions for effective learning.
6. It is possible to describe brain function in terms of a left/right division. The left side favours language, mathematical processes, logical thoughts, sequences and analysis; the right side, creative activities, rhyme, rhythm, music, visual impressions, colour and pictures.

Based on these precepts we can devise a list of recommendations:

- Be sure to drink water from time to time when studying.
- Move from time to time; some determined efforts to encourage increased blood flow are perhaps better than leaving it to chance.
- Do not attempt to work beyond the limit of your concentration; break up activities with short contrasting activities.
- Use activities which challenge different 'brain' strengths – left/right brain.

- Try to have insight into the bigger picture and seek out patterns in and between different areas of your study.
- Work in an environment where you can experience relaxed alertness, orchestrated immersion, always attempt to work with active processing (mental activity).

The work setting

The physical location of your workspace, its layout and other environmental considerations, can affect the progress of your work to a very great extent. This is also true of other factors, such as the time of day, or the need for you to do other pressing activities (looking after others for example).

With any group of students, if we ask the question 'Where do you like to get your work done?' there will be a wide range of answers, which will include more than a mention of the room where the work takes place. Some will include music, or no music, some will include the lighting of the room or the temperature, others will talk about the need for coffee, or the need to work late into the night. Some of the responses are likely to make others think about their own preferences. For example, it might be that a large subset of a particular group of students express the need to work late into the night. For others this would seem impossible and highly undesirable, as would the need for some to have musical accompaniment to their studying.

The reality of the situation is that we all have different needs and preferences. As with our preferred learning style we will all have a preferred learning context. It is very helpful for you to establish, early on, a setting and way of working, apart from whether you take notes in different colours, or whether you like to make an audio recording of your notes for later revision, which suits you, and which you can develop and manipulate to meet your full requirements.

You may have a clear picture of the setting that is conducive for work in your particular case. It could be that you work best in a solitary location with as many potential distractions excluded as possible. It may be that you prefer the comparatively busy setting of a quiet study area of a library. Below are some comments and descriptions given by first year undergraduates of their preferences and requirements.

- Sally (24), Combined Studies: I need to know that I have got everything else out of the way. If I've got washing to do, or arrangements to make I do it all before I start work. If I don't it will keep on coming back to me and getting in the way.
- Dave (19), Engineering: I always draw the curtains because my table is next to a window and any slight movement outside will distract me, I'm a very nosey person.
- Jayne (19), Early Childhood: Biscuits and hot chocolate at very regular intervals. I set myself short targets, like finish reading this chapter and then I can have a reward.
- Claire (18), Applied Biology: I can only really get down to work late at night. I think I find it almost exciting to know that most people are tucked up in bed while I am

getting things done. Sometimes I end up very tired the next day, but I seem to manage.

- John (21), History: I can't work at home, there are too many other things to catch my attention. I go to the library, it's open 24/7 and there's the added attraction of books being on hand, especially the reference copies of the course books, which I can't afford to buy.
- Wynter (20), Italian Studies: Sometimes a couple of us arrange to work together, not doing the work together, but being in the same place, then at certain times we stop and chat about something different to work, have a coffee and then get back to it. It breaks up the time well, but it's tempting to have too many breaks.
- Andrew (19), Maths: I have to have everything just so. Books, notes, everything ready to use. I have spare pens, lots of paper and a bottle of water. I go to the toilet before I start. This way there is nothing to stop me and I can go on and on.
- Jenny (32), Social Policy (part-time): I always have a set time on every week day, usually 9.30 to 12.30, when the children are at school, and nothing can get in the way. Everything else has to be fitted in as and when. It's hard, but I can usually stick to it.
- Nick (19), Education and Drama: I play music on my laptop, quietly, but it's always there. I use my laptop for everything – notes, essays, the internet. I couldn't work without it.
- Martin (18), Computer Science: I only work in one-hour blocks. I might do a few at a time but I set my phone alarm and always stop after an hour. I get a drink and walk around a bit … check for post or something like that.

These comments and insights in some ways refer back to the question of learning styles, but some of them go beyond that. There are comments above which suggest that the frame of mind of a learner can have a big effect on how effectively they are able to work. Sometimes the effect is obvious. If you know that there are certain chores which have to be completed this may well play on your mind to the point where you cannot concentrate fully on your studying. The recognition that the home environment is simply too distracting for work is not a learning style consideration, it is sensible admission that working at home is not a suitable option, in your case, for serious study.

The actual physical location of where you choose to work, along with all of the associated thoughts, worries and environmental features that come along with it, has a great impact on your ability to concentrate and get on with the important work that you have to complete. In the best conditions for you, you are likely to do your best work.

SUMMARY

- For the purposes of this book, we will consider that learning is an individual and complex process of construction which leads to:
  - the acquisition of knowledge
  - the understanding of complex ideas
  - the development of skills (both intellectual and physical)

- the development of a range of attitudes and beliefs based upon exposure to new knowledge and related concepts.

- An understanding of one's own learning processes is possibly the most important insight into study that a learner in higher education should have. For this reason a basic understanding of metacognition (insight into your own thought and learning processes) is something that all learners should have, at least in some measure. At the same time, insight into personal strengths and preferred learning styles is also very important for successful learning.

- Engagement with new knowledge, concepts and skills, through mental activity, lies at the heart of learning. The detail of how mental activity is organised and undertaken can vary widely. Effective learners are able to identify and capitalise upon their personal preferences and strengths in order to achieve their learning goals within whatever constraints they may encounter.

- The physical setting for your work and the timing and other arrangements which you make should be with your best learning interests in mind. Just because others work with loud music, or in the library (but presumably not both), does not mean that this will be most suitable for you.

Next

Since reading will form such an important element of your study we will look in the next chapter at ways in which reading can be made more efficient. The content of this first chapter will have bearing on some of the suggestions and strategies which are presented.

Activities

Learning: Think of a time in your recent educational experience when you feel that some particular element of study, or learning event, seemed to go very well. List the features of the learning situation.

Deep and surface learning: Think about your learning in a school or college context and decide which approach you were taking to a particular task. Whichever category you place yourself in on that occasion try to consider the reasons why you operated in that way. For example: deep learning – 'I found the topic intriguing and wanted to know more'; surface learning: 'I had to get the assignment done by the next day'.

Learning style: If you have not already completed the learning style inventory in this chapter consider an investigation of your own learning style. Think about it and try to place yourself on the V–A–K (Visual – Auditory – Kinaesthetic) spectrum. It is unlikely that you will be wholly within one classification or the other. Most of us have mixtures of preferred style. When you have done this you might like to compare your intuitions with the result of a more formal investigation. Either use the inventory included here or search out a more detailed version via the internet. You will also be able to find out more about styles in general and your own preferred style in particular.

Setting: Think about where you do most of your studying. List the five most important features of the setting. List five features of a work environment that would definitely not suit you. Go through each aspect of your work surroundings and timing, and consider whether this really does suit your needs. If you think that something about your setting is not suitable make plans for changes and try them out next time you work.

2 Reading for Academic Purposes

LEARNING OUTCOMES

What this chapter has in store:

- A consideration of the central role of reading in your study
- The idea of 'active reading'
- The importance of what is known as 'clear thinking' whilst reading
- The description of different strategies for effective reading
- The idea that you should always challenge what you read
- The importance of keeping a record of what you read

Reading is likely to take up a vast proportion of the time you devote to your university work. This chapter will show you that there is more to reading than understanding the shapes of letters and the words which they build. There are few readers who could not improve the way that they read, especially in relation to studying – reading for pleasure is in many ways quite different. This chapter will introduce you to some of the approaches which have been used by successful student readers, with different preferences and learning styles, and you may well discover a way to improve the way that you approach your reading.

Active reading

Reading will be a crucial element of your study in higher education. In previous study your reading may well have been directed and supported by teachers and tutors, and this may continue to be the case for you now, initially at least, but there is a much greater expectation and requirement, if you are to be successful, to read more independently and more widely than you may have previously. Some say that there is an art to reading effectively at tertiary level. Isaac Disraeli, the literary father of prime minister Benjamin, pointed out that reading effectively is a skill to be developed much as learning to think and to write effectively, he wrote, *'There is an art of reading, as well as an art of thinking, and an art of writing.'* (Disraeli, cited in *The Oxford Dictionary of Quotations*, 1981)

Often the ability to read, that is, to decode the text on a page into understandable language, is taken as being all that needs to be accomplished. Decoding is one element of the process (for you this will now be totally automatic and unconscious), but understanding what you have decoded, and being able to do this in a highly effective manner, is a crucial element of the complete skill of reading, especially in advanced educational settings. Young children are often able to read convincingly and fluently to their teacher, but when questioned concerning the content of what they have read their lack of comprehension becomes obvious. As we saw in the previous chapter, understanding is at the heart of what you have chosen to be involved in, and the ability to make sense of what you read is the foundation of understanding. For some of us this comes easily, but for others time and effort need to be taken and approaches to help with reading need to be considered and developed.

While your reading techniques may have been adequate in the past, tertiary level study often requires a new and better approach if you are to cope efficiently with the quantity of reading material with which you will be presented. Many students mistakenly believe that reading faster will improve their ability to study and achieve their deadlines. Speed reading by itself will not be sufficient for effective study. What is required is effective reading. You will be more likely to achieve this if you take an active approach to reading and do more than simply acknowledge the words on the page. Reading actively involves the use of a range of strategies, the first of which is clear thinking.

Clear thinking

Before looking in detail at what makes reading effective, we will consider what is sometimes thought of as a prerequisite to reading. That is, thinking clearly about what it is that you are going to read, and then, what you are reading. The ideas set out in this section are based on the work of Alexander (1999). The work is not widely published and forms a small part of the documentation relating to an Open University module.

The ability to think clearly lies at the heart of making sense of what can be confusing and contradictory information in complex academic texts. Clear thinking is a technique which helps the reader of a text to be able to see patterns and structures in what is read. It is one of the skills of higher level study that you need to develop if you are to be successful.

The more sources that you refer to in your reading for any investigation that you are undertaking in your study, the more likely you are to come across contradictory views. Dealing with these views will form an important part of your work. You need to be able to distinguish between information which you can rely upon as being accurate and reputable, and information which is possibly dubious in some way or another. You will have to extract the key ideas from what can be unstructured materials and you will have to arrive at a position where you have an understanding of the topic and of the points presented. On this matter, to which we will return in Chapter 5, the use of material from online encyclopaedias with no real academic pedigree is not a good idea. Even sites such as Wikipedia, which is widely recognised as a good starting point, should not be used as an authoritative source. The content is contributed by users themselves and the authority of any particular user is not always clear. The information is also open to amendment by others.

The importance of context

The most fundamental principle of clear thinking is always to keep ideas in context. Suppose, for example, that you find some contradictory information from two sources. Can you find out, or deduce, something about the respective writers?

- What are their particular perspectives?
- What are they trying to accomplish by publishing the material?
- What are they basing their views upon?

The perspective of the author is an important part of the context of the ideas you are reading. In some cases it might be relatively straightforward to pick up on the author's particular standpoint; it may be made clear in the text, or the author might be acknowledged as a member of a political party, or religious group; the writer may be a journalist who works for a well-known publication which takes a well-known view of the topics under discussion. In other cases the process is not so simple. At times like this you might be well advised to undertake a little further investigation; this can be carried out fairly quickly, in most cases by making use of the internet.

By considering what the writer is attempting to accomplish by the publication of the work in question you will gain more insight into the work itself. For example, is the article a well-balanced consideration of the topic, or does it give what many would consider a one-sided perspective, in which case the purpose of the writer might be to propagate the view in question and diminish any views which might be considered to be contrary. Most reputable writers will make their purpose clear, and state in an introduction or preamble that they are writing to put forward a set of views based upon a particular philosophy or standpoint. Others may be providing the findings of research into a phenomenon and the research may have been carried out in such a way as to ensure its lack of any sort of bias. In cases like this the reader should consider the conduct of the research and make decisions about its approach and whether or not it achieves what it set out to achieve. Writing can be persuasive and biased in very subtle ways and the skill of a clear thinking reader is to detect this at an early stage.

We have considered that writing might be based upon research, and if this is reported fairly and honestly there will be few problems with it. Other writing may be based upon a range of other 'sources'. We have to be aware of unreliable evidence. If writing is reporting facts we have to be certain that the facts are what they seem. It is not unheard of for opinion to be presented as fact.

Facts and values

Facts can be described as ideas which are universally true. A dictionary would give a definition along these lines. (For example, www.dictionary.com 'fact' definition one: something that actually exists; reality; truth.) Everyone has their own perspective and their own view of the world, and we each have our own construction of reality. Since we all live in the same world, and experience many of the same ideas, objects, people and events, and since we have shared languages and cultures there is inevitably a good deal of overlap in these views, a good deal of agreement and shared reality.

At one end of the spectrum some ideas are virtually universally agreed, for example, that we are not able to walk on water, fly under our own steam to the moon, and the planet Earth is not flat. This almost complete agreement is as close as we can get to the notion of an 'absolute fact'. Often, we are happy to go along with a general agreement between people who have thought a lot about something or who are generally considered to know a lot about the subject in question – an expert in the field. When we treat something as a 'fact' it means that we consider it to be universally agreed, but even then it is important not to be rigid in our thinking and to recognise that there is a possibility that there is someone who might want to challenge it.

At the other end of the spectrum, it is clear that some ideas are the views of one individual, based upon their experiences, feelings and perceptions. For now we can discount the views of the mentally ill, although in a wider, more philosophical, discussion it might be of interest to consider the views of those held to be unbalanced in some way, as their views are also based on their feelings and experiences. Somewhere in the middle of all of this are views shared widely within a group, but contradicted by the shared views of other groups. These include what are generally called 'values'. An important part of the context of some material you will look at must be not just the views of its authors but how widely those views are shared and by whom.

Observations and theories

Another approach to clear thinking is to consider the principles behind what is generally considered as the 'scientific' approach. A scientific approach does not explain everything and it need not be applied only to questions of science. It too applies only in some particular contexts. The chief value of a scientific approach is that it will lead to the description of an area of understanding which is relatively reliable, in part because it has been developed in a measured and systematic way, and usually because it has been tested on subsequent occasions.

Essentially, the scientific approach to establishing truths combines two different types of knowledge:

1. Observations, direct or indirect, which are experienced by someone.
2. Theories or explanations which link those observations.

The value of a theory is that you can use it to make predictions. You can predict that other observations will fit the same patterns. Of course any theory has its limits. We need to be clear about just where a theory applies.

The test of an observation is how accurate, complete and reliable it is. We need to know how carefully the observation was made. Often, the observations we are hoping to trust are not our own. They may be reported to us by someone else, or may be in something we have read. There may be a chain of reports before the observation reaches us. At each stage of reporting there is the possibility that the story has been changed, that an observation may be replaced by theory, or that crucial aspects have been cut out. The test of a theory is how well it explains the observations it is linking.

We have already pointed out that a scientific approach need not be limited to scientific experiments. The basic principles apply to everyday experiences as well, and can help clarify our understanding of them.

You may meet a person on several occasions, and consider them to be bombastic or even rude. Your conclusion concerning the nature of the person might be that they are unpleasant or arrogant; you will have developed a theory based on your observations. However, there could well be other explanations for the behaviour that you have observed. For a number of different reasons the observed behaviour could be out of character. There is a definite difference between observations and theories developed from them and it is helpful to bear this in mind in your study.

When is one theory 'better' than another?

We know that it is possible for a number of theories to exist which purport to describe the same phenomenon. A particular theory takes precedence over another when it explains more fully, and makes more connections between, the observations that it is based upon.

An example of this could be the apparent conflict between Newton's Laws and Einstein's work on relativity; in reality both theories have relevance in different contexts. New theories often evolve alongside older theories, and the two can coexist for some time. Eventually the newer theory is able to explain more and more of the observations that it is based on and this theory takes the lead and becomes the accepted wisdom. The older theory may well still have validity in some circumstances, but this will not stop it from being eclipsed by its new rival.

The test of a theory is how accurately it can connect a collection of observations, and in how wide a range of situations it is applicable. Many theories can never be considered as fixed and true. The best that can be hoped for is that it will be the most acceptable in the views of those who have been able to investigate and consider in detail the phenomenon in question. There is only a very limited sense in which most theories can be considered as the final answer.

In your reading there will certainly be contradictory and incomplete information. Alexander (1999) suggests it may help you, in your attempts to make sense of and summarise what you find, if you:

1. Try to separate observations from the theories and explanations about them.
2. Consider how likely they are to have been observed accurately and connected coherently. (Are they reporting events and observations, or theories about them?)
3. Look for the perspective of whoever is making a statement. (Are there any values they might have which affect what they are saying?)

Strategies for effective reading

As we saw at the start of this chapter, reading will be an integral part of your study and it is important to become as effective a reader as possible. To be effective, you have to read with a purpose, with a plan and with concentration.

Effective readers are organised; they do not just look at words, they search for their meaning. They assimilate what is being read with what they already know; they are active readers who remember and draw conclusions from the material as it is being read. If you are reading in an area new to you, it is important that you first form some framework of what the material is about in your mind. This is done by surveying the text in advance of getting down to reading it in detail and is sometimes known as pre-reading. This can be seen as activating schemas (see Chapter 1).

Pre-reading

Pre-reading is a useful technique for two main reasons. First, when you pre-read you gain an overview of the content and tone of what it is you have read. This allows you to make a judgement about whether or not to proceed to the next stage of reading in more detail. It may well be that, having gained an overview, you decide that further reading is not necessary. You may want to leave it completely, or you may want to come back to it at a later time. Secondly, by pre-reading you begin to activate your prior knowledge and prepare yourself, unconsciously in most cases, for the acceptance of new information. In a sense you are preparing the ground for the sowing of new seeds.

To pre-read a whole book it can be helpful to seek answers to some simple questions:

- Look at the contents page – does it seem to contain useful material?
- Read the introduction or preface – what is the author's purpose? How is the text structured?
- Glance at the chapters – are summaries included? What do the first and last paragraphs tell you about the chapter?
- Survey the index – are there relevant words listed? What topics are given most coverage?

To pre-read a chapter:

- Skim through and examine headings and sub-headings.
- Look at any illustrations.
- Read the summary at the end if there is one.
- Read the introductory and concluding paragraphs.

Find the topic sentence

An awareness of paragraph structure can help you to identify the main point in a paragraph from the detail or supporting evidence. As a general rule we can say that a paragraph contains one main point; there will, of course, be exceptions to this rule. Generally, if you are reading a text which has no subheadings, you can survey this by reading only the first and last sentence in each paragraph. Either one of these is usually the topic sentence. Topic sentences introduce or sum up the main point which is expanded in the paragraph.

[Note: The topic sentence of the paragraph above comes at the end.]

Look for key words and key phrases – skim-reading

The skill here is to concentrate on vital words or phrases, without which the meaning would be lost, glossing over or ignoring the less important words or phrases. Important statements or definitions are often put into italics or bold. Sentences or phrases which are ordered with numbers or letters should be considered. When sentences begin with 'first', 'secondly', 'finally' they give cues to important sub-points in the text. When skimming it is helpful to give attention to charts, diagrams and maps; an author often uses them to present important ideas visually.

Reading for different purposes

You will be reading for three different purposes at university:

- To gather material that must be understood and recalled in detail.
- To understand and evaluate the author's purpose in writing and the supportive arguments or evidence presented.
- Background reading.

Pre-reading and finding the topic sentence may be all that is required for background reading. For material that needs to be understood and recalled in detail, you may need to develop a more systematic approach. There are a number of reading systems which could serve this purpose. Which particular approach to detailed reading you eventually choose to follow will be a matter of personal choice and will be dependent upon several factors, including your particular learning preferences (see Chapter 1). Here we will look at a selection of different systematic approaches and it will be for you to work with one or more of them and then, importantly, develop your own approach, or even set of approaches, based upon your preferences and your particular reading need at any given time.

Many competent readers make use of the types of approach set out here. They do it instinctively and in more or less detail according to their particular purpose. It is the actions of competent, accomplished readers which form the basis of the different models being considered here.

SQ3R and SQ4R

The first system that we will consider is called the SQ3R method. The derivation of its name will become clear as you read on. There are five stages to pass through, each one dependent on the stage preceding it. The description of SQ3R below assumes that we are dealing with a chapter in a book, but the system can be applied in any reading context.

1. **Survey:** Glance over the headings in the chapter and read the final paragraph. Look for a central theme. Try to identify some core ideas. Find words highlighted or italicised by the author, read any definitions in boxes or in the margins, read any key sentences which are highlighted in any way and read the chapter summary or synopsis if there is one – this will be either at the beginning or the end of the chapter.
2. **Question:** Go back to the beginning of the chapter and turn the first heading into a question. This will arouse your curiosity, increase your comprehension, bring to mind information already known and help you to understand the section more quickly. For example: 'Difficulties which arise when using the internet' could become 'What are the difficulties which arise when using the internet?', and 'The evolution of number theory' might become 'How did number theory evolve?' or even 'Describe the evolution of number theory'.

3. **R**ead: To find the answer to your question, read to the end of the first section. Here you are looking for material to clarify arguments and assumptions, to evaluate them and to answer your own questions. Your reading is an active search for answers. When you have read, or perhaps read more than once, the section in question you should be able to formulate an answer to the question which you posed yourself.

4. **R**ecite/**R**ecall: Look away from your text now and attempt to recall the answer to your question. Use your own words and give an example. If you are able to do this then you have taken in the content of the section. If not, then glance over the section again. A good way to do this is to write down short key phrases as notes on a piece of paper. These can then form the basis of the notes that you might choose to make at a later stage.

5. **R**eview: Look over all your notes to get a summary of all the points and their relationships with each other. Check that your recall was correct and check your memory by repeating the main points under each of the headings from the chapter.

Using the five steps of the SQ3R method is likely to result in faster reading, highlighting of important points and assisting in the process of installing them in your memory. It is an example of engagement (see Chapter 1). Another benefit from this method is that exam questions will seem familiar because the headings you turn into questions are often those set in tests.

This approach stresses engagement and activity, which, as we know from Chapter 1, are crucial elements in the process of developing understanding. Engagement and activity are features of all of the reading strategies suggested here.

SQ4R is a minor variant of SQ3R. The variation has the potential to be important for some readers. The fourth R refers to w**R**ite, or **R**ecord. Yet another version of SQ4R includes **R**elate as a stage in the process. In view of what Chapter 1 says concerning constructivist learning and the importance of activating prior knowledge and the notion that all new knowledge and understanding are built upon what the learner has already learned, the stage of actively relating new information to other already acquired knowledge or understanding is important. Quite how important, or how explicit to make this stage will depend upon the individual learner.

Muscle reading

This system comes from the United States. It is based on SQ3R and it specifies more text highlighting or more note-taking. There are nine stages involved, in three phases, and it is suggested that the system is easier to remember if three short sentences are held in the memory. They are:

- Pry out questions.
- Root up answers.
- Recite, review and review again.

Phase One: Pry out questions *Preview:* Read the headings and the summary, if there is one, and look at illustrations and graphics – diagrams, charts, pictures.

Outline: Read the chapter outline if there is one; if not, create an outline using the headings and subheadings in the text. This outline can be written in a notebook or on an index card and kept in the book.

Question: Write down a set of questions that you think the chapter will provide answers for, the headings in the chapter could be used to generate these questions.

Phase two: Root up answers *Read:* Read to find the answers to your questions. Do not read for too long at a time. Focus your attention by visualising the concepts mentally or by drawing pictures or symbols to help you to understand the text. Some people favour reading out loud as a way of helping to make sense of what is being read.

Underline: When you have finished a section, go back and add notes in the margin or highlight major points, although library books should not be treated in this way. Sometimes it is worth photocopying sections of library books for this purpose.

Answer: As you read through the section and come to the answers for your questions, write them down.

Phase Three: Recite, review and review again *Recite:* Talk to yourself, aloud or silently, about what you have just read. Many people find that putting new information into their own words is helpful in coming to internalise and understand new material.

Review: When newly encountered ideas are reviewed within twenty-four hours of reading the material there is an increase in the amount retained. To do this, read through your marginal text markings or your notes.

Review again: This one is difficult to sustain, but if you can review your notes weekly or monthly there is pronounced learning benefit.

PREP

PREP is made up of three main steps:

1. **P**review
2. **RE**ad to understand
3. **P**rocess to learn

Step 1: Preview   This is the preparation stage, in which the reader is encouraged to look through the text and 'see the lie of the land'. Questions which should be asked at this stage include:

- Does this look interesting?
- Is it suitable for my purpose?
- Which section seems most promising?

Step 2: Read to understand   Whilst reading, certain questions, relating to the detail or ideas that you want to be made clear for you, should be asked; the questions that you pose will be related to your purpose for reading (see 'Reading for Different Purposes' earlier in this chapter). You will also use suitable techniques for helping you to engage with the text. For example:

- Underline or highlight important words, sentences or passages.
- Write marginal notes.
  (These points are only suitable where marking is allowable, i.e. the book in question is not a library book. For some library books it might be a good idea to photocopy important sections which can then be marked or highlighted as necessary.)
- Keep a brief record of the most important points from the text in note form. (This might be more detailed if you are using a library book.)

Step 3: Process to learn   In this final stage more activity is called for, leading to more engagement with the information and ideas in the text. Activities can include:

- Writing a short summary.
- Creating visual study tools – diagrammatic representation of the ideas and information.
- Creating mnemonics or simple and memorable rhymes.
- Reciting the main points of your notes.

This model does not include the idea of discussing with others, or exchanging thoughts about a text which has been read by more than one member of a group, but it would be a sound, socially constructive, approach to take. Tutors often build this into seminar sessions, when some advanced reading has been set. In other cases students meet, either formally or informally, to discuss what has been read.

S-RUN

The principles of this system are very close to those underpinning the preceding systems. The difference is in its brevity. In many ways S-RUN can be seen as a précis of what has gone before, and for some it will be refreshingly manageable.

The four stages of this system are:

- **S**urvey: Survey the chapter, read and consider the title and the introduction, as well as all of the headings, charts, graphs and diagrams.
- **R**ead: Read the chapter.
- **U**nderline: For each section, underline material that explains the section's heading(s).
- **N**ote-take: Write brief notes on the material. Write a summary of the main points of the chapter.

Reading for assignments

It can be helpful to develop a systematic approach to your reading for assignments. One such approach could be:

- Select a book or an article from the reading list that gives an overview of the topic.
- Decide what you need to find out. Write down some questions to focus your reading.
- Check authors, publication date, contents and index pages to determine if the material is relevant to your needs.
- Record details of author, title, place of publication, publisher and date now so that you will not have the trouble of trying to find the material again when compiling a list of references.
- Skim-read relevant sections and compare them with other material before taking notes. Record page number with any notes you take.

Avoid overuse of highlighters when reading photocopied material or your own textbook. Brief notes will be much more useful. These can be written in the margin of photocopied material or your textbook.

Finally, remember to read with a purpose and vary your reading rate to suit the complexity of the material. As an advanced student you should be examining the ideas and arguments critically as you read. The development of your ability to be critical in your assessment of the accepted body of knowledge in a discipline is a skill you will be encouraged to develop throughout your university education, and one which forms a part of the armoury of graduate skills which you will acquire through successful university study. Consider how arguments are constructed and presented. This is something you will be aiming to achieve in your own writing. We will return to this later.

Smart reading

All of what has gone before in this chapter is designed to lead towards helping you to develop the skills and approaches of what, in modern parlance, has come to be known as being a 'smart reader'. Smart reading is about being focused and about asking questions of the text *as it is read*. Smart reading pays attention to making good use of contents pages, introductory and concluding sections and indexes. These are the parts of texts where an overall sense of what a particular piece/book covers can be gained in return for a minimum amount of time and effort. Once a sense of the content, approach and quality of material provided by a particular source has been achieved by browsing the different sections and locations, anything which is not wholly appropriate can be passed over and it is then possible for you to devote more of your precious time to the material which is most pertinent to the purpose of the reading. As a smart reader you will have a clear picture in your mind of what it is you are reading for. You will have considered the question, or the task, and 'unpacked' the detail. You will have a definite view of what it is that you need from your reading and you will be able to keep well focused by making use of the techniques above in one measure or another, in a range of different combinations and in a way that you will have tailored for yourself.

One additional point which some of the literature concerning smart reading stresses, but is not explicitly made in the sections above, is that reading a piece more than once is very likely to be necessary. The expectation with academic reading, as opposed to the reading of fiction or other leisure reading, should not be to be able to digest every subtle nuance of the text in one reading. It is not unusual for the text to appear complex and impenetrable on first reading. Sometimes the reason for this is the nature of the writing; some authors can be over-complicated in their style and write in over-elaborate ways. (This is also something that we will look at later when we consider your own writing.) Sometimes the reason is that the text concerns complex concepts and arguments that cannot and should not be reduced to simple bite-sized pieces. Your task as an academic reader is to understand what you are reading and this is quite likely to involve making use of the techniques described here. It will also frequently lead you to return to read passages, or even whole chapters or articles, more than once. This is a perfectly normal and appropriate approach to take.

Making a record of your reading

In all of the above strategies for reading there is a place for recording or note-taking. This can be a very personal, even an idiosyncratic, activity and we will consider this in detail in a later chapter. At this stage, however, it is worth mentioning the idea that you should keep a clear record of what you have read. This does not refer to keeping a record of the ideas and information from your reading, but to keeping bibliographic details of the texts in question. Providing accurate references in your written work, as we will see later, is very important, and when you come to finish a piece of work and find that you do not have a record of where the specific quotes come from, or the title and year and place of publication of a particular book, you will find it difficult, frustrating and extremely time-consuming to attempt to re-trace your steps and find the essential missing details (See Chapter 6 to find out what details you will need to record.)

In the past the advice given in this situation, especially for extended work such as dissertations, was to keep a card index box with a record card for each book, chapter, article. The card could also include short comments or reminders concerning the text in question. This rudimentary, paper-based, database worked well for generations of students and academics, but now there are technology-enhanced versions of the card index file which serve as excellent tools for keeping and managing references.

Bibliographic software

The aim of bibliographic software is to allow you to input, store, organise, retrieve and format lists of references in a simple and straightforward way. A database of references is created which can then be saved, searched and used alongside word processors. Within the word processor it is possible to import and format references as an assignment is written. Good quality bibliographic software allows the reference list to be formatted in a number of different styles to match the requirements of tutors, departments or even publishers.

Universities invariably support one of the well-known programs for dealing with references and bibliographies. You should investigate what is available for you at your institution. Bibliographic software, such as EndNote, Procite, or RefWorks, is capable of more than keeping and manipulating records of references. Many students, academics and other writers make extensive use of both the basic and the more advanced features of the systems to assist in their writing and accurate referencing.

Challenge what you read

As a student you may find that you underestimate your ability to challenge or question what has been written by published authors. The process of unconscious thought you will rehearse centres on the notion that you are simply a novice student and the writer is an established academic, or similar expert. There are many reasons, however, why what appears in print, even in reputable locations, can and should be challenged. Here are some of the reasons.

- The author's expertise: in spite of having a range of qualifications and experience in a particular area of expertise, it is simply not possible for a writer to know absolutely everything about complex fields of study.
- Time and place: what you are reading could be out of date. Books and academic articles may well have been written some time ago, and knowledge and ideas change over time, rapidly in some cases. It is very important to be aware of the date of publication of what you are reading. It might also be the case that the precise context of what you are reading is different to the situation that you are considering – facets of systems in another country for example.

- Knowledge: the nature of knowledge is such that demonstrating something to be correct and true is not always possible. Through a process of scientific enquiry, taken in its broadest sense, it is only possible to disprove something. For that reason some philosophers and academics consider that knowledge is at best only tentative, and always open to change and contradiction.

In your reading you should also pay attention to particular, potentially problematic, approaches or use of language, for example:

- Ambiguity: if something is not clear or is in some way ambiguous, pay more attention to it. See if you have initially not understood what is written, but can tease the meaning out. If it really is unclear or ambiguous, then it needs challenging.
- Inconsistency: if you detect flaws in the presentation of an argument, do not accept it.
- Unintelligent use of language: vacuous expressions, which are woolly and open to misinterpretation, should be cause for alarm in academic writing. Writing should be clear and thorough. Some words work against this. Words like nice, good, bad, few, many, are not precise and therefore not helpful for the reader. Words of this type can be interpreted differently by different readers. Where they are used they should be defined, or quantified in some way, for example: 'By few, we mean fewer than 25% of the sample.'
- Generalisation: in much research it is not possible to investigate every case of a phenomenon and so moving from a specific case to a general case is a valid activity. But only when it is firmly justified. Treat all generalisations as suspicious until you are convinced otherwise.
- Economy with the use of evidence: evidence can be presented in a variety of impressive ways which sometimes persuade the reader that it is fair and balanced when in reality it is not complete and has been presented in such a way that the full picture is obscured. Sometimes it is helpful to consider what has been omitted. (In a different context this was once famously referred to as 'being economical with the truth'. (Sir Robert Armstrong, a 20th century civil servant, paraphrasing Edmund Burke, an 18th century Irish politician.)
- Consensus: phrases such as 'we all know that' should give cause for concern. It is possible that the writer does not have evidence to support a particular claim and instead is appealing to the reader to agree with the point without having substantiated it with evidence.
- Authority: just because an expert supports some view does not mean that it is correct. Even experts must have good evidence.
- Common sense: one person's common sense is not necessarily the same as another person's. It is a mistake to assume that common sense is a universal phenomenon, applying to everyone equally. If a writer tells you that it is 'common sense' to accept a particular point, challenge it.

Final thoughts

All of the techniques and models set out in this chapter are used in one way or another, in a variety of combinations, by readers of what are sometimes very complex texts. Often they are used instinctively by readers and have been developed in response to their reading needs. In other cases they have developed as a result of teaching, or reading on the subject of study, and in almost all cases they have become a personal, modified version of what is presented here. You will see that all of the models presented have similarities and areas of overlap. All of the separate techniques here are used in some measure by accomplished readers to acquire information; accomplished readers will also have a wide range of other reading techniques not included here. There is no one correct way to read, but developing an appropriate and accomplished technique should mean that increased knowledge, understanding and retention will be the outcomes of your academic reading.

SUMMARY

- Reading will form an important element of your higher level study.
- Your reading might be in need of a review of techniques.
- There are a range of techniques available to help in the process of gaining new information and understanding from reading.
- Be systematic and logical in your approach to reading and recording the important elements of what you read.
- Keep detailed bibliographic notes, including title, author(s), publisher, date of publication and page numbers for specific quotes.
- Challenge what you read.

Next

The stage of your work following on from, or often taking place at the same time as, reading will be making a record of what you have read. This should be a far more sophisticated process than copying sentences or even paragraphs from your reading to your note book. The way that you choose to record your reading and the important ideas and explanations that you need to internalise, can make a big impact on the progress that you make, especially when the time to prepare for assessment arrives.

Activities

Topic sentences: Look at a selection of paragraphs taken randomly from different sources. Identify the topic sentence for each of them.

Pre-reading: Choose an article associated with your subject, or your next assignment, and pre-read it. Remember this does not mean read it word for word. It should take you between five and ten minutes and when you have finished you should have an idea of the content and the main points/arguments. Look back at the pre-reading checklist before you start if you need to.

Reading: Read a short text related to an area of your study, look for evidence of the points considered in this chapter and write a few short phrases or sentences describing them.

Think about:

- the perspective of the author
- the presentation of facts, values and theories
- the sources relied upon in the presentation of ideas.

Look out for:

- ambiguity
- inconsistency
- unintelligent use of language
- generalisation
- economy with evidence
- the authority of the writer
- appeals to common sense or consensus.

3 Note-taking and Recording for Learning

LEARNING OUTCOMES

What this chapter has in store:

- Some thoughts about the reasons for taking and keeping a record of your lectures and your reading.
- A look at the many different approaches to record keeping taken by different learners.
- Examples of a range of note-taking strategies, including graphic organisers.
- Thoughts about the use of technology for record-keeping.

Good note taking is a form of critical reflection on an argument the author is trying to set out. Poor note taking is an arbitrary selection of some of the things an author has said. Taking brief notes means you have to think about the material you are trying to understand. Good notes should be a result of thinking and analysis. They should be in your own words, and they should be brief. (University of Warwick, 2006, History Department Undergraduate Handbook)

In all likelihood you will spend a good deal of time reading and making a record of what it is that you have read. This could be why 'reading' a subject at university is the standard formal way of saying what it is that you are studying. As you will be spending a fair proportion of your time on this recording activity, and given that you want to make the best use of your time, it is important to know that you are in fact being efficient. If you are satisfied with your current approach, then all is well and good, but it still might be to your advantage to leaf through the pages of this chapter and see what it is that other effective readers and note-takers do.

We have considered some aspects of reading for academic purposes in Chapter 2. Now we can put together some of the points covered earlier with some techniques for recording notes from reading, lectures or other sources. First we will consider the reasons why keeping a record of your work in one form or another is important. We will also consider, again, that there is not one single best approach to recording and the precise approach taken by individuals is a matter of personal choice. This choice is most often best made from a position of knowledge. Knowledge of, first, preferred learning style (see Chapter 1), and secondly, a knowledge of the different approaches that have been found effective by others undertaking the same type of academic study. There is also a point to be made about setting and fitness for purpose. One method of recording that may serve well in one setting – such as sitting alone in private – may not work so well in a library work area, seminar room or lecture theatre.

Let us first picture a novice student faced with a reading and note-taking situation. This is the first occasion in a new setting where reading in preparation for a forthcoming seminar has been required and the student is keen to do the job well and arrive on the day with the reading completed, ready to follow the seminar and to contribute if necessary. The reading is of an article from an academic journal, it is complex, in that it contains difficult new ideas in a new area within the subject, and it is written in a formal tone almost to the point of being 'un-user-friendly', especially as this is the first time that this style has been encountered. This reading task is of a quite different nature to any faced before. In the past, reading for study has always been set by a teacher who has given guidance about which points to pay attention to and particular questions have usually been set. Much previous reading has been from textbooks which have been written in a very different style to that found in academic settings. What approach is taken?

Instinct tells the student to read and take notes, and that is all. So, he or she reads and writes furiously for two hours or more and at the end of this time the article has been read, every word, and almost every word has been re-written on the student's note pad. The apparent note-taking has taken the form of copying out huge chunks of the text. The end result is that the article has been read and writing based upon the reading has taken place, but the notes are simply a slightly reduced version of the main text and would serve very little purpose in the future. Also, there is a strong likelihood that much of the content of the piece will have been lost to the hapless reader. This is because no real engagement with the text has taken place. There was no thought about which ideas were of most importance, no decisions about which points to make a note of and no real mental processing of the information. The exercise amounted to a process of copying, which some people seem to be able to undertake without registering the all-important content of the text being copied. With this in mind, and taking into account what has been said about engagement, individual differences and considering different idiosyncrasies, it might be that for some individuals this approach to academic reading would prove to be successful, but in the great majority of cases it would not.

The purpose of record-making

These are several reasons for making a record of your reading or other sources of information.

1. It is a record of your reading:

   - gives a record of important ideas for future use
   - gives a record of where information is located

2. It helps in the process of writing:

   - helps with the flow of ideas
   - helps in planning, you can see what you have got
   - helps in organisation – reorganising notes, order etc.
   - helps in getting started

3. It can be important for understanding:

   - a good example of engagement: process of thinking and prioritising (what to note)

4. It helps in remembering:

   - writing a shortened version involves thinking (engagement), helps in transferring ideas etc. to long term memory (see Figure 1.2, Chapter 1)
   - notes taken diagrammatically or pictorially can benefit from use of visual memory (visual learners)
   - useful when revision time arrives
   - short version of well-organised material ready to re-read and engage with

Making, keeping and referring to well-organised notes is an important element of the learning process. If you do not take notes you must consider how you will replace this part of your learning experience. For almost all people, not taking notes of some type and being satisfied with either 'just reading', or 'listening very carefully' does not work.

Some ideas and principles

Whatever the situation in which note-taking is undertaken, there are some sound principles that can lead to the effective recording of the information and ideas in question, and lead to the successful achievement of some or all of the purposes of note-taking set out above. Some ideas seem to be a reflection of common sense, others will seem unsuitable or even unmanageable in your particular situation, but they are all tried and tested and relied upon by many students in many different situations.

- Be methodical: date your notes, number each page, have a clear title.
- Think before you begin: decide on your focus and what it is that you want to learn from your reading.
- Keep your notes brief: certainly do not copy out large chunks of text; paraphrase and write in your own words.
- Write phrases as opposed to whole sentences.
- Do not write out too much from a source: notes should be a much shortened and refined version of the original.
- Make use of headings and sub-headings.
- Number points: 1, 2, 3, ... or a, b, c, ...
- Highlight key words or ideas in some obvious way: capitals, underlining, use of colour, highlighter pen.
- Make connections between points in different places on the page: use arrows or lines.
- Be absolutely clear about the sources: keep a full bibliographic note of the source and, if it is different, where you accessed it.
- Be absolutely clear when writing direct quotations: use a different colour for example and note the page number from the original.
- Use icons or symbols to indicate particular items in your notes: a quick sketch of a book to indicate the title of recommended book, or a reference to follow up; a bold or stylised question mark to indicate a point of confusion or a question that needs to be followed up.
- Use abbreviations: especially for words related to your subject area which you will use repeatedly.
- Try to be neat in your note-taking: if you are to make use of your notes at some future point you do not want to be attempting to decode hieroglyphic-like scrawls or to unpick the meaning of a scramble of words squashed together in a corner of the page.
- Store notes logically and safely: notes are only useful to the extent that they assist in your learning and are available for easy consultation at a later date (times of revision, for example). Number, label and even date the files or boxes where your notes are kept.

Linear versus non-linear

According to your preferences, you may feel most at ease with writing notes in a strict sequence which matches the order in which the ideas and information are presented in what you are reading. The alternative is a non-linear approach, which can be undertaken in a variety of diagrammatic ways. The definition of non-linear, according to where it is looked up, can be as simple as 'not in a straight line', but more interestingly it can include and refer to the word 'chaotic'. Certainly it is not good for your note-taking practice to aim at an end product that is chaotic – it is possible that this strikes a chord with you! – but for many learners, at all levels, a diagram of some type is the preferred method of noting the important points from a text, or even a lecture.

The human brain works associatively as well as linearly – comparing, integrating and synthesising as it goes. Association plays a dominant role in nearly every mental function, and words themselves are no exception. Every single word and idea has numerous links attaching it to other ideas and concepts. (See 'Schemas' in Chapter 1.) This advanced version of non-linearity may well be mimicked in the style of note-taking preferred by some, and there is no reason why it should not, as long as the principles above still apply, especially the notion of easy access.

There was a time when the use of formal shorthand, Pitman script or something similar, was widely taught and used in business settings. Some academics and students would learn to use this style of rapid recording as a means of keeping notes. With the advent of word processing technology the use of shorthand seems to be dying out, and it is not often seen at all in offices or in academic settings today. It is possible that learning the basics of this style of writing might be of use to some students and perhaps it should not be ruled out simply because it has gone out of fashion elsewhere.

KEY PRINCIPLES

Associative/association: the human brain works in an associative way. Ideas are associated with each other when there is a link of some sort. The link is often to do with meaning but there can be any number of different ways that ideas are linked, including memory, timing, likes and dislikes.

Graphic organiser: any of a range of different diagrammatic approaches to recording information.

Concept map: a specific type of graphic organiser in which ideas are linked pictorially according to meaning. Introduced by Novak and Gowin (1984).

Diagrammatic approaches – graphic organisers

There are some formally recognised visual and diagrammatic, or quasi-diagrammatic methods which can be used to establish a framework of understanding relating to reading or the content of a lecture. As a family these visual tools are referred to as graphic organisers.

Graphic organisers are a pictorial or diagrammatic way of representing and organising information and are often used as a means of recording what has been read. Graphic organisers help to convert and reduce a mass of information into a structured, easily accessible and easy to read display, often in a non-linear format. When finished, the end product conveys complex information in what can be an easy to understand format. For example, an academic article can be reduced to a set of important points (facts, ideas, arguments, references) which can be represented in a visual format on a single sheet of A4 paper.

The different approaches to a visual format for recording or planning have a variety of names. Some are referred to as maps, and this is a good analogy to use. Others include more of a hint concerning their make-up or purpose: concept map, for example, or semantic web. We will look at some of these titles and consider the layout of the variously described systems, but for an individual user there is no real need to follow sets of rules. For the individual the particular style of graphic representation must be something which suits the user and the purpose the end product must serve.

Developing understanding by creating graphic organisers

The process of converting information and ideas into a visual format is likely to provide opportunities for increasing understanding and insight into the central themes or topics in question. To create the map, attention must be paid to the relationships between the separate items included and links must be made between them in a logical and meaningful way. Choices are made as the map is constructed concerning the priority given to the information, in order to establish which aspects of the content are the most important and require greater emphasis. Positioning of items on the sheet should also be a consideration. There is no right or wrong way to construct any of the different styles of map. Decisions concerning structure and layout are always personal, based on choice and reflection. This is one of the reasons why working in this way can be beneficial to learning. The need to engage with the content of reading is paramount if a coherent and useful map is to be generated. It is this engagement, as we know, that is a crucial element of the process of learning.

Working with graphic organisers can also help with the generation of new ideas and links between ideas. Graphic organisers can be used to structure writing (planning an assignment for example), to help in problem-solving, decision-making, studying, planning, research and brainstorming. We will look again at the use of maps and organisers in the later chapter dealing with writing.

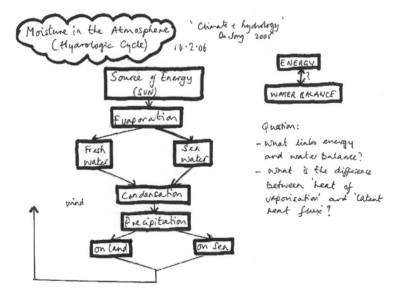

Figure 3.1   Example of a simple flow chart based on a short section from a book

Constructing a graphic organiser

There are different types of organisers and many have specific names, as we will see. For individual use, however, there is no need to adhere to a specific design. The process of creating a visual representation of information and ideas can, and should, remain a personal constructive activity. Graphic organisers can be drawn free-hand or one of many different software tools might be used. (See Appendix 2 for a short list of software titles and web addresses.) Adding colour as a means of coding and illustrating various links or similarities, or including symbols in a graphic organiser is a way of increasing the ease of use of the overall display.

Some examples of different approaches to graphic organising follow.

Flow diagram (see Figure 3.1)   Of the non-linear approaches under consideration here, the flow diagram is the most linear in nature, although there is great scope for creating links and loops to connect and relate ideas together. Flow diagrams are used in certain subject areas as a matter of course – computer science is an example – and some topics in many other subject areas lend themselves well to this approach. In the creation of formal flow diagrams there are certain conventions about the shape of particular boxes and their purpose, but for an individual

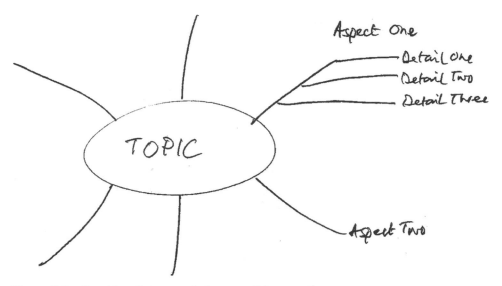

Figure 3.2   A spider diagram: six legs on this occasion

creating a model of the content of an article, for example, these rules need not be followed. The process, as with practically all of the ideas and suggestions included in this book, is completely open to individual interpretation. You are encouraged to develop a way of working which best serves your purpose and matches your preferences.

Spider diagram (see Figure 3.2)   A spider diagram is best suited to noting the different aspects of a single theme or topic. Precisely how the diagram is set out is a matter of choice, but often the layout can begin to resemble a spider's web. The process of building out of a passage of text, often a short passage, even as short as a single paragraph, is a means of focusing on the single topic and drawing out all of the main elements of the topic and noting them succinctly. It is often the case that a series of diagrams of this type might be used in a lecture, or in the reading of a longer text. Also, a spider diagram can be used to give a different representation of a particular point or item of focus on the topic within a set of notes made in a different way. This is, of course, true for any graphical approach.

Concept map/mind map (see Figure 3.3)   These two titles are not fully interchangeable, but the two approaches can be seen as similar in nature.

A concept map, first conceived by Novak and Gowin (1984), is a freely drawn diagrammatic representation of the related elements of a particular topic. Links are

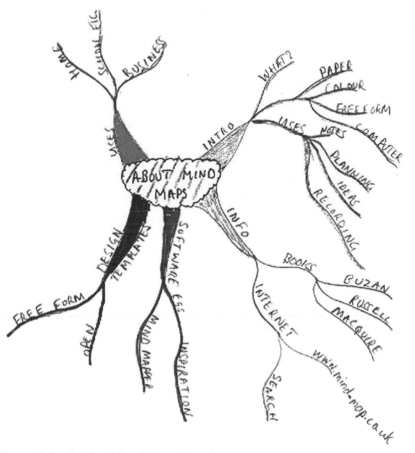

Figure 3.3   A Mind Map® based on the concept of mind mapping

drawn between separate items, which are conceived of as conceptual connections, that is, the line connecting any entries on the diagram represents a meaningful connection between them. In most cases the nature of the link is written on the line itself.

A mind map, originally devised and developed by Tony Buzan (see Buzan, 2002), has a slightly more formalised structure. Mind maps tend to allow for a topic to be explored as the map extends outwards. There are not usually links within and across the map and colour is used to highlight aspects of the map which may be grouped conceptually or are in other ways similar.

Mind maps and concept maps both typically feature key words or phrases. Both forms of mapping also allow for additional material to be added as a topic unfolds – either from texts, or from the spoken content of a lecture. Readers interested in the genesis and development of the two, very similar yet different approaches could consult the original sources, which are included in the list of references.

It is sometimes considered that mapping of the type described here is more suitable for creative, arts-based subjects. This is patently not the case. The use of mapping as a tool depends far more on the preferences, learning styles and general disposition of the person choosing to make the use than on any consideration of the topic of the map. There are many scientifically minded students, working on topics from across the whole spectrum of subject disciplines who find the use of mapping for planning and problem-solving extremely beneficial. Some even go as far as to say that they could not work without one.

Pattern effect   Pattern effect notes take on many of the points from the sections above dealing with graphical representations. Pattern notes are necessarily idiosyncratic and often reflect the personality of the creator in some small way or another. Certainly pattern notes cannot be prescribed; they are a combination of style, preference, motivation and a need to model what is being considered in a way other than by linear writing. Pattern notes will contain key words, key phrases, words in boxes of different shapes, lines and arrows, pictures and diagrams, perhaps a mini flow chart and a section which shows the conceptual links between sets of ideas. There will be dotted lines, solid lines of different thicknesses, underlining, capital letters for emphasis, words which are highlighted or coloured in some other way, and there may even be Post-it ® notes or similar which can be moved from place to place as the pattern evolves. There may well be sketches or iconic drawings to represent different ideas and there will be the use of personal shorthand.

In some respects it is not a sound idea to include an example here, as there is a danger of its being seen as a template, but the two, very different examples offered in Figures 3.4 and 3.5 may be helpful.

Converting linear notes to a non-linear format

As part of a reviewing process it is sometimes useful to go through notes taken and rework them into a diagrammatic form. This serves two purposes, though for some it is considered excessively time-consuming. First, as a result of the mental activity and engagement that this task will require, it serves to fix the ideas that you are dealing with more firmly into long term memory, and secondly it provides an alternative

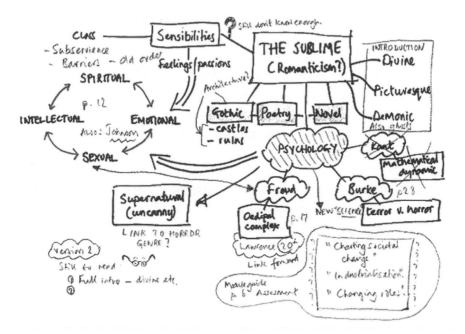

Figure 3.4 Personalised diagrammatic representation of a learning topic (1)

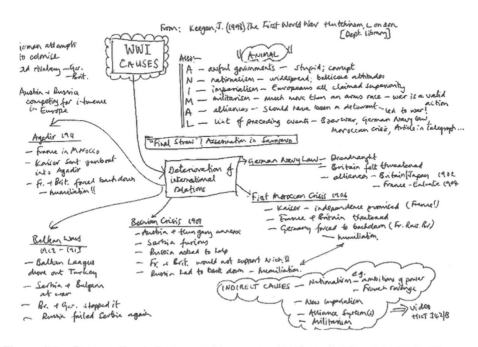

Figure 3.5 Personalised diagrammatic representation of a learning topic (2)

representation of the ideas and information which will be of use when the time for revision arrives.

For many a fusion of approaches seems to work best. It could be that a flow diagram as an additional element of a list of bullet point notes suits a particular situation. There are no rules. All that should be kept in mind is that, however you choose to keep records of your reading or your lectures, the end product must be useful for you and serve all of the purposes of such activity.

The methods outlined above can all be used for keeping notes, or for planning assignments. We will look later at techniques for planning and for ensuring that you develop arguments, as appropriate, as you outline and investigate different topics in your work.

The Cornell System

There is a formalised method of note-taking, devised, as the name suggests, by a department at Cornell University in the United States, which may appeal to some students. The system requires that a page is set out in a precise way (see Figure 3.6) and a set of guidance notes is provided. The system is recommended for note-taking in lectures, but it can easily be used when taking notes from other sources.

How to use the Cornell Note-taking System

- Use one side of the paper only.
- Record in the **note-taking area**.
- Try to get things down in outline form.
- Use diagrams and different colours to emphasise ideas and make connections between ideas.
- Leave some white space for adding ideas later.
- The left hand margin, or **cue column**, is used to reduce your notes. Here, write down key terms, formulas, page numbers, references etc.
- The bottom margin is for **summaries**. Here you summarise your notes and write down your reflections and thoughts to question later.

The benefits of the system are:

- It helps to emphasise the important facts and ideas.
- It can be used to study for exams by covering the recording area and testing your knowledge.

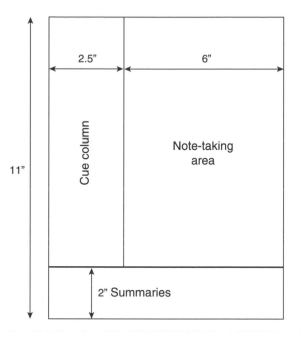

Figure 0.6 The layout of a page for the Cornell Note-taking System

Technology for recording

With the arrival of small handheld technologies for recording, such items as a digital voice recorder, a tablet PC, an MP3 player/recorder or a PDA (Personal Digital Assistant) have become increasingly popular for keeping a record of what is said. The more traditional voice recording options will create a digital file of all of the speech within range, and an entire lecture can easily be captured for later playback. In some cases it is possible to convert the sound files to text files and the content can then be read as well as listened to. It can be useful, perhaps especially for those who have auditory learning preferences, to be able to re-listen to what has been said. These recording devices can also be used in smaller, even one-to-one situations such as small group tutorials, or individual consultation meetings. In most cases it might be advisable at least to mention that you intend to record your meeting, perhaps even ask permission. It might, for some, be a useful exercise to transcribe, or note-take from the recording as a further way of engaging with the content and keeping a personalised record.

There is a danger that having a sound recording of a lecture might be seen as all that is needed. This is certainly not the case. We know that engagement with ideas is at the heart of learning, and simply storing a 'copy' of a lecture will not lead to any understanding of its content. The sound recording is only as useful as the use that is made of it: for re-listening, for note-taking and for verification.

Many tablet PCs have the ability to convert handwriting, which is written on to the screen with a stylus, into text. Even the handwritten notes can be saved and stored digitally. It might be wise to think carefully about some form of secure back-up for files of this type, and even, perhaps, keeping a printed copy. It is possible that as technology advances even further, as it is certain to, there will be newer, more effective, and more secure ways of keeping records of information from the human voice, and from textual sources. The reverse is also true. It is currently possible for texts to be 'read' from computer screens, a development for visually impaired users, and this system could be of advantage for those with a preference for listening rather than reading.

Final thought

The very last word for this chapter can go to Tony Buzan, a well-known advocate of using the 'whole' brain and a key player in the development and use of mind mapping. He says that:

> The brain remembers well by colour so if you write everything in blue ink that is monochrome. Monochrome is a visual representation of monotone, from which derives monotonous, or boring. Boredom makes the brain go to sleep. (Buzan, 2002)

SUMMARY

Keeping records of your lectures and your reading is important because:

- The process of taking notes helps you to engage with the content of your work. In turn this helps in the process of transfer to long term memory.
- Engaging with the content of your work encourages a flow of ideas.
- You have a record of your work for future use.
- Your notes are helpful when the time to plan written work arrives.
- Notes taken diagrammatically or pictorially can benefit from the use of visual memory.
- Your notes and other records become extremely useful when time for revision comes around.

Remember:

- There are a great many different ways to keep records of your work. Your job is to find the method which suits you best.
- When taking notes it is important that you do not copy out sentences or passages word for word, or copy a mass of factual information. Doing either of these will not serve a useful purpose. You will not be thinking about the

content, just the letters and words, and you will not find the end product useful at later stages.

- Lastly, remember there is not one correct method for note-taking. We all develop our own systems for taking notes, and different approaches can be equally effective. How ever you choose to take notes, it is important that you do not allow note-taking to become a lengthy, boring and passive way of learning.

Next ➡️

We will look in the next chapter at ways of finding a way through the maze of different types and locations of information which you will need to become familiar with and with which you will need to become deeply engaged.

Activities

Finding the main idea from a paragraph: Choose a selection of paragraphs randomly from any of your reading material. Identify the topic sentence. In your own words, write one sentence which sums up the main point/argument of the paragraph.

Reviewing your notes: Look back at some of your notes and consider how useful they are, or will be in the future. Consider:

- Ease of reading
- Brevity
- Organisation
- Titles and labels
- Sources clearly identified
- Use of your own words rather than mostly copied word for word
- Main points featured and easily identified
- Understandable
- Use of graphics and colour.

4 Finding the Information You Need: Using Libraries and Library Systems

LEARNING OUTCOMES

What this chapter has in store:

- Detail of the classification and filing systems used in academic libraries (Dewey; Library of Congress)
- Explanations of storage locations in libraries (reference sections; stack)
- Detail of the possibilities of bibliographic databases in different subject areas
- Examples of the additional services available in academic libraries
- The use of library facilities and subscriptions for accessing information electronically, both in the library and remotely

Librarians are almost always very helpful and often almost absurdly knowledgeable. Their skills are probably very underestimated and largely underemployed.

Charles Medawar

In a sense this chapter could be seen as being out of order. We have already considered reading and note-taking in the previous two chapters, but you do actually need to have located the material to read and record notes from. Given that for many students the purchase of all of the books needed for the course is an unobtainable luxury, to be able to use a library and its associated systems is an essential objective to have in mind. This chapter will review the major elements of an academic library. Having read it, you will be in a position to apply what is written here in the context of the library, or libraries where you will find yourself working.

Traditionally the university library has been the first port of call for searching out academic literature. For a number of reasons this is changing, most notable amongst them being the rise in the availability of academic resources, in particular, academic journals, through the medium of the internet (see Chapter 5). Libraries are still, and are likely to remain, the focus of much searching, reading, studying, photocopying and, of course, lending. Many of the books you will need to consult will only be available in the library.

There is no doubt that the library will continue to be an important centre for the sort of information that is needed for undergraduate study. The internet and other computer-mediated sources are important in academic study, and will become increasingly important over time. Access to 'electronic' information is the topic of the next chapter.

There is a lot to be said for becoming familiar with the layout of the university library. In particular you should know your way around the specific sections dedicated to your subject area. This may not be limited to one location. Many universities have more than one library and the resources are stored in a variety of ways, not always simply by subject. Even in a single building it is possible that books of interest to you may be in different locations, on different floors of the building, or in some cases stored in an area not accessible to all users.

Classification systems

The Dewey Decimal System

For many years the Dewey Decimal System of classification for all library books held sway. The system has its roots at the beginning of the public library movement in the nineteenth century and it was the only system in use for most of the history of modern libraries. It was devised by the American Melvil Dewey, who was born in 1851. He originated the Dewey Decimal Classification System in 1873 and it was published and patented in 1876. The system was based upon existing, but less extensive, classification systems, some of which used the decimal style sub-division system for refining the precise classification of an individual work. The system was new and valuable because it was the first to put books in order according to discipline rather than the alphabet. The system is reported to be in use in 95% of school and public libraries, and 25% of academic college and higher institutions (OCLC, 2003).

The system uses arabic numerals (1, 2, 3 …), as well as the roman alphabet (A, B, C …). There are ten main classes that are subdivided into ten divisions each (see Table 4.1). Each division can be broken down into ten sections. In total this gives a set of approximately 1,000 sections of knowledge, as some are not used. It is possible for subjects to appear in more than one class. For example, a book on mathematics could be placed in the 372.7 classification, or in the 510 classification – it could be a book for teachers, dealing with how to teach mathematics, or it could be a mathematics textbook. Any individual book is given its own unique classification based upon the subject matter of the book, which is gradually refined to the point where the subject of the book can be

Table 4.1 The top level Dewey classifications and the major sub-categories

000 Generalities	**100 Philosophy and Psychology**
010 Bibliography	110 Metaphysics
020 Library and information sciences	120 Epistemology, causation, humankind
030 General encyclopaedic works	130 Paranormal phenomena
040 Special topics	140 Specific philosophical schools
050 General serials and their indexes	150 Psychology
060 General organizations and museums	160 Logic
070 New media, journalism, publishing	170 Ethics (moral philosophy)
080 General collections	180 Ancient, medieval, oriental philosophy
090 Manuscripts and rare books	190 Modern western philosophy
200 Religion	**300 Social Sciences**
210 Philosophy and theory of religion	310 General statistics
220 Bible	320 Political science
230 Christianity and Christian theology	330 Economics
240 Christian practice and observance	340 Law
250 Christian pastoral practice and religious orders	350 Public administration
260 Christian organisation, social work and worship	360 Social services; associations
270 History of Christianity	370 Education
280 Christian denominations	380 Commerce, communications, transport
290 Other religions	390 Customs, etiquette, folklore
400 Language	**500 Natural Science and Mathematics**
410 Linguistics	510 Mathematics
420 English and Anglo-Saxon languages	520 Astronomy and allied sciences
430 Germanic languages (German)	530 Physics
440 Romance languages (French)	540 Chemistry and allied sciences
450 Italian, Romanian, Rhaeto-Romanic	550 Earth sciences
460 Spanish and Portuguese languages	560 Palaeontology and paleozoology
470 Italic languages (Latin)	570 Life sciences
480 Hellenic languages (Classical Greek)	580 Botanical sciences
490 Other languages	590 Zoological sciences
600 Technology (Applied Sciences)	**700 The Arts**
610 Medical sciences (medicine, psychiatry)	710 Civic and landscape art
620 Engineering	720 Architecture
630 Agriculture	730 Sculpture
640 Home economics and family living	740 Drawings and decorative arts
650 Management	750 Paintings and painters
660 Chemical engineering	760 Graphic arts (printmaking and prints)
670 Manufacturing	770 Photography

Table 4.1   *(Continued)*

680 Manufacture for specific use	780 Music
690 Buildings	790 Recreational and performing arts
800 Literature and Rhetoric	**900 Geography and History**
810 American literature in English	910 Geography and travel
820 English literature	920 Biography, genealogy, insignia
830 Literature of Germanic language	930 History of the ancient world
840 Literatures of Romance language	940 General history of Europe
850 Italian, Romanian, Romanic literatures	950 General history of Asia (Far East)
860 Spanish and Portuguese literatures	960 General history of Africa
870 Italic literatures (Latin)	970 General history of North America
880 Hellenic literatures (Classical Greek)	980 General history of South America
890 Literatures of other languages	990 General history of other areas

identified from the number alone. The stage of classification which follows this is the use of letters, which are used to make the book individually identifiable. This is not foolproof, but in almost all cases this system works well, and combined with accurate cataloguing, obvious shelving techniques and clear labelling, allows for books to be stored and found efficiently.

It is possible for books with the same subject content but with different titles to have the same Dewey classification except for the three letters, which signify the name of the author or the organisation responsible for the publication. For example, the three books below all have the same decimal classification. The difference between them is indicated by the letter suffixes, which relate to the author:

> Student record book: personal challenge./ Trident Trust.
> 374.08 TRI

> Teaching and learning in further and adult education./ Walklin, Les.
> 374.08 WAL

> Transforming teaching and learning: developing 'critical skills' for living and working in the 21st century/ Weatherley, Colin.
> 374.08 WEA

A typical example of a classification would look like this:

> Using ICT in Primary Mathematics Teaching. Mary Briggs and Alan Pritchard
> 372.7 BRI

However, the precise designation of a particular book to a specific classification is a matter for an individual librarian, that is to say that there is a certain amount of judgement involved in identifying the exact classification. The same book could be placed in a slightly different place in different libraries, as below for the Briggs and Pritchard example, where there are some striking similarities but no unanimity:

University College Canterbury Christchurch	372.34 BRI
University of Manchester	371.39445
University of Southampton	372.7 BRI
University of Leeds	372.7 BRI
Liverpool John Moores University	372.7 BRI
St Martin's College	372.7044 BRI
University of Central England	372.7044 BRI
University of Warwick	375.512854 BRI
Sheffield Hallam University	510.70285 BR

These differences are interesting, but at a practical level unimportant. The important consideration to be made is internal consistency, that is, that within a library there is a consistency which means that when a user becomes familiar with the system there will be no anomalies or surprises.

The Library of Congress System

Another system for classification is the Library of Congress System. The Library of Congress is the unofficial national library of the United States and the research division of the United States Government. It is situated in the American capital, Washington D.C. The library has 530 miles (850 km) of shelves and holds more than 130 million items, which is second only to the British Library (over 150 million items).

The classification system used in the Library of Congress is favoured by many academic institutions throughout the world. If you are to make effective use of your library it would be useful to understand the principles involved in the system and also to take some time to become familiar with the divisions and subdivisions within your subject area. The top level classifications are as shown in Table 4.2.

Each of the classes is further subdivided. Table 4.3 shows an outline of classification B, General Philosophy, with its range of subdivisions.

Library of Congress call numbers

The ability to work with Library of Congress classification numbers, more commonly known as 'call numbers', is a skill which develops with practice. A little introductory

Table 4.2 The top level classifications of the Library of Congress System

A	General works
B	Philosophy, Psychology, Religion
C	Auxiliary Sciences of History
D	History: General and Old World
E	History: America
	This class is not divided into letter sub-classes.

	11–143	America
	151–889	United States

F	History: America
	This class is not divided into letter sub-classes

	1–975	United States Local History
	1001–1145.2	British America (including Canada); Dutch America
	1170	French America
	1201–3799	Latin America; Spanish America; History of Brazil

G	Geography, Anthropology, Recreation
H	Social Science
J	Political Science
K	Law
L	Education
M	Music and Books on Music
N	Fine Arts
P	Language and Literature
Q	Science
R	Medicine
S	Agriculture
T	Technology
U	Military Science
V	Naval Science
Z	Bibliography; Library Science; Information Resources (general)

Classes I, O, W, X and Y are not in general use.

level information will assist in the process. Below is a typical call number, in this case it belongs to a book entitled: *The Case for Religion* by Keith Ward.

BL 51.W2

Call numbers can begin with one, two or three letters. The first letter of a call number represents one of the 21 major divisions of the Library of Congress System. In the example, the division 'B' is 'Philosophy'. The second letter, 'L', represents a subdivision of Philosophy, namely 'Religions, Mythology, Rationalism'. All books in the BLs will be about one or more of these three topics.

Table 4.3   The subdivisions of the B classification of the Library of Congress System

B	Philosophy (General)	
BC	Logic	
	1–199	Logic
	11–39	History
	25–39	By period
	60–99	General works
	171–199	Special topics
BD	Speculative philosophy	
BF	Psychology	
BH	Aesthetics	
	1–301	Aesthetics
	81–208	History
	301	Special topics
BJ	Ethics	
BL	Religions, Mythology, Rationalism	
BM	Judaism	
BP	Islam, Bahá'ísm, Theosophy	
BQ	Buddhism	
BR	Christianity	
BS	The Bible	
BT	Doctrinal Theology	
BV	Practical Theology	
BX	Christian Denominations	

The first set of numbers in a call number define the subject of the book. '51' in the example teaches us more about the book's subject. The BL 51 group of books are on the subject of Religion.

The call number finishes with the 'cutter number' (named after Charles Cutter, founding member of the American Libraries Association). It is a code representing the author, or organisation's name, or the title of the work. The cutter number is usually a second set of numbers (or number), preceded by a letter. In this case the 'W' stands for Ward.

As a further example we can look at the book we classified with Dewey numbers, *Using ICT in Primary Mathematics Teaching* by Mary Briggs and Alan Pritchard. We can see how the call number's meaning is defined:

QA 135.6.B74 2002

Q	Science
QA	Mathematics

QA101–145   Elementary Mathematics, Arithmetic
B74   B relates to the name of the first author
2002   Year of publication, if included

This book is to be found in the Science section, more specifically the mathematics section, in the numeric range 101–145; 135.6 defines the book more specifically according to its main topic (ICT and mathematics in primary education); the B74 locates it within the 135.6 section. When included, the last four numbers give us the additional information of the year of publication.

With this system books are stored first according to the two letters at the start of the call number, secondly in numeric order, thirdly according to the letter relating to the author and lastly according to the number attached to the letter of the author's name.

Clearly the above is only a brief synopsis of the system and most users find that they become fully attuned to particular sections and classifications in the library where most of their work is carried out. Libraries will have introductory information available if you need more than the basics to begin searching for and finding books. One problem sometimes encountered is actually moving from a catalogue where a classification number has been found, to the place on the shelf where the book is stored. Again this requires practice and familiarity with the layout of the shelves. Labelling forms an important part of library navigation and so it is important to take note of the labels and to begin to understand the patterns involved in the layout of your particular library. If in doubt find a librarian, or other assistant, and ask.

Catalogues and indexes

Library catalogues are there to help users efficiently locate a specific item among an expansive library stock. The days of well-thumbed card indexes have gone and all but the smallest of libraries now have some form of online catalogue. (Birmingham University has an online card index, which is made up of scanned cards arranged into a sophisticated database, which is a novel idea and saves for future use and research the catalogues used by students and scholars over many years.)

Often named OPAC (Online Public Access Catalogue), the catalogue, or rather the range of catalogues associated with each library will be accessible via dedicated computers actually in the library building, but also, in almost all cases, via a web-based portal. What this means in practice is that it is possible to access and search the library catalogue from anywhere with an internet-connected computer. Not only is it possible to establish whether a book is present on the library catalogue, i.e. whether the library

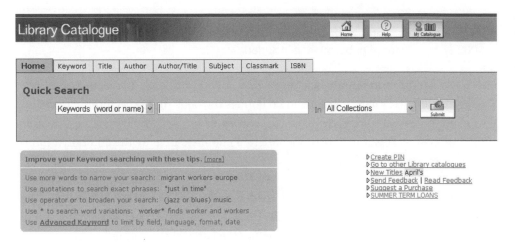

Figure 4.1   A typical homepage for a university library catalogue (OPAC)

has a copy, but there is also a range of other options related to the library and its services that can be completed on-line. Amongst these will be such things as:

- Renewing your books on loan.
- Making a book reservation.
- Checking your personal loans.
- Requesting books via the inter-library loan service.

Other options may be changing passwords and other related actions. There will also be some library-specific options, possibly requesting that a book might be transferred from one campus to another, or making course or module-related requests for special arrangements which have been put in place by the library and course tutors.

Possibly the most useful and time-saving of the features associated with online access to catalogues is the ability to save a journey to the library, which in some cases might take some time. If the book that you need is on loan then you know not to make the journey and you will, if you choose, make a reservation for the book which will be recalled for you. You will be notified by e-mail when the book is ready for collection.

Online access to the library catalogue requires that you have basic skills in computer use. You will need to be able to make a search of the system at the very least. If you are familiar with techniques for searching an electronic resource, the internet for example, or any sort of database, you will understand such terms as 'key word'. If you have no experience of searching in this manner you may well need to use the guidance given on-screen, which will give you all that you need to get started.

In essence what you will do is ask the catalogue a series of simple questions. For example, 'Find all of the books in the catalogue written by A. J. P. Taylor'. This would be an example of an 'Author' search. Similarly it is possible to carry out a 'Title' search. If you do not know the full or correct title it is possible to search for titles which include certain words, or to carry out simple 'key word' searches. If you know that there is a book covering the topic of functional programming languages but the full title escapes you then a title key word search for titles including the words 'functional', 'programming' and 'languages' may well be all that you need to track it down. You may need to do a little detective work, or even lateral thinking. You may think that you remember the title fairly accurately, but sometimes this is not the case and you should try variations on the theme.

A search in the OPAC system of a big university library for these three words ('functional', 'programming' and 'languages') led to the identification of five titles. A search for books with just two of the key words ('functional' and 'programming') led to twenty titles. Sometimes, especially if you are not clear that you have the title right, a search with fewer words is a better option for finding the right title. In this case the actual title was *Elements of Functional Languages* and with a few simple variations on the theme the book was eventually traced.

The progress of a search might be as follows:

1. Title search for: 'functional', 'programming' and 'languages'. Result: Five titles, none of which was for the right book. Title search for: 'functional' and 'programming'. Result: Twenty titles, none of which was for the right book. Key word search for: 'functional' and 'programming' Result: Seventy-one titles, the correct title, *Elements of Functional Languages*, was listed at number sixty-two.
2. In a search for the same book, but with less information to hand, you might remember that the author's name was something like Henderson, or Hensman, you could carry out a similar set of searches.
3. A search for the three letters 'Hen' as an author netted an unmanageable 1,264 results. A search for title *and* author, at the same time, with 'Hen' in the author field and 'functional' in the title field took a little longer to finish but the end result was four titles, the fourth of which was actually: *Elements of Functional Languages* by M. C. Henson.

For many online catalogue users the process appears intuitive and, in conjunction with a minimum of onscreen guidance, they are able to function well and find what they are looking for. Other users do not find the process so straightforward and either need more practice, or support from elsewhere. This support can come from two main sources:

official and unofficial. That is, from the library itself, or from a 'more knowledgeable other' (see Chapter 1). Help from the library could take the form of asking a librarian for a minute or two of their time to set you on the right track, or it could mean signing up for a tutorial session. University libraries, in most cases, provide training for all of the services they provide. Often at the beginning of a university course there is a library induction session which will introduce new students to the building, the system, the subject librarian and the range of resources available. There will also be opportunities for more detailed support, often in a semi-formal session, to learn more about specific activities – literature reviews, electronic databases, for example. Searching will certainly be covered at times like this.

Informal support can take different forms. It could be turning to the person using the computer next to you in the library and asking a short question. It could be talking to a fellow student who may be familiar with the subject area and the names and topics associated with it. In line with the notions of social learning and the principles of scaffolding discussed in Chapter 1, the 'chat with a friend/colleague' approach is sound though it is not always possible.

Probably the best way to learn how to use the system efficiently is to practise with it. If you have a particular need, the way to meet it, in terms of finding the resource in the library that you need, is to set aside a little time to experiment with the catalogue facilities and, sometimes by trial and error, come to a better understanding of how it all works. If this is combined with input from library staff, or perhaps fellow students, there is no reason why you should not become well versed in the use of the catalogue and able to track down whatever you are looking for.

Journals and other periodicals

All libraries, but especially academic libraries, will hold thousands of books, but also many thousands of journals, reports and other printed materials. For every academic discipline there will be a range, a very wide range in most cases, of journals which publish current articles based on research and other academic and scholarly activity. These journals will also be catalogued, and the catalogue will be available for searching in one way or another. If we look at one discipline as an example, we will see the size of what we might be dealing with. In an attempt to track down academic journals dealing with chemistry, for example, this is what happened.

A catalogue search for journals with the word 'chemical' in the title found ninety-nine titles, ranging from *Accounts of Chemical Research* to *Theoretical Foundations of Chemical Engineering*. A similar search, this time for the word 'chemistry', found 156 titles. To the novice chemistry student this would be an impossible list to deal with. However, with good advice from module tutors, who will make suggestions and recommendations in taught sessions or in the module documentation, and with experience, it will be possible to identify and locate appropriate journals. Sometimes particular journal articles are referenced in your reading and you may want to read the article in question. It is then, armed with the full bibliographic reference from your reading, that you can interrogate the journal catalogue and establish, first, if your university has a copy of the journal in question, and secondly where it is located.

There is a period of change currently taking place in the realm of academic publishing and libraries are having to make decisions about whether or not to continue with subscriptions to what are quite expensive journals when there is an electronic subscription available. For this reason it is sometimes the case that a library may well have copies of a particular journal, with every edition of every volume published, but only up to a certain date. Simply finding that a particular journal is available in the library will not be enough information. You need to know which volumes and dates are held to be sure that the one that you want will be there. We will look at access to electronic journals in detail in Chapter 5.

Once you have become familiar with the most relevant journals to your study it would be a good idea to look from time to time on the shelves where the latest editions of journals are placed. It is a fairly common policy for libraries to put the newest edition of each journal that they receive in a prominent position in the library, maybe in the main concourse, or perhaps in the subject-related areas within the building. By browsing the new journals from time to time you will get a sense of what is new or what is particularly topical in your subject area. Tutors will be very impressed with (appropriate) references to the latest editions of reputable journals related to your work.

It may be useful here to mention 'Athens', which is a system of allowing access to a wide selection of academic databases by means of one point of entry. That is, you need only one login name and password. In most universities this will be the same as your university name and password. When you are using computer access within the university the use of Athens may not appear obvious to you, but when you try to access the same sources remotely, you will be denied access without the appropriate Athens authentication. We will return to the use of Athens in Chapter 5.

Reference materials

If you have used libraries to any great extent you will have an idea of the types of materials they hold apart from books. In public libraries there is a section named 'Reference' or something similar and in this section is a range of encyclopaedias, dictionaries, year books (such as *Who's Who?*) and a selection of less obvious inclusions such as local bus and train timetables. What separates out the reference section from the main collection is usually that it is not possible to borrow books from the reference section except in very special circumstances. In academic libraries the same conditions apply to reference sections, and the reference sections are usually far more expansive. There may well be the usual selection of dictionaries and associated compilations of information, but there is a good deal more under this heading and there are also books and other materials which are designated 'Reference Only' stored on the shelves with loan copies of the same material. One of the small annoyances in some libraries is to arrive at the check-out counter with a book from the fifth floor only to be told that you have brought down a reference copy which is not for loan. To be fair, these copies usually have a distin-guishing label on their spine, but it can be all too easy to miss this visual cue.

Sometimes libraries will place a particular book on what is referred to as 'Temporary Reference', usually at the request of a tutor, at a time when it might be in high demand and there are insufficient copies for the number of students following a particular module.

What will be held in the reference section?

The reference section in an academic library goes far beyond what would be found in a public or school library. There are untold treasures of information and information sources hidden away in every subject area which the lay person could not imagine. Often in academic libraries there is a general reference section, including many of the items found elsewhere – dictionaries, yearbooks, travel schedules and timetables, but there will also be a section of reference materials for each subject section. There are many general sources and even more which are subject-specific.

The following description is of the arrangements for the History reference collection in a typical university library. The library serves a medium-sized undergraduate pop-ulation and a thriving higher degree programme, there are also a number of researchers and doctoral students associated with the department. The library resources, both actual and electronic, are a very important element of the department's teaching and research programmes. There is a dedicated History librarian working full-time in the library who is in regular contact with the academic staff in the depart-ment. The library uses the Library of Congress system for most of its collection, and Dewey Decimal for one area, which was inherited from a former local college when the two institutions amalgamated.

For History there is one sequence of factual reference works, which includes ency-clopaedias, handbooks, indexes and atlases. These are classified as [ref] D – F and are not for loan. In the online catalogue these items are found with all of the other stock and are not stored separately. The classification number is prefixed with [ref] which identifies their status. These particular reference books are shelved together at a point close to the entrance to the History section of the library.

There is a second sequence of reference (not for loan) items which is made up of bibliographies. These are classified as [ref] ZD – ZF (the Z implies a bibliography, as you can see in Table 4.2). These items can be found in the library online catalogue, most easily by using the classification numbers.

The third reference sequence is of printed abstracts and indexes to periodicals. These items are shelved with a larger set of indexes, periodicals and similar material in a location adjacent to the main History collection in a part of the library used for Arts-related reference materials. These items are annual publications which index the periodicals, books, theses and exhibition catalogues published that year. Many of these annual publications are also available online via bibliographic databases such as Historical Abstracts, American History and Life, and others.

There has been a huge growth of full text resources which have become available on line in the past five to ten years. Many of the well-known (to history scholars at least) reference materials and other compilations, such as Early English Books Online (EEBO), Eighteenth Century Collections Online (ECCO), Evans Digital (the American version of EEBO) and Making of the Modern Economy (MOME) are available via the internet. There is access to over a third of a million historical texts across all of the sub-disciplines of the subject. Access to these online resources is straightforward for students registered at the university and a feature of the majority of them is that they are 'word-searchable', which is an incredible time-saving device. Many are also available in what is called 'page images'. That is the original pages of old documents, books and other artefacts are viewable in their original format, not simply a transcript, which is highly desirable in many aspects of historical investigation. These services give an unprecedented depth of access to the printed record and enable research methodologies that would previously have been impossible for students in places remote from the physical location of the originals; this in practice, of course, means almost all university locations. EEBO and ECCO are available to universities for a modest annual subscription. Some of the databases require outright purchase, and they can be very expensive. It is said that you could buy a small house for the cost of the full set of The Making of the Modern Economy (MOME), a fully comprehensive 'witness to the theories, practices, and consequences of economic and business activity in the west over four centuries. A fully searchable database of approximately 12 million pages and more than 61,000 titles & editions' (Saur Verlag, undated)

Another type of resource also available via the internet, though many of these online resources are not strictly library reference works, is document collections, for example, Empire Online. There are many of these and access is, for some at least, free of charge.

This description has given an overview of the sort of material which is generally available in one subject area. Other subject areas have similar structures with subject-specific variations and idiosyncrasies. The total amount of material available to students is far beyond what any library could have hoped to provide in the past. This is very good news for the most part, but there are of course pitfalls to accessing materials online, which we will consider later.

Library arrangements: loans, reservations and recalls

There is a range of types of loan available in university libraries. Some books, as we have seen, are not available for loan at all, others on a weekly, monthly and sometimes termly basis. Obviously not all loan arrangements are the same. It is useful to know specific arrangements for the libraries that you will use, partly because many libraries impose fines for breaching the regulations on returning books (and you may not be allowed to borrow anything further until you have paid).

The main library arrangements of which you should be aware are:

- **Reference Only**: items not available for loan.
- **Temporary Reference**: an item designated as reference for a limited period, such as leading up to exams when the demand will be high and copies in short supply.
- **Short Loan**: sometimes the loan period may be as short as twenty-four hours for certain items, for similar reasons as Temporary Reference.
- **Reserve Collection**: items are sometimes collected together at the request of a tutor and made available either as Reference Only, or on a Short Loan cycle. These materials will relate to a particular module or assignment.
- **Staff Collection**: some items may be designated as for loan to staff only.
- **Early Recall**: if an item is in demand by other students libraries will sometimes ask for it to be returned earlier than the due date. Fines may well be imposed for lateness.
- **Renewals**: renewals can often be made without visiting the library, either by phone, or more likely via the library website. If an item is in demand it is often not possible to renew it; similarly, in some cases, if it is overdue.

Library communications   In many cases university libraries will contact you by e-mail. They will use your university address, and some of the communications might be important – relating to fines for example. If you do not regularly check your university e-mail account, possibly because you use an alternative address, or you are not in the habit of using e-mail, you might well not receive the messages sent to you. If you use a different e-mail account it would be sensible to create a forwarding rule in the university account to ensure that everything is delivered as it should be.

Inter-library loans

Accessing books and materials from other libraries, sometimes referred to as 'Document Supply Service', is a way of obtaining whatever it is that you need if it is not available in your home university. Before initiating a loan of this type it is important to be sure that the library does not have the item in either printed or electronic format.

Inter-library loans incur a cost to the library, and many libraries pass this on to students, albeit at a subsidised rate. You will need to be aware of the arrangements in place. Obviously different libraries will have different policies and practices. Some universities may require that an application is authorised by a tutor. Below are two examples of charges:

First 150 requests per year	£4.00
Requests over the 150 limit	£16.00
Urgent action requests	£12.00

Staff, Researchers, PhD, M*Phil Students*		*Students MA, MSc, MBA, Dip Course, UG 1,2,3,4*	
Photocopy	£4.50	Photocopy	£2.00
Loan	£7.50	Loan	£2.00
Urgent action	£16.00	Urgent action	£6.00
Renewal	£2.80	Renewal	£2.00
Worldwide search	Price available on request	Worldwide search	Price available on request

The range of material is wide and includes books, articles, reports, theses, conference proceedings, patents, government documents and other less obvious items. Having access to degree theses can be useful, especially if you are working on a project in an obscure area of your subject. Most theses come as microfilms from the British Library Document Supply Centre (BLDSC) and libraries will have the appropriate equipment to read work in this format.

Using the libraries of other universities.

There are arrangements in place which allow registered university students to use some of the facilities at other university libraries. This is useful during vacation times for example. In most cases this does not extend to full borrowing rights, but some access, and the use of a photocopier, can be of great use. It is often possible to use the quiet study facilities too.

There is an extended version of this system called UK Libraries Plus, which enables certain groups of students additional rights. This scheme allows students who are part-time, distance learning, full-time postgraduate or on work placements to borrow material from other libraries.

Archives and stacks

A stack room is an area set aside in a library for out-of-date periodical and other archived materials. In almost all cases stack rooms are not accessible by library users and materials have to be requested. Stack rooms are kept locked and secure for a variety of reasons.

Items held in stack rooms are usually ones that are not requested on a regular basis but are needed to form a part of the whole collection of the library's assets. Whole collections of journals from many years ago, periodicals, newspapers, old books which could well have importance to particular areas of study but are not generally used are stored in the library stack, as are items which are fragile and considered to be in 'poor health'.

Most universities will have copies of all higher degree research theses (PhDs and dissertations by research) which have been successfully submitted for awards. The precise way that they are catalogued, stored and accessed will vary but in general they will be open to access and copying, according to some conditions. They are not generally available for loan. For example they may appear on the Library Catalogue with a specified classification: 'RES DIS' is one example.

Specialist librarians

In most big university libraries there will be subject-specialist staff. The role of these people is to manage the stock, liaise with departments, offer support and consultancy, respond to requests for new materials and to be available whenever possible to answer immediate queries. They are an excellent resource though, unfortunately, sometimes in short supply. A simple face-to-face question, or a short e-mail, can often save a great deal of time. There is, again in the bigger libraries, a subject helpdesk, which is a place where immediate requests can be dealt with. It is worth taking the time to get to know your subject librarian and, if it exists, the subject team supporting the specialist librarian. You should get to know the arrangements in place in your institution and take advantage of what is available in order to help with time-efficiency in your work.

More than just a library

Compared to libraries that you will have come across before university, the library that you will now use will be far more than a warehouse of books for loan. There are many other roles and departments included under the same roof, or at least under the auspices of the university library. This will vary from place to place, but often university libraries are repositories for specialist archives. An example of this is the Modern Records Centre at the University of Warwick, where there is a large collection of documents and archives relating to trade unions and similar organisations, employers' and trade associations, industrial relations, pressure groups, political parties and organisations, business and management, individuals involved in the history of industry and the trade union movement, and education insofar as it has had an effect on trade unions and related areas.

There are many collections of the papers, letters and other materials relating to the entire works of particular authors, politicians or musicians. These are often donated to a university because of the value to heritage and research and universities are only too pleased to accept providing that there is adequate accommodation and there is sufficient funding to maintain them. Examples of these would be the personal papers of influential politicians such as Winston Churchill or the original musical manuscripts of Benjamin Britten.

This chapter has presented an enormous amount of information and it is fairly certain that you will not need to be totally *au fait* with all of it. The best way to become library-efficient, is to visit your library, practise and seek help when necessary.

SUMMARY

- Despite the rapid rise in internet access to a very wide range of academic and other materials the library will remain an important, even crucial, element of undergraduate study for the foreseeable future.
- Knowing your way around the library that you will use, both in the physical sense, and in the sense of familiarity with the classification system in use is important and the sooner you achieve this the better.
- There are two main classification systems in use in academic libraries: the Dewey Decimal System and the Library of Congress System.
- There are different levels of access to materials, including 'Reference Only' 'Short Loan' and 'Standard Loan'.
- Libraries provide access to an enormous range of electronic data via the internet, including many journals, some of which they may also have as paper copies.

- There are specialist librarians for each subject area, often working with a small team.
- Libraries are more than warehouses for books. They contain both other materials and a wide range of related services.

Next

We have considered libraries in detail here, and also touched upon electronic access to materials. In the next chapter we will look in more detail at the ways in which computers can mediate our access to a wealth of vital information. We will also consider the possible dangers and pitfalls of blind faith in the integrity of some online sources.

Activities

Classification: Do you know the classification headings for your subject in the university library? If not, make a point of finding out. Also, get to know the location of the books and journals (which may well be in a different location) relating to your subject. Find out the name of your specialist librarian; you might want to go as far as introducing yourself.

Searching the library catalogue: Set yourself a search task related to your subject. For example, locate a copy of one of the following in your library:

- *Biological Indicators of Water Quality*. Edited by A. James and Lilian Evison, 1979.
- *Engaged Learning with Emerging Technologies*. Edited by David Hung and Myint Swe Khine, 2006
- *Artaud and the Gnostic Drama*. By Jane Goodall, 1994.
- *Tropical African Development: Geographical Perspectives*. Edited by M.B. Gleave, 1992.
- *Statistical Analysis: A Computer Oriented Approach*. By A.A. Afifi, S.P. Azen, 1979.
- *Mozart and Salieri: The Little Tragedies*. By Alexander Pushkin; translated by Antony Wood; foreword by Elaine Feinstein, 1982.

Access to journals: Is it possible to gain access to one of the following journals in your library, either as a paper copy, or via electronic means?

- *The Journal of International Accounting, Auditing & Taxation*
- *The Journal of the Law Society of Scotland*
- *Nuclear and Chemical Waste Management*
- *The Australasian Journal of Philosophy.*

5 Computers and the Internet as a Source of Quality Information

LEARNING OUTCOMES

What this chapter has in store:

- A note about access to second-hand books.
- Some detail concerning the access to electronically stored information afforded by university libraries.
- Information about the use of Athens for remote access to useful sources of information.
- A consideration of the use of the internet for locating appropriate sources of information for undergraduate study.
- Information about search engines, both those which are broadly focused, and those which are more specifically targeted.
- Detail of search techniques and strategies.
- A word about plagiarism.
- A brief look at Virtual Learning Environments.

In the previous chapter we considered the way that libraries can give access in traditional ways to virtually all of the information and other material that you will need. We considered that the university library is and will continue to be a very important element of the provision made for students. We also considered systems mediated by access to computers within the library. This chapter takes this further and sets out the enormous range of possibilities that access to computers in general, and the internet in particular, can give.

Second-hand books

Before we look in detail at the role that the internet might play in your study, it might be helpful to look at how the worldwide second-hand book market has suddenly become accessible through electronic technology in a way that has never been possible before. Books are expensive, and in the past looking for a book in a second-hand bookshop, even one close to the university, was not a very satisfying pastime. There are now dedicated websites which will track and supply used books. They claim to be able to source any requirement, and in my experience this has always been the case. Other reputable internet booksellers, such as Amazon, almost always have access to second-hand copies of the new books which they sell. Even when a book is quite new it is often possible to find a cheaper used copy for sale. If you are one of the breed who like to have their own copies of the books that they use, then the burgeoning second-hand internet bookshop market will be of great interest to you. The service is usually very good, cheaper than buying new and very swift in delivery.

Databases

KEY PRINCIPLES

Database: a collection of data arranged for ease and speed of search and retrieval; in modern usage this refers exclusively to information which is stored in a computer.

Standalone databases

A standalone database is a compilation of information which is usually contained on a single compact disc or CD (although sometimes more than one CD is needed). The information is usually specific to one area of a subject, and is searchable. The range of databases available in this format is very wide, and each subject area will have several available. The difference between an online database and a standalone database is that the standalone variety does not need access to any other source of information except what is stored on the CD(s). An online database needs access to either a computer server in the institute via an intranet, or to the home of the database via the internet. There are advantages for each system. An online database can be updated on a very regular basis, a standalone database cannot, although many companies will issue updated discs from time to time. Some information sources do not need updating: historical data such as population statistics will not change, for example. Standalone databases will still work even if there is a problem with an internet connection. Online databases can be accessed by many different users at the same time, this is not always the case with standalone databases.

Below is a selection from the list of available standalone databases from a typical university library. The full list contained over eighty different titles across all subject areas.

- Allgemeine Deutsche Biographie & Neue Deutsche Biographie
- Barrington Atlas of the Greek & Roman World
- Civil Court Practice 2000
- Dictionary of National Biography

- Encyclopedia of Philosophy
- Gray's Anatomy
- Historical Atlas of Islam
- International Trade by Commodity
- National Gallery – complete illustrated catalogue
- Newnes Interactive Electronic Circuits
- Oxford Dictionary of Quotations
- Soldiers who died in the Great War
- Thesaurus formarum totius latinitatis cetedoc – index of Latin forms
- Works of John Ruskin

Online databases

One of the great advantages, in the field of study, provided by ubiquitous electronic communication is the unfaltering availability, both on and off campus, of online information – specifically academic sources of information provided by online databases and similar reputable and well-maintained repositories.

Online sources have the advantage of being available from wherever you are, provided that you have Internet access and the appropriate login requirements (see 'Athens' below.) Standalone, subscription databases are regularly updated, but there is sometimes a risk of some information being less than totally up to date. With online sources this possibility is minimalised.

Athens

The Athens Access Management System (AMS) controls access to what are known as web-based subscription services. There is a cost involved for subscribing institutions, but this is not passed on to individual members of a university.

For the sake of ease of use, the Athens system has been developed for the academic community and allows a registered user access to a very large number of information databases, electronic journals and other information, all of which would normally require separate registration and login procedures, with just one user name and password; in most cases, for university users, this will be the same as your regular user name for university services.

Athens provides easy access to almost every source of high level academic-based information you are likely to need. It is a rare exception to find a site of relevant information in the academic sphere which is not accessible via Athens.

If you are not made aware of this facility when you arrive at university, it will be worthwhile contacting the library to find out more.

In the same typical university library the listing of online databases runs to hundreds of titles. For the letter A there are over twenty titles, and this number is more or less matched for all letters of the alphabet with the exception of K, Q, X and Y.

Database subject headings typically include:

- Arts
- Business
- Economics
- Education
- European Union
- Law
- Medicine
- Official Publications
- Sciences
- Social Sciences
- Statistics

Electronic journals

KEY PRINCIPLES

Journal: a periodical published for a special group such as a learned society, or profession.

Almost all academic journals have some measure of electronic availability. Some will allow access, for subscribers (in your case the university and its members), to the full texts of all of its editions, others allow access without subscription to the abstracts of the articles. (An abstract is a short introductory paragraph which is written to precede an article and gives a general impression of the content, and if appropriate, the findings of the research reported.) By reading an abstract it is usually possible to decide if you need to consult the full text of an article. The importance of making use of both current and past academic journals cannot be overemphasised, and tutors will expect that you consult the appropriate journals for your discipline.

We have considered in Chapter 4 the way that libraries are increasingly moving towards subscription to electronic versions of academic journals. There are many obvious advantages to being able to access online versions of the articles that you need to read. Below is a set of details taken from one university website (the University of Warwick). By quickly reading through them you will achieve an overview of many of the issues surrounding the use of e-journals rather than paper journals. You would need to look through the information provided by your institution to know exactly how the system will work in your case.

How to find electronic journals

Many journals are now available in electronic format. You can access these journals from the Library's Web pages. Choose 'Electronic Resources' and navigate to the Journals page.

From the **Journals** page you can choose to access our electronic journals in a number of ways:

By title
Use the search box to search for the title you require. Remember that this is a list of titles only and therefore you cannot do an article search.

By e-journal collections
Services such as Science Direct and Ebsco Host EJS, among others, enable you to search by journal title or, by using key words.

Journal browse page
This page allows you to browse the e-journal collection alphabetically. It also presents a list of the home pages of publishers with whom we have arranged electronic access for some or all of their titles.

By subject
Select a subject category and you will be presented with a list of subjects within that category. From there you can access a list of titles.

Alerting services
Many electronic service providers offer a free alerting service. You can sign up to be informed of new content in a specific subject area or of the publication of the latest edition.

Full-text electronic access to a number of journals is also available on some of the online services to which we subscribe.

Viewing and saving
Many full-text electronic journal articles are now being provided as Portable Document Format (PDF) files. To view these you need to have Adobe Acrobat Reader software installed on your computer. PCs on the campus network should have this software available. If you are using a PC on the campus network you can either save (download) the article to your own workspace or have it printed on an IT Services network printer. However, if you are using a Library PC you may have the option to save to your H: drive, e-mail to your address or you can save the article to a suitable device.

(Continued)

Access from off-campus

It is possible to access the electronic journals from off-campus. This is most easily done via Athens.

Athens

An Athens username allows you to use from anywhere in the world any Athens database to which the Library subscribes. All University of Warwick members can access Athens, the username and password required is the same as your IT Services login name and password. Find out more about Athens from IT Services.

To find a paper copy of the same journal you would first have to establish whether your library has copies of the journal and then find the appropriate copy on the shelves. There is always the chance that the one you are looking for is missing. If your library does not hold the journal then you would have to apply for an interlibrary loan copy via the document supply service (see Chapter 4). This could take some time.

Official reports

According to your area of study, the importance of governmental and other official documents may vary. However, the government of the UK, and many others around the world, will concern themselves, to lesser and greater degrees, with virtually every subject.

In the UK the government releases Parliamentary Papers, often referred to as Command Papers. (They are known as Command Papers because they are released formally 'By Her Majesty's Command'). Command Papers are documents released by the government and presented to Parliament. They include: White Papers, Green Papers, treaties, reports from Royal Commissions and various government bodies.

Government departments publish an enormous range of other documents, many of which are relevant to academic study. These can also be accessed online via the UK Official Publications (UKOP) website (www.ukop.co.uk/). UKOP is the official catalogue of official publications in the UK since 1980. UKOP has over 450,000 records from over 2,000 public bodies, and it is the most comprehensive source available for information about official publications in the UK.

Electronic reference collections

In the previous chapter we considered the reference collections held by libraries. In the past these collections of dictionaries, encyclopaedias, yearbooks, timetables, compilations of lists and other items were strictly limited to what the library in question could afford, and what space they could use. With the advent of electronic access mediated by the internet cost is still a consideration, but space no longer limits the works that are accessible.

Libraries routinely subscribe to a very wide range of reference material providers to allow registered users at the university to take advantage of instant online access. (Using the phrase 'very wide range' is perhaps to understate the reality!)

Table 5.1 gives a representative impression of the range and style of reference material which is available electronically. The full list of material would be much longer.

The use of the internet for academic study

The internet is undoubtedly a rich source of quality information. However, it is much more than this too. Amongst other things it is a source of misinformation, inaccuracy, bias, mischief and unadulterated rubbish. This is without considering the offensive, the obscene and the downright illegal.

The nature of the internet and the World Wide Web

This is not really the place to expand upon the internet's history and the nature of the phenomenon itself, but for those readers new to the medium a background to and explanation of the internet's make-up might be useful and of interest. Other readers might choose to skip this section.

The internet is very large computer network which is made up from other smaller networks of computers. It is actually made up of millions of computers which are connected in many different ways and which, through the worldwide telecommunications system, can make connections with each other and transfer different kinds of information from one computer to another. The telecommunications system which the internet makes use of consists of the infrastructure of underground cables and overhead wires, exchanges, satellite links and radio links which has been developed over many years by many different international, national and local authorities and companies.

The internet is huge. The network of computers making up this worldwide community runs into millions of 'members', and the number of computers with the capability to connect with the network runs into many more millions. The internet holds a vast store of information with great possibilities for education.

The World Wide Web (WWW) is, in a sense, the visible element of the internet. The WWW is the interface between users and the network of computers where the many millions of websites with their many millions of items of information are to be found.

Table 5.1   A selected example of the range of online general reference material commonly available in university libraries

Heading	For example
General collections of reference resources	General, multi-purpose materials: Info Connect: comprehensive reference resource HERO: Dictionaries and Reference Works: Dictionaries, thesauruses, encyclopaedias, fact books, maps, etc. Ref Desk – single source for facts on the net
Acronyms and abbreviations	Acronym Finder: contains more than 186,000 acronyms
Almanacs	Annual publications, which include calendars with weather forecasts, astronomical information, tide tables and other related tabular information: World Almanac
Biography	Nobel Prize Archive: Nobel Prize winners since 1901, with links to other sites
Currency	Currency converter with rates updated daily
Dictionaries	Online linked dictionaries covering all languages
Encyclopaedias	Large numbers of both general and subject-specific encyclopaedias
Flags	Database-style resources of national and other types of flags, with links to other sites
Grammar	English Grammar Online
Maps	UK maps World maps
Measures	Dictionary of Units Megaconverter: a growing set of weights, measures and units conversion/calculation modules
Postcodes	Postcode Finder
Quotations	Brewer's Dictionary of Phrase and Fable 1894
Telephone directories	Telephone directories around the world
Thesauruses	Getty Thesaurus of Geographic Names Merriam-Webster OnLine Collegiate Thesaurus Roget's Thesaurus Online
Travel	Railway timetables UK public transport information

Table 5.1   *(Continued)*

Heading	For example
Universities	UK Site Map
	Universities worldwide
Weather	The Met Office
	World Meteorological Organization
Words	Omniglot – Guide to writing systems
	Wolinsky Web – Word Play
	World Wide Words

The internet offers a range of facilities, allowing users to obtain information and resources, to communicate and to publish information. The World Wide Web provides relatively straightforward access to the vast quantity of information and resources available on the internet and is the facility people use to 'surf ' for information. The internet is made up of millions of 'pages' of information. The collection of pages created by one individual or organisation is known as a website. Each page, which can include text, images, sound, animation and video, and links to other pages or locations, has its own unique address, known as a URL – Uniform Resource Locator.

Though the addresses of websites sometimes appear as a jumble of letters and numbers, there is a simple logic to the way that they are constructed.

An address familiar to many readers is:

[http://www.ucas.ac.uk/]

Let us unpick the elements of this address:

HTTP	Hypertext Transfer Protocol	The most common format (protocol) for the transmission of internet information. Other protocols include: HTTPS, FTP, DNS and POP3
WWW	World Wide Web	This page is accessed via the 'friendly' interface of the internet.
UCAS	University and Colleges Admissions Service	This page belongs to UCAS
.ac	Abbreviation for 'academic'	This page is located in the academic domain
.uk	Abbreviation for United Kingdom	The domain is located in the United Kingdom

Table 5.2   The web address 'http://www.ucas.ac.uk/apply/guides08.html' compared to a postal address

	Address for the Internet	What does this mean?	Equivalent for an item of mail
What is it?	http://	Hypertext Transfer Protocol: one of the different ways in which information can be transmitted over the internet	Letter, parcel or telegram
Where is it going?	www.ucas	The World Wide Web server for the Universities and Colleges Admissions Service	Country and city
Additional information	.ac.uk	An academic institution in the United Kingdom	District
More precisely?	.apply	A part of the UCAS server with information about applications	Road name and number
Final destination?	guides08.html	A web page document which is called 'guides08' and contains information about making applications for the year 2008	Name of person

The address below belongs to a specific page of the UCAS website:

[http://www.ucas.ac.uk/apply/guides08.html]

By looking at the URL in more detail we can see that there is a section of the UCAS site concerning applying, denoted as: 'apply'. There is a further section which contains a guide for 2008 applications, a document entitled 'guides08.html'. The 'html' indicates that the document was created in a language (hypertext mark-up language) suited to display via the World Wide Web. Equally the document could have been created as a Word file and the '.html' would have been replaced by '.doc'.

An analogy with a simple postal address can be made (see Table 5.2).

By 1991 the World Wide Web, notionally invented by Tim Berners-Lee as a means of simplifying the exchange of large amounts of data concerning particle physics, became available to those who were able to equip themselves with computer and a modem. A modem is a device which can be connected simultaneously to a computer and to a telephone system and used to convert information from a computer into a form which can be transmitted via the telephone system's infrastructure. Modems are gradually being replaced by routers, as internet users take advantage of the availability of broadband and high speed connections. One distinct advantage of broadband connections, apart from the increased speed, is that the telephone landline remains open and usable at the same time as internet use.

One definition picked from the results list of an internet search for the phrase 'World Wide Web' (and there are many to chose from) is:

> wide-area hypermedia information retrieval initiative aiming to give universal access to a large universe of documents. (attributed to Hughes, 1993)

This can be enlarged upon as follows:

- **wide-area**: The World Wide Web spans the whole globe.
- **hypermedia**: It contains a range of media, including text, pictures, sound and video. The individual elements are connected by hyperlinks which connect pages to one another and allow for swift movement from one location to another.
- **information retrieval**: Viewing a web document is very easy thanks to the help of web browsers, which are the point of contact between the user and the web. Web browsers allow the user to retrieve pages just by clicking a mouse button when the pointer on the screen is over a *link*, or by entering appropriate web addresses. Information may be retrieved from the web extremely quickly, by any suitably set up computer with an internet connection.
- **universal access**: No matter what type of computer is being used, or what type of computer the information is held on, web browsers allow for apparently seamless connection to, and movement between, many different computer locations.
- **large universe of documents**: Anyone can publish a web page. No matter what obscure information you want to find, there is certain to be someone who has produced and published a web page about it. It will not necessarily be exactly what you want, it might not be accurate or written in an appropriate style, but it will be there. There are many millions of web pages in existence now, and many more are being added each day. (The importance of evaluating web-based resources will be dealt with later.)

Services provided by the internet

To all intents and purposes the World Wide Web is the friendly, public face of the internet. However, the web is just one of the services that the internet provides, although it is the best known and probably the most widely used.

Some other services provided by the internet are e-mail, FTP, usenet, newsgroups and mailing lists, instant messaging, chat rooms and video conferencing. Let us look at each in turn.

e-mail allows users to send and receive written messages via a telephone line. For an entire new generation e-mail is ubiquitous. It forms the essential element of communication in many spheres, including work, hobbies and family life. The use of e-mail has made communication, from desk to desk in the same office or from home to home across the world, a very different experience from pre-computer times.

FTP (File Transfer Protocol) is a way to transfer files from computer to computer via the internet. You might typically use it to transfer ('upload') a web page from your own computer (where you are writing it) to a web server so it can be accessed by the world; or you may use it to transfer ('download') a file from a public archive to your own computer. There are many FTP clients (programs) available. Most internet users work very efficiently without having to know about FTP.

Usenet (also called internet news) is a huge network of discussion groups. Newsgroups are like notice boards where people log in to a particular group to read and contribute remarks or questions. There are thousands of newsgroups covering any and every topic and interest. The groups are set up within broad categories such as sci (science), biz (business), comp (computers), soc (society) and alt (alternate); for each broad category there are a great many more specific titles.

Mailing lists usually consist of a group of people who exchange e-mail about a subject that interests them. Mailing lists are a means for individuals to communicate and network. For example, a mailing list called 'natlangs-forum' allows people with an interest in languages in all sectors of society to write to the list about relevant topics, alert one another to useful websites or ask for help and advice.

Instant messaging is an internet service that allows a user to communicate in real time (synchronously) with other users who have the same instant messaging software installed on their computer. Instant messaging includes something called 'presence technology', which means that when a user opens their messaging software they can see who, on their contact list, is also online. With instant messaging a written conversation proceeds in a similar fashion to a telephone conversation. It is possible to send and receive documents, pictures and sound files and most applications have video possibilities with the use of a web cam. This type of messaging has become a staple of the teenage generation, but it is not exclusively theirs.

Chat rooms allow a number of people to 'meet' on the internet and have live, text-based conversations in real time. It is similar to having a telephone conversation with one or a number of people, except that the participants type instead of talk. Some chat rooms are unrestricted and unmonitored; the more reputable chat rooms have controls, in the hands of the users, in that they can block contact from specified users, and also in the hands of a chat room moderator who can make checks for content-related matters.

Video conferencing enables two or more people, in different locations, to talk to one another while also being able to see each other. It is also possible to arrange for the exchange of audio, video, images or any other digital file to allow users in different places to work simultaneously on the same document. There are useful business and educational applications for video conferencing, as there are for the other features of the internet.

It can be seen that the make-up of the internet which has been outlined above can be divided crudely into two broad categories: information and communication. Beneath each of these headings there are, naturally, sub-divisions. Information can be *accessed* or *published*, and communication can in general terms be of two different types: *synchronous*, happening at the same time – that is the people communicating are actually sitting and responding to messages as they are written (*chatting*) – and *asynchronous*, where messages are written and sent but not necessarily read or responded to until later – e-mail is an example of asynchronous communication.

The World Wide Web and the other areas of the internet we have looked at can be classified into one of these headings. Web viewing is clearly concerned with access to information, or, when used to create pages and sites, to publishing information. Exchange of e-mail is asynchronous communication, whereas video conferencing and instant messaging are examples of synchronous communication.

Search facilities

The internet is undoubtedly an incredible source of information the size of which extends beyond what we can easily conceive. Without the ability to find specific information on demand the internet would be no more than a universe-sized haystack and we would have less chance of finding what we were looking for than finding a needle in a standard haystack.

KEY PRINCIPLES

Search Engine: A search engine is a program that searches documents held on the internet for specified key words and returns a list of the documents where the key words were found. The term 'search engine' really refers to a class of programs, but it is often used specifically to describe systems like Google, Alta Vista, Excite and many others, that enable users to search for documents on the World Wide Web.

(Continued)

(A typical search engine works by sending out what is known as a spider to collect as many documents as possible. Another program, known as an indexer, then checks these documents and creates an index based on the words contained in each document. Search engines use a complex algorithm (set of instructions) to create the index in such a way that only meaningful results are returned for each query. The whole process happens incredibly quickly.

Certain ideas need to be considered when using an internet search engine for academic purposes:

- First, most search engine companies make money by placing certain sites at, or near, the top of a result list. The search engine companies make most of their money through adverts, not from the number of searches carried out.
- In most cases search engines are not capable of indexing more than about one-third of the information held on the internet.
- Many search engines lag behind in indexing new sites, which might mean that whatever you locate could be more than two years old, and more recent sites might not be located.

For these and other reasons it is important to be aware that internet searching for academic information can only sensibly be seen as a part of the full picture.

We will look at some of the practicalities of internet searching later. For now, we will consider some of the academic-specific search facilities available. These particular tools for searching are designed specifically for use in research and other scholarly work, and in most cases should be a first port of call for information in most academic disciplines. There will of course be times when a common, and well-respected search engine such as Google will also serve your purpose well.

Google Scholar Most experienced internet users are aware of the search engine Google. It is by fairly common assent the most used of the search engines which are freely available. The success of Google has allowed the company running it to diversify into other areas of interest. Such sites and facilities include Google Earth, a tool for exploring the world via the medium of scalable aerial and satellite photography and maps which is searchable and navigable in a variety of ways, and Google Maps, an atlas which allows for searching by different terms and provides fine detail of all of the major centres of population in the world. There is also Google Scholar, which as the name suggests, is designed for use by the academic community. We are told on the Scholar website that:

Google Scholar provides a simple way to broadly search for scholarly literature. From one place, you can search across many disciplines and sources: peer-reviewed papers, theses, books, abstracts and articles, from academic publishers, professional societies, preprint repositories, universities and other scholarly organizations. Google Scholar helps you identify the most relevant research across the world of scholarly research. (http://scholar.google.com/)

The claims made by the site are certainly not highly exaggerated. Google Scholar has been generally well received by its target users and is recommended as a good starting point by many university departments.

It is certainly worth looking at the website for Google Scholar, and reading about the way that it operates. Having some knowledge of the ways in which items are located will give you insight into the usefulness of the system and allow you to make judgements about its value to your specific subject area. It is also worthwhile asking your tutors about the use of Google Scholar in your research, and also about other more specific alternatives.

More specific searching options   Google Scholar is designed with specific academic and scholarly users in mind, but it is a general, rather than a domain-specific search tool. As we saw in Chapter 4, there are many internet databases which are subject-specific and more targeted. Here we will look at two examples from one subject area (Education) as an illustration: the British Education Index (BEI) and the Education Resources Information Center (ERIC).

The **BEI**, which is based at Leeds University Library, provides a broad range of infor-mation services relevant to the work of students, researchers, policy-makers and practi-tioners in the fields of education and training. The services go beyond the tracking of documents and information. There are five sections to the index, the first of which, the index itself, will be of most use to undergraduates. The five sections are:

- The British Education Index: a database of information about UK literature which sup-ports study and research in education, and which has a system for notifying those who register with information concerning new additions, that is newly published materials relating to specific topics.
- The British Education Internet Resource catalogue: a database of information about pro-fessionally evaluated internet sites which support educational study and research.
- The Education Conference Programme Service: a detailed searchable record of pro-grammes and event archives for conferences in the area.
- The Education Conference Listings Service: provides a calendar for education- and training-related conferences and gives information about conference locations, content and other details.
- Education-line: a database of the full text of conference papers, working papers and electronic literature which supports educational study and research.

The BEI has developed over the years from a set of regularly updated hard-bound encyclopaedic reference sources to a set of very sophisticated and invaluable tools for many scholars in the field of educational studies. The hard-bound copies took up a good deal of shelf space and were unwieldy; the internet-based twenty-first- century version takes up no space at all and is exceedingly manageable.

ERIC, based at the Education Resources Information Center in the United States, is an internet-based digital library of education research and information. It is operated and sponsored by the Institute of Education Sciences (IES) of the United States of America Department of Education. ERIC provides access to bibliographic records of journal and non-journal literature indexed from 1966 to the present. ERIC also contains a growing collection of full-text materials in PDF format, which means that it is possible to obtain documents in the original format in a very simple and timely way. When compared to the use of the inter-library loan service described in Chapter 4, this system is a clear winner.

ERIC is an American version of the BEI. Used in conjunction with each other they can provide detail of almost everything which has been published in the last forty years or more concerning the practice and theory of education in the western world. This is a remarkable resource to be able to access.

The two examples from the educational domain are more than matched in every other subject. You will in many cases have the particular points of access to the corresponding systems relating to your subject area drawn to your attention. It will serve you well to investigate them and make use of the facilities available. This will become more important to you as your course proceeds and you are given greater responsibility for discovering materials and references for yourself. This will be especially true if you are required to undertake a research project, something which often makes up an important part of final year undergraduate work.

More about search engines   Many internet users, even the most experienced, are at times surprised to discover more about the many different functions, or even tricks, which are available in most search engines. We will consider some of the basic and some of the more advanced general features of search engines here. One message that you should perhaps take from this section is that you should investigate the features of your preferred means of internet searching, and experiment with ways of making your searching more efficient.

Which search engine you choose to use is largely a matter of preference. Many users stay with the search engine they first came across and are happy to work with it. This is not a bad approach, because consistent use of the same system will develop a familiarity with the features of the system and allow you to develop personal ways of searching. If you do not have a preferred search engine, or if you want to shop around for one which might suit your needs better, there are many to choose from.

In deciding to make use of a particular search engine, good advice would be to choose one which gives least interference from advertisement. For search engines to be free to use there does need to be a source of revenue, and different companies approach this in different ways. Engines which regularly provide sponsored links and which in a very subtle way give priority to certain sites need to be looked upon with care. Some engines appear biased – often in the direction of their paymasters – and these too should be treated carefully.

In general it is probably best to use a well-known and reputable search engine for your general searching, and one which is recommended for your particular subject area for more specific work. It is not feasible to provide an exhaustive list here of specific engines for specific subjects, but in conversation with fellow students and tutors it is quite likely that you will be directed towards one which is well suited to your area. A subject specialist librarian would also be a good place to enquire. If this fails, then you could turn first to Google Scholar, which we have considered earlier, or you could use your preferred search engine to seek out something more appropriate.

Carrying out a search

What follows is a guide to searching for both those experienced in the routines, and those who are relatively new to internet searching. As mentioned earlier, it is still possible for even the most rugged and experienced internet users to learn new shortcuts and different techniques. For this reason it might still be worth looking through the following sections even if you put yourself in the 'experienced' category. Much of what follows refers to the use of Google, but it will all have relevance, perhaps in a slightly modified form, to the use of all engines. The help facilities for all worthwhile search engines will provide the fine detail that you may need in specific cases.

There is, as we would expect, a site dedicated to looking for specific search engines. It is called Web Search Engines and is found at: www.web-search-engines.net/. A simple browse of this site might find a subject specific engine to suit your needs. Naturally, anything that you find should be considered carefully and examined for bias and the prevalence of advertising. On this site it was straightforward to find sites such as:

- Infomine (http://infomine.ucr.edu/), described as: a database of scholarly social sciences, humanities and general reference instructional resources, built by librarians from the University of California.

and

- BUBL (http://bubl.ac.uk/) a UK-based service which uses the Dewey system of classification (see Chapter 4) and describes itself as a: 'Catalogue of selected Internet resources covering all academic subject areas. All items are selected, evaluated, catalogued and described by experts' (BUBL, undated).

Table 5.3   The effect of increasing the number of key words when searching for information

Key words	Hits
rainfall	19,000,000
rainfall South America	2,530,000
rainfall South America records	1,650,000
rainfall South America records 1900	208,000
rainfall South America records 1900 government	143,000
rainfall South America records 1900 government meteorological	37,200
rainfall South America records 1900 government meteorological Argentina	686
rainfall South America records 1900 government meteorological Argentina Brazil Chile	365
At this stage it is quite likely that the first site on the list, belonging to the World Meteorological Organisation, will hold the information that is needed.	

Key word searching   A simple key word search for one word will undoubtedly return an enormous number of hits. You can go a long way towards narrowing down your search by using more relevant key words. Five or six is probably enough for most searches to return a manageable number of hits. Even if you are not sure that they are relevant, experimenting with different combinations of words is quicker than getting a whole lot of hits and ploughing through them. If a key word search with five or six words turns up more than at the most forty hits, it can be quicker to try again with a revised set of words. In some cases you may feel confident that you are homing in on the information that you are searching for with more than 40 hits. See the example above. The example in Table 5.3, which concerns searching for information about rainfall patterns in South America over the last 100 years, will illustrate this.

The list of ten key words at the last stage of this search has become unmanageable, but it was arrived at in a methodical way. It is likely that working in this particular way is less efficient than a search for a specific phrase.

Phrase searching   Search engines allow for specific phrases to be entered and searched for. To search for a specific phrase, type in the whole phrase within double quotation marks, e.g. '"South American rainfall"'. The search engine will only find pages which include the phrase, as you have entered it. Finding an exact phrase can make all the difference to a search. Use phrases that you would expect to find in a work concerning what you are looking for and that are specific to the area you are working in. This will help you to target your searches accurately.

The phrase '"South American rainfall"' returned 172 hits. By combining a search for a phrase with a key word, the focus of the search is increased further. The same phrase with the addition of one word outside of the double quotation marks – for example, '"South American rainfall" Records' – returned a reduced number of hits, 132.

Searching a website or page   When it seems that you have found a suitable website it is sometimes a good idea to search the page or the site in question. Some sites have obvious search facilities and, combined with good links for navigating around the site, this makes specific information more easily located. You can also use a feature in the web browser software (such as in Netscape, Internet Explorer or Mozilla, for example) to find all instances of a specific word or phrase. On an open web page, click on the 'Edit' option on the toolbar and choose the option 'Find on this Page' or similar. A dialogue box will open where the word or phrase should be typed. (Often Ctrl F will open this dialogue box.)

Advanced search techniques

Avoiding words and phrases   Some searches bring up an enormous number of hits which are totally irrelevant owing to the fact that your search term is closely associated with something other than what you are searching for. One example might be searching for information concerning cams (a device familiar to engineers). A simple key word search for 'cam' brings up 75,100,000 hits, many of which appear to be related to web cams. If you conduct the same search but exclude pages that contain the word 'web', the number of hits is more than halved – still too many, but it illustrates the point. The usual way to exclude pages containing certain words is to insert a minus sign (type a hyphen on your computer keyboard) before the word that should be excluded: 'cam - web'. Each search engine will have specific search features which should be explored and then used to increase your searching efficiency.

Domain-specific searches   With Google there is an option to search only UK pages. If you are looking for something UK-based on the internet (searching for my name for example) you could type my name and then select pages from the UK only. For other countries you can limit the search to a specific country by typing 'site':

followed by the domain name for that country, for example '"Alan Pritchard" site:fi' will find all the web pages in Finland that include that name. (Remember to use double quotes around words you want to be linked.)

You can narrow domain-specific searches even more. For example, you can search all the academic websites in the UK by adding 'site:ac.uk' to your search criteria, or just a single university by typing the university's website address, e.g. the Warwick site can be searched by adding 'site:warwick.ac.uk' to the search criteria.

Language-specific searches   Google offers the option of choosing to find only pages written in a specific language. Click on 'Advanced Search' and select this option. It is not 100% accurate, a few pages in another language can slip through, but it can be useful sometimes depending on the search that you are making.

Image searches   Also in Google you can search for images. Just click on the 'Image' tag near the top of the page. Typing in the box will select all the images associated with that word or phrase. For example, typing in '"Alan Pritchard"' will give you a selection of images related to the name; only one of them is actually me.

What search engines do not do

Upper and lower cases   Google, along with many other search engines, is not case-sensitive. For example, if you type 'ANNIE' or 'Annie' you get the same result.

Plurals   Search engines do not routinely convert plurals to singulars or vice versa, so if a plural of a particular word does not return what you are looking for, try doing the search again with the singular. For example, typing, '"aspect of practice"' will not work if you are looking for 'aspects of practice'.

Spelling   Google is good at picking up misspelling and suggesting a correct spelling – unless the word you type in is still a real word but a different one from the one you meant. For example, 'aspect of practise' will not be highlighted as a possible spelling mistake because of the existence of the word in two forms – noun and verb.

UK/US spelling   If you cannot find what you are looking for it might be because it is spelled differently in the United States. Remember '–er' instead of '–re', '–ize' instead of '–ise', '–or' instead of '–our' as word endings. Some words use 'k' instead of 'c' and 'e' instead of 'ae' or 'oe'. Some words drop entire syllables (e.g. 'orient' instead of 'orientate', 'pressure' for 'pressurise'). Since about half the pages on the Internet are of American origin, it is worth making sure you are searching them too.

The California State University library has a tutorial entitled 'The Information Jungle', on its website which explains and compares different search engines (CSUSB, undated). If you would like more information and some comparisons of different search engines this would be a good starting point for you.

One point which cannot be stressed enough here is that the use and efficiency of any search engine can be improved if you take a little time to experiment with its features. This approach, combined with looking at the 'Help' or 'Tips' section of the engine's site is likely to help you to become a more effective search engine user. Alongside this approach you can of course talk to others about their preferences and their personal shortcuts.

Website evaluation

We will consider the evaluation of websites in some detail here, as it is a very important aspect of safe internet use in its broadest sense, which includes avoiding the dangers of using highly suspect factual information. There are certain aspects of web-based resources which have a bearing on the style and quality of a site. With these in mind, it is possible to approach web-based information with caution and an awareness of the potential pitfalls of internet use.

Website attributes

There is a list of website attributes, concerning the quality of any particular site, which is quoted, both on official websites and in other reputable locations.

The suggested list of headings against which the attributes of websites might be assessed is as follows:

- Authority
- Purpose
- Audience
- Relevance
- Objectivity
- Accuracy
- Currency
- Format
- Links

These headings are enlarged upon below by means of sets of questions which might be posed in order to gain more insight into a particular site and to enable an evaluation based on more than initial impressions. Some of the questions are taken from the same source. The heading Ease of Use has been added.

It would be a good idea to go through each of the questions below and use them in relation to a website known to you. Ideally you should be able to internalise the ideas set out here and use them each time that you consult the internet, especially if the quality of your work depends upon the validity of the information that you are using. Opinions from a website with the address: 'www.honestjohnknowsitall.com' are quite likely to be of lower academic value than carefully orchestrated arguments from a reputable source located in a university, for example. It is your job to be absolutely certain which of these two opposites, and all of the shades between, you are making use of.

Authority

You need to consider:

- Who has written the information?
- What is the authority or expertise of the author?
- Are there contact details for the author?
- Where does the content originate from?
- Is it clear who the author is and who has published the site?
- Are they qualified to provide information on this topic?
- Is the material biased?
- Where is the content published?
- What is the domain name of the website?
- Is it published by a large organisation, or on a personal website?
- Does the website cover the topic fully?
- Does it provide links and references to other materials?
- If links to other materials are provided, are these evaluated or annotated to provide further information? Do these links work?
- Does the site contain any advertising?
- Does any advertising influence the content?

Purpose, audience and relevance

You need to consider:

- What are the aims of the site?
- Does it achieve its aims?
- Who is the intended audience for this content?
- Is the content easy to read and understand?
- Is the site specifically aimed at children?

- If so, is the level and tone of the content appropriate?
- Is the site specifically aimed at adults?
- Is the site relevant to me?
- Does the material provide everything that is needed?
- Could more relevant material be found elsewhere, in a book or magazine for example?
- Is the site trying to sell something?

Objectivity

You need to consider:

- Is the information offered as fact or opinion?
- Is the information biased in any obvious way?

Accuracy and currency

You need to consider:

- Does the information appear to be accurate?
- Are additional references given?
- Can the information be verified from other sources?
- Are the spelling and grammar correct?
- Is the content dated?
- When was the content last updated?
- Are all links up to date and valid?
- Are any areas of the site 'under construction'?

Format

You need to consider:

- Does the site contain information in the format that I want?

Links

You need to consider:

- Does the site give me advice/ideas/other choices?

Ease of use

You need to consider:

- Is the site easy to use?
- Is the site well structured?

- Is it easy to find relevant information?
- Is the content in an easy-to-use format?
- What facilities does the site provide to help locate information?
- Does it have a search facility?
- Is the menu navigation logical?
- Does it provide a site map or index?
- Does the site load quickly?
- Is the site attractive in design?
- Is the content copyright, or can it be used providing the source is acknowledged?

These questions are all pertinent, and certainly deserving of attention. Obviously some of them are of greater importance than others. If you can be sure that the information is wholly *bona fide* it matters less that it is written in an unusual font, for example. Experienced internet users often run through these points, or at least some of them, when they visit a site for the first time; in many cases this is, at least partially, carried out informally and even unconsciously. It is possible to disregard a website almost immediately in some cases based on what could be described as intuition. This intuition is based upon experience and the use, in some measure, of the questions above.

Website location

An important pointer to the pedigree of a website, and a means of answering some of the questions above, can be found in its address (URL). As we saw earlier, certain elements of a web address give details of its location. The example given was that an address which includes the characters '.ac.uk' has its source in a British academic institution, usually a university. Tables 5.4 and 5.5 give details of other elements of web addresses which give insight into their background and ownership.

We have seen that there is a set of simple skills which, if used, will give important clues as to the validity and reliability of individual sites. For many internet users the notions of website evaluation considered above become second nature, and in practice, with effective searching, sites of poor pedigree, of blatant commercialism, or of no clear academic value do not impede the progress of efficient and productive searching for relevant academic information.

In some cases internet searches will lead to the sites of reputable academic journals. Access to these sites is restricted in many cases to registered users. As we saw in Chapter 4, registered students will have access to these sites and to the electronic journals which they hold via the Athens system.

Table 5.4   Top-level domain codes

Domain code	Meaning
.ac	Academic institution – mostly this refers to universities but there are exceptions. Used exclusively in the UK and so only found in the form '.ac.uk'
.co	Commercial body in the UK. Used almost exclusively in the form '.co.uk'
.com	Originally intended for 'commercial' bodies, but any person or organization, commercial or otherwise, may register and use '.com'
.edu	Educational institutions. Mostly used in the United States, Canada and Australia, but also seen in other countries
.gov	Government departments, agencies and branches. Including local authorities
.mil	Military bodies
.net	Bodies and computers that represent part of the internet's infrastructure
.nhs.uk	UK National Health Service trust or department
.org	Designated for miscellaneous bodies that do not fit under any of the other top-level domains. Mostly used by non-profit organisations

Table 5.5   Some country domain codes

Country code	Country
.au	Australia
.br	Brazil
.ch	Switzerland
.cn	China
.de	Germany
.fr	France
.jp	Japan
.uk	United Kingdom
.us	United States of America – this is very often missing, since the very first web addresses were from the United States

Online encyclopaedias – a word of warning

Using material from online encyclopaedias with no real academic pedigree is not advisable. Let us look at the example of Wikipedia, which is widely recognised as an excellent source of information across an enormous range of topics. However, Wikipedia's content is contributed by the users themselves and the authority of any particular user is not always clear. The information is also open to amendment by others. This is recognised by the nature of the Wikipedia organisation and there are a number of safety measures in place to try to maintain the integrity of the site. To this end there are Wikipedia workers known as 'recent changes patrollers' who have the task of 'averting vandalism'. The fact that this role exists indicates that so-called vandalism – probably the malicious or at best, mischievous, alteration of content – does take place. For this reason alone there can be no absolute guarantee that the information you find is 'safe and sound' and from a reliable, reputable source. None of this, however, detracts from the value of Wikipedia as an introduction to a topic and as a source of further reference.

If you are interested in this facet of online access to information you could carry out a phrase search using 'the dangers of using Wikipedia'. You will find articles to read that strongly advise against the use of Wikipedia in academic work for submission.

Plagiarism and Essays for Sale

Plagiarism is the use of material written by others without correctly acknowledging its source. Plagiarism is cheating and is a serious academic misdemeanour. In extreme cases a student's registration will be withdrawn and they will be required to leave the university.

Plagiarism can be intentional, which is serious, and it can be unintentional, which is possibly a sign of extreme foolishness. Whichever version of plagiarism appears in the work of a student when submitted for assessment it is highly likely to be detected, and action is very likely to be taken. For minor unintentional plagiarism, such as failing to acknowledge the source of a short quotation, leading the reader to think that the words were written by the student, the action taken is likely to be the loss of marks. This could of course lead to the piece of work failing with the consequent results attached to a failed assignment. The dire consequences of extreme intentional plagiarism have already been mentioned.

You should be absolutely certain that any work you submit for assessment cannot be considered as any form of plagiarism. To be sure of this you must not copy any work from any source without properly acknowledging its source (we will look again at plagiarism and at referencing systems in Chapters 6 and 7).

The advent of electronic technologies has made it easy for the unscrupulous to copy texts from one source to another in order to pass them off as their own. However, there are similar new technologies which are capable of detecting this very action. Universities provide plagiarism detection tools for their staff to use, although in many cases astute academics need no help to sniff out plagiarism.

Most internet-aware students will have come across the idea at least that it is possible to buy essays from sites which have been set up specifically to assist in the process of cheating. It may be tempting to investigate these sites and even to peruse a sample essay from your subject area, but even this is fraught with danger and simply not worth the risk. Experienced tutors recognise the signs of plagiarism very easily. They know the literature of the subject that they are teaching and are astute at picking up on the many indicators in a piece of written work which sound alarm bells and lead them to make detailed checks of individual work. It may be the case that some plagiarised work slips through the net, but much more does not.

Virtual Learning Environments

A Virtual Learning Environment (VLE) is usually a web-based system for providing teaching and learning resources combined with other features such as notice boards, discussions, group and individual e-mail. At their best VLEs are an effective and meaningful means of online interaction between students and teachers, and a repository for resources including administrative detail (meeting times for example), lecture materials (additional notes and handouts), readings and links to other external sources (academic websites such as appropriate journals, even specific articles). At their worst, they are no more than an electronic storage facility for lecture handouts. Many VLEs also have facilities for student tracking and assessment. That is, it is possible for tutors to see who has accessed certain aspects of the site, who has contributed to discussions, or responded to requests for ideas or help; sometimes VLEs are used to set tasks, tests and the like which can contribute towards assessment scores for a particular module.

You may have been exposed to the use of a VLE in school or college, but in general they are not widely used at this level. Universities, however, are increasingly making use of them and it is very likely that your institution will have some plans at some stage of development for the implementation of a system of virtual learning.

There are a number of commercially produced systems (Blackboard, WebCT, Moodle, Boddington), some of which are available free, but many universities have developed their own systems, tailored to needs identified internally. Some institutions consider that a VLE is a tool for distance learning courses. This is clearly true, but there are also many situations where VLEs can be of great value in more traditional university teaching settings. If you are in a position to make use of a VLE in your study it will be important to become familiar with the system.

There are many advantages to the use of a VLE, most notably in terms of access to resources, tutors and fellow students. Being able to access materials, or to contact others directly from remote locations, can be of great benefit. It means that travel time can be reduced and economy of time and effort improved. Some see VLEs as an excuse for reducing student–tutor contact time. This may indeed be a side effect, but it would be a shame if that were the only reason for their introduction. Some tutors, even whole departments, do not make use of VLEs. This is for a whole variety of reasons ranging from the individual tutor being against the 'new' idea, to the simple fact that there is no system available. It is likely that the use of VLEs will increase over time, and that you will be introduced to one during your period of study.

SUMMARY

- It can be an advantage to own certain books that are important to your course. Books are very expensive, but the worldwide availability of second-hand books via the internet makes many of the books that you might need more affordable.
- The university library is the gateway to far more than stored paper-based materials.
- The Athens system allows access to the vast range of academic and scientific material which supports serious academic work. Athens access will be mediated by your library in all probability.
- The internet is an excellent tool for locating appropriate sources of information for study at all levels, but it must be used with extreme caution.
- Different search engines are more or less useful when searching for academic material. Precise search techniques can make a big difference to your success in finding what you are looking for.
- There are some specific search locations for academics to use, Google Scholar is a good example.
- There is an increased danger that you might find yourself inadvertently, or otherwise, guilty of plagiarism when accessing electronic sources. Extreme care must be taken to avoid this.
- There is a trend across most sectors of education, especially undergraduate courses, towards the use of Virtual Learning Environments.

Next

Since almost all of your work will be leading towards assessment, the next chapter will look at this area in detail. To begin with, the more conventional essay-style submission will be considered and then the lengthier dissertation. Other types of assessment, including exams, come in the chapter that follows.

Activities

Searching: If you are relatively new to the use of the internet for academic purposes you might like to experiment a little. Choose a key word related to your subject and carry out a simple search with a search engine, Google (www.google.com) for example; note how many 'hits' are made. Carry out an identical search with another search engine, alltheweb (www.alltheweb.com), for example, and compare the number of hits with the first search. Can you account for the difference? Investigate the advanced search options and experiment with different engines. Try to limit the search to academic institutions in the United Kingdom for example (see above). Experiment with Google Scholar, the version of Google specifically for academic work.

Website evaluation: Choose a website related to an aspect of your subject and evaluate it according to the criteria listed below. You could find a site at random with a simple key word search, or visit a site that you know about already.

1. Is it clear who has written/provided the information?
2. Are the aims of the site clear?
3. Does the site achieve its aims?
4. Is the site relevant for my purposes?
5. Is the information at an appropriate level?
6. Can the information be checked?
7. When was the site produced?
8. Does the information appear to be biased in any way?

6 Assessment: Essays and Dissertations

LEARNING OUTCOMES

What this chapter has in store:

- An explanation of the purposes of assessment
- Help with style and other considerations in academic writing
- Explanation of some of the process words used in assignment titles, and the vital importance of understanding and fully answering the question
- Specific guidance for writing essay-style assignments
- Guidance relating to writing dissertations
- Detail concerning the importance of accurate referencing

We have seen in earlier chapters that there is a vast amount of work to be done when you are studying and learning at university. The preceding chapters have outlined the process of learning, and many of the study techniques that you will make use of in your work. For many, the focus of all of their work is the assessment; all that they do is driven by the looming spectre of assessed assignments and exams. It is good to have assessment in mind, and it is advisable to be looking towards doing as well as you can when assessments are made. But to see the essence of your study as what could be considered as 'hoop-jumping' would be to miss many of the opportunities for wider experiences that are perhaps not the sole focus of the assessment of your course. For this reason you should understand your assessment and work hard towards being prepared for it, and being successful, but you should not let assessment shroud your academic, or social, life in dark clouds. This should be possible if you take an approach to your assessment which involves understanding the processes, learning the techniques, paying attention to detail, such as timing, and not leaving anything to the eleventh hour.

The purposes of assessment

Without delving too deeply into the realms of curriculum theory, it is possible to find definitions of assessment and pointers to the perceived value and purposes of assessment. In all university regulations there will be information concerning assessment. Statements such as 'The purpose of assessment is to enable students to demonstrate fulfilment of the objectives of the programme of study and achieve the required learning outcomes at least to threshold standard' (Manchester Metropolitan University website) or 'The purpose of assessment is to provide an opportunity for students to demonstrate, develop and share their critical understandings of current theory and practice in the area of ...' (University of Derby website). The fine detail of assessment and what it will actually mean for you will be given you by module tutors and module handbooks.

The Quality Assurance Agency for Higher Education (QAA) provides guidance for universities, and their code of practice for assessment includes the following definitions for: Assessment, Diagnostic Assessment, Formative Assessment and Summative Assessment:

- Assessment is a generic term for a set of processes that measure students' learning, skills and understanding.
- Diagnostic assessment enables attributes or skills to be identified in the learner that suggest appropriate pathways of study, or learning difficulties that require support and resolution.
- Formative assessment is designed to enable the learner to obtain feedback on his/her progress in meeting stated objectives (learning outcomes) and reviewing goals.
- Summative assessment provides the means whereby a clear statement of achievement or failure can be made in respect of a student's performance in relation to stated objectives.

(QAA, 2000)

For lay people the notion of summative assessment that best encapsulates their understanding is the end of year, or course, examinations, under strict exam conditions, after which a judgement of pass or fail is made. This is often seen as the most important outcome of a course. It is the award of a qualification, dependent upon the outcome of final summative assessments, which, in most cases, focuses the attention of students. Any one who has taught a university module will know that students are always keen to know about the assessment requirements right at the very start, and this is understandable.

Often in universities there is more emphasis laid upon summative assessment, but diagnostic and formative assessment also have a place. In many cases, feedback is given at midpoint assessments in a module. For example, if an assignment is submitted, marked and returned at some stage in a module, and there is another, similar, assignment later in the year, students should expect to be given formative feedback which will enable them to improve their performance for the next point of assessment.

Assessment at university can take on many forms. The traditional essay and the end of year exam still hold a major place in many courses, but there are other forms of assessment which are commonly used across a great many subjects and courses. Some subjects favour particular approaches to assessment, some subjects require practical work which is written up in the form of a report, others might favour a portfolio submission as a record of learning and development. All subjects might require essay-style submissions and within one subject area a range of different assessment requirements is likely to be in place.

An important point to keep firmly in mind, before we discuss assessment any further, and certainly before you begin to write for assessment, is that your tutors will not want you to write in a fancy, over-complicated, pseudo-academic way. This is something that we will return to in this chapter and in the one that follows. You must write in a way that is clear and communicates well. Some students seem to think that to write a university assignment they must use sentences with endless multiple clauses, and words with as many syllables as possible. This is strictly not the case. To write at a university level you must write clearly and precisely. This may well mean choosing simpler words if they actually do the job that is needed, and it may also mean sometimes writing in sentences which might be long, with multiple clauses, but clear. The sentences might also be short. This theme will re-emerge over the next two chapters.

KEY PRINCIPLES

Assessment: Any of the processes which are implemented with the purpose of measuring the current progress of learners; examinations and assignments are the most common forms of assessment.

Formative assessment: Assessment which may be used to make a judgement of the future needs of individual learners.

Summative assessment: Assessment which takes place at the end of a period of study to make a final measurement of achievement.

The essay-style submission

It is very likely that as a new undergraduate you will have written many essays during whichever route you have followed to your university studies. Precisely how well honed your skills are will depend upon the support that you have been given over the years, including constructive (formative) feedback, and the amount of practice that you have had. In many ways essays written at university are no different from those written for other courses at a pre-university level. The structure of a good essay written for GCSE coursework will, in all probability, be very close to the structure of an undergraduate essay. The differences are likely to be the length, the complexity of the arguments involved, the more extensive reference to other sources, and the use of language at a more sophisticated level. (We have already noted that 'language at a more sophisticated level' does not mean language which is unnecessarily complicated. We will consider style later.)

In Chapter 2 we considered some of the possible failures in the academic writing of others which you should look out for in the course of your reading; such things as: ambiguity, inconsistency, unintelligent use of language, generalisation, economy with evidence, the authority of the writer and appeals to common sense or consensus. In your writing you must try hard to avoid these things. If you do not, then you should not be surprised if your tutor picks up on it and challenges your work for these reasons. You might find it helpful to re-read the section of Chapter 2 which deals with this. It is the final section, entitled 'Challenge what you read'.

The basic structure of an essay

There are essentially four main sections to an essay, some of which are likely to have sub-divisions. They are:

- Introduction
- Main body
- Conclusion
- References and bibliography

The first three sections may call to mind advice given by primary school teachers concerning the beginning, middle and end of a piece of creative writing. The fourth section, references and bibliography, takes on far more importance at this level of work than many newcomers seem to recognise. There will be more on references later.

Introduction   The introduction will do exactly as the title suggests, it will introduce the topic, the question to be answered and your approach to answering the question. You will give your interpretation of the question and set out the content you will cover. In most cases the introduction will equate to approximately one-tenth of the overall length of the essay.

You should aim to provide a context for the ideas which will be dealt with in the main body of your essay. There is, naturally, more than one way of doing this. It may be the case that there are certain terms in the title of the essay which need to be defined. This should be done in the introduction so that there is no mistaking what it is that you are writing about. In some cases, mostly in the areas of history, politics, sociology, economics and other related subjects, it might be necessary to locate your essay in time, that is, give a brief idea of events, movements, or people who may have had influence on the topic that you will be covering.

Main body   The main body of your essay will be made up of a series of paragraphs, each one dealing with a particular theme or topic, and each one linked to the next. All of the points you make should be supported by arguments, analysis and supported by quotations from source material – that is, the ideas of other writers which must be acknowledged and correctly referenced. You need to analyse the material and give your views. Your views do have a place in the academic submissions that you make. Your views will be considered, and you will have arrived at them as a result of your study and understanding; they will not be something picked from the air, or read in passing in a newspaper.

In the main body of your essay you need to make use of the skills of selecting, organising, interpreting and analysing material which is relevant to the question. You should present your ideas in a clear, logical and coherent structure. This structure should have been finalised during your planning.

If you are writing about a controversial topic, with conflicting ideas and positions, you must consider both sides of the argument equally and deal with all of the relevant ideas, not just those which appeal to you or seem most important or credible.

The worth of your work will be judged on how well you balance viewpoints on the basis of available evidence, how well you evaluate the material and how well you find faults in the arguments of others. The way that you develop an argument will also be a major consideration. Some consider that the ability to develop an effective argument is at the heart of academic study, and it is certainly an important graduate skill. Your ability to construct and develop an argument may well set you above your peers, and make the difference between a piece of work that is 'ok' and one that is 'very good'.

To structure an argument you must:

- Be wholly consistent
- Link ideas together, and
- Proceed logically and step by step to a sound conclusion.

The paragraphs making up the main body of your essay should be structured in a way similar to the pattern below:

First paragraph – introducing your argument   As we have seen, all assignments which are in the form of an essay will need to present and develop an argument. This is true for all types of essays. It is actually very difficult to think of an essay-style question which will not, in some measure at least, expect you to present, develop and sustain an argument. Essays which simply describe do not get good grades; when the word 'describe' appears in an essay title it will usually be in conjunction with other words, 'Describe and account for ...', or 'Describe and interpret ...'.

The first paragraph deals with the first topic that your introduction said that you would address and the first sentence should introduce the main idea of the paragraph. (Compare this idea with the notion of the topic sentence which we considered in the section dealing with efficient reading in Chapter 2.) The next sentences should develop the topic of the paragraph and include evidence, details, quotes and references. The last sentence of the paragraph should lead to the next paragraph. For example: 'Having considered the background to the ... we will now look at each of the causes in detail' or 'The next point to consider is ...'.

Second and successive paragraphs – developing your argument   An argument needs to be built one step at a time, and each step will need a new paragraph in your essay. Each paragraph will need to build on the points from the previous paragraph. Paragraphs are essentially the bricks of your essay and the better you are able concentrate on making each brick present a point clearly, with links to the brick before and the brick which follows, the better your essay will be.

A paragraph should have a single main idea, point or argument. Each time that you move to a new idea (or point or argument), you must begin a new paragraph. It is allowable to include closely related ideas in one paragraph as long as it does not make an excessively long paragraph, or over-complicate your writing. It should be a straightforward task to sum up the content of a paragraph with a single brief statement. Think back to what was said about topic sentences in Chapter 2, covering reading for academic purposes.

For each paragraph there should be

- A topic sentence which sums up the main point being made. In most cases it is wise to put this sentence at, or very near, the beginning of the paragraph (though we have seen that sometimes it is placed at the end to sum up the content). Again, the first sentence should introduce the topic of the paragraph and it should be linked with the paragraph which it follows, for example, 'The next aspect of ... is ...' or 'Now that the causes have been outlined the effects will be considered'. This type of sentence maintains the flow of your writing.

- An explanation of any terminology that might not be clear, or which has not been defined earlier.
- Evidence, or other comments, to support the point being made. This could be in a range of different formats. For example, a brief background to the topic; development of the argument of the paragraph, setting out the reasoning behind the argument; the provision of evidence to support or even challenge the argument of the paragraph. This evidence, of course, can be in many different forms – facts, statistics, quotations, brief anecdotes, all with full and appropriate referencing.
- An evaluation of the evidence that you have presented. If possible you should compare it with evidence from a different source. It might be advisable to do this in a new paragraph, but you should explain in the opening sentence what it is that you are doing.
- Analysis of the causes or reasons for what you have presented.
- A discussion of the points made, including any consequences resulting from them – counter-examples, for example.
- A concluding sentence. This sentence will relate directly to the topic of the paragraph, and in most cases look forward to the next paragraph or section of your work. There will be times when a conclusion to a paragraph is not needed.

This seems a lot to fit into one paragraph, but much of what should be included will be brief and to the point. You must beware of writing overlong paragraphs which are difficult to follow. At every point you should be thinking about the reader, and how you can make reading your work a straightforward process.

Conclusion   The conclusion is the section of your essay where you sum up all that you have written. You give the conclusions that you have drawn from your reading and the analysis of the evidence that you have presented. Essays should lead to a well-founded conclusion, drawing together the ideas examined in your writing. Where the title specifically asks for a personal opinion, the conclusion is the place to include it. Many essay questions either explicitly ask a question, or a question is implied. Questions need answers. When the title of an assignment asks a question the biggest single fault made by students is not to answer it.

The length of the conclusion will equate to approximately one-tenth of the overall length of the essay and balance neatly with the introduction.

Questions as essay titles

- Why did the North industrialise more rapidly than the South, and what difference did this make?
- Where do scientific hypotheses come from?

- What can oral history tell us about the memory of Italian fascism?
- How satisfactory is the de Broglie–Bohm theory as a resolution of the measurement problem?

All of the essay titles above are essentially posing a question. Apart from supplying an introduction and a discussion of the elements which make up the question (for example, showing that the North did industrialise more rapidly than the South; defining and giving examples of scientific hypotheses; defining oral history, memory and Italian Fascism; explaining the de Broglie–Bohm theory and defining the 'measurement problem'), there must be an answer to the question which is adequately treated in the last part of the essay.

When preparing for and writing your assignment you should refer constantly to the title. By keeping the title at the forefront of your mind you are far less likely to stray from the task of doing what it is that the title asks of you. Look at the title often and re-read it each time you sit down to continue with your work, or each time that you pause to consider your progress. You might even go to the extreme of writing it out and sticking it to the top of your monitor so that you cannot avoid seeing it.

How To Get Started

It can be daunting when faced starkly with a title, and for some the effect is a little like being a rabbit caught in headlights. The danger, at first sight of the question, is to think that you should leave it for now. Doing this just means that the headlights will become more intense as the deadline comes nearer.

In most cases the titles for assessment are given at the start of a module, often in the module guide. It is considered by some that it is not worth thinking about the title, or which one to choose, at the start of a module because the material relevant to it will not have been covered. There is some sense in this point of view, but it is a good idea to have at least some preliminary thoughts. One reason for this is that if you wait for a few weeks you will find that the books you need from the library are on loan and if you reserve them you will be some way down the queue. Some students attempt to borrow every book on a reading list as soon as it is published. This is understandable if a little unfair, not to mention annoying for those who are less speedy in their response.

There are probably as many ways of preparing to start writing an assignment as there are ways of reading and taking notes. That is to say that everyone will have a preferred way of working and they will stick to it, even if this involves waiting to the last minute and then sitting up for most of the night to finish. Naturally this approach could never be recommended, but we know that it is used by some – sometimes, seemingly, to good effect. By far the best way to prepare is to start early and to be methodical. The nature of the method has to be personal, but the following outline sequence is recommended:

- Select the title or question.
- Divide the overall task into smaller individual tasks.
- Record your thoughts, ideas and sources, in one place and write a plan.
- Collect source material together.
- Write a first draft.
- Read your work and make corrections.
- Produce a final draft and proof read it one last time.

Assignment preparation sequence

Select the title or question   Choose the question or title and be clear what the topic is. Talk about it with others in the group. If it is not entirely clear, check with your tutor. Most tutors would prefer to clear up any possible confusion at the earliest possible stage. Often a short e-mail will help sort out any problems, but your tutor may have a preferred means of contact which you should use.

Divide the overall task into smaller individual tasks   Sometimes it is helpful to divide the overall task into smaller units which can be accomplished in order. Each time a smaller task is completed there can be a feeling of achievement. The tasks could be: visit the library and find books from the list or search for other related titles; begin a tentative plan; make notes from readings; look for more material if necessay; write a first draft of the introduction; draw up a timetable for completing the essay.

Record your thoughts, ideas and sources, in one place and write a plan   At the initial planning stage it can be very useful to write down, or record in the form of a diagram, as many ideas as you can which will have an impact on the content and structure of your work. Some of the ideas may well be disregarded later. From this brainstorm-style activity it should be possible to draft an initial plan. The way in which you do this is a matter of personal preference, as so many of these things are. You might favour a list, or you might prefer to work on a larger than normal sheet of paper and produce something in the style of a concept map, on which you can easily include links and associations which will help in the sequencing of your work.

The way that you write your plan may well be linked to the way that you choose to make notes from your reading or from lectures. We saw in Chapter 3 that there are useful and acceptable diagrammatic and graphical approaches which can be taken. This is equally true with assignment planning. Some of the graphic organisers mentioned in Chapter 3, in particular the flow diagram or the concept map, lend themselves very well to the task of planning.

The simplest form of essay plan would be organised with headings for each section of the essay: Introduction; Point One; Point Two; Point ... ; Conclusion. For many this type of plan, with notes of guidance and references for each section, will be an adequate guide for writing the essay in conjunction with notes from readings and other source material. For others more is necessary. As we have seen with many of the suggestions for techniques and strategies throughout this book, assignment planning is a personal and sometimes idiosyncratic concern. If you do not have a particular way of planning your writing, or if you are not satisfied with what you currently do then you should try another approach. You need to determine what will work best for you and this will depend, as before, on your preferred learning style. (You may well think that planning an assignment is not strictly speaking part of your learning, but it is. It is an important element of your engagement with the content of your course.) If you consider that a linear approach will suit you best then set out a sheet of paper with the main heading for your work, and begin to write points under each heading. If you want to try a more visual and schematic approach then choose a larger sheet of paper and write the assignment title centrally in reasonably large writing. At this point you have more choices. You could work in a brainstorm fashion, writing down ideas as they occur to you. Or you could work in more of a linear way by writing down ideas under the headings of Introduction; Definitions; Main Point One etc. The advantage of the open graphical approach is that you can draw links and make connections between ideas and you can include a way of sequencing what you have added to the diagram as you work though it.

As an exercise you could write a short plan for a piece of work in both of these ways, that is, as a list, and then as a diagram. Consider which you feel to be most useful and then develop work towards perfecting your preferred approach.

Collect source material together   Search for and gather together appropriate information. In the first instance you should consult the recommended texts and articles. Following that, you should undertake a search of your own, making use of the library catalogues and journal searching facilities, or a careful search using an appropriate internet search engine. Read and make copious notes – not forgetting all bibliographic and location details. Again, the nature of your reading and note-taking is a matter for you to decide. We have considered this in Chapter 2.

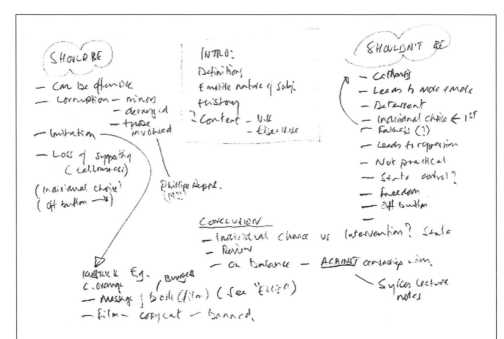

Should the portrayal of sex and violence in films and on television be censored more heavily?

Introduction

Sex, violence and censorship, all subjects which stir up high emotions
Define all three – see refs.

Case against censorship

Point One: The judgement of the individual should prevail

Point Two: Portrayals of sex or violence can be cathartic

Point Three: Visions of extreme violence can act as a deterrent

Point Four: Censorship adds to the repression surrounding matters of sex

Point Five: Censorship in one area can lead to censorship in other areas
Point Six: It is not practically enforceable

Case for censorship

Point One: Sex is private and not for public consumption

Point Two: Some people are offended by images of sex and/or violence

Point Three: Can lead to corruption

Point Four: Those involved in the creation of scenes etc. might be damaged/corrupted

Point Five: Scenes of violence can lead to imitation [Clockwork Orange]

Point Six: The glorification of violence can lead to desensitisation and callousness

Conclusion

Case against censorship is strong

[Review and decide]

Figure 6.1 Two different plans for the same essay question

Write a first draft   As you start to write you should stay close to your plan initially, which will have been written in accordance with the accepted structure. As you progress it is likely that you will want to amend your plan and either include or exclude certain points.

At this stage it is worth considering the precise way in which you will write. In the not too distant past it was unusual for students to do anything but write their work by hand. Some would use a typewriter for the final version, but this was not very common. Now the expectation is that your work will be word processed. Some universities make this a requirement, others prefer to say that it is advisable or preferred. For most students this will not present a problem. Some students will carry out their preparatory work by hand and move to a computer for the final stage of the process. There are so many advantages to using a word processor for the whole sequence that it is sometimes difficult for a dedicated computer user to understand why some will choose pen and paper. Writing drafts on a word processor offers enormous flexibility. Text can be removed, new sections can be added later, the order can be altered, ideas can be written down as they occur and used later, a spell checker can go some way to eliminating errors, the thesaurus function can help when a word does not seem quite right, references can be added to a list as the work progresses, ready to 'tidy up' later, copies of your work can be saved in different locations to ensure that it does not get lost. Despite these many advantages, it may well be that you prefer handwriting. However, if your university makes it a regulation that your submissions should be word processed you should begin straight away with becoming familiar with the technology, and for the reasons suggested by the list of advantages above, become a competent word processor user.

There is a potential danger, of course, if you rely entirely on the word processor and do not take safety measures. There have been many occasions when a student has asked for an extension owing to the need to redo their work because of a computer crash or some such disaster. It is said that there are two groups of people in the world: those who have lost work on their computer, and those who will lose their work. It is really important to understand where your work is saved and to have more than one copy of it at all times. For example, the files for this book are saved on the computer where it is being written. They are also saved at the end of each writing session on my university network. This is done by connecting to the university intranet from outside, logging on to the system and uploading the files. To be even more cautious they could also be saved periodically to an external, removable hard drive, a CD, memory stick, or even a floppy disk. Whatever you do, have a system and be rigid with its application. If not, you will lose work, or at the very least, you will be confused about which is the most recent version.

When writing it is important to write in an appropriate academic style. This means using correct English, avoiding colloquialisms, not using contractions and generally making your writing straightforward to read and clear to follow and understand.

We noted earlier that it is common for some students to feel that they have to write in a complicated way because they now are at university. This is not true. Good academic writing is not over-complicated. It may at times be a little complex, because complicated ideas and arguments necessitate detailed explanations, but it should never be over-elaborate or turgid for its own sake. When writing your aim should be to be simple, straightforward and concise. If you keep this notion firmly in mind your writing will not confuse, or even amuse those who read it by its overcomplexity. For example, compare the two paragraphs below:

> English Robins (Erithacus rubecula), under typical meteorological and nutrient availability conditions, are a solitary, non-migratory sub-species; however when prevailing underlying contextual situations extend to extreme conditions with respect to climate and nutrition, this isolatory tendency may be seen to be reversed.

> Robins are usually solitary birds which are present all year round. In time of harsh weather or lack of food they can be seen in pairs or small groups.

Your writing must convey information, ideas and arguments accurately, but there should not be a need for it to be translated into understandable language.

Read your work and make corrections   It can be tempting to think that you have finished before the final stages are actually complete. If you are a last minute writer then you may well be very short of time for the all-important final stages. Conversely, some people find it hard to stop re-reading and making corrections and alterations. There needs to be a sensible middle way.

You need to read your essay and confirm for yourself that it answers the question, or completes the task that was set in the title. If it does not, then you will receive a very poor mark, no matter how well written the work might be. You will need to be satisfied with the sequence, the arguments and counter-arguments, the referencing and every other aspect of what you have written. It is likely at this stage that you will alter parts that are not exactly as you want them to be. You should make a final check of spellings and grammar; marks can be deducted for poor presentation, including spelling, grammar and use of English.

Produce a final draft and proof read it one last time   When you are satisfied, you should produce the final version, by printing it in most cases, by writing it out in others, and you should then proof read it. This may seem like a tedious process, but many slips are picked up at this stage. Spell checkers are not infallible, and cannot pick up a wrong usage where both words exist ('there' and 'their' for example). Also, it seems it is all too easy to write the opposite of what you actually mean, by just accidentally missing out the word 'not', for example.

There are many ways of proof reading. Professional proof readers, we are told, often read the text backwards so that they can concentrate on spellings and other structural features and avoid being diverted by the content. This is probably going too far, but you do need a system. It is very easy to read your work and see what you *think* you have written. It does seem that no matter how many times we proof read a document there will still be mistakes that slip through our net. For this reason it can be a good idea to ask a trusted friend to read your work for you, possibly on a reciprocal basis. The proof reader does not necessarily need to be conversant with the subject matter. Indeed it could be a test of your writing that an 'outsider' can make sense of it easily. Another good approach is to read your work aloud. By doing this you need to translate what you see into coherently structured speech. Often you will pick up on unnecessarily clumsy constructions, or sentences that are far too long for their own good.

The process list for essay writing in Table 6.1 summarises this section and might be of use to you if you prefer to have a checklist approach to completing tasks. It is taken from an online writing guide for students in higher education (Gillett, 2007).

Important words used in essay titles

There are certain words and phrases used in essay and assignment titles which are not always easy to understand. They are words with common usage which take on specific meanings in the context of academic writing and may lead to confusion (and low marks) if they are not understood and responded to appropriately. It is helpful to spend time thinking about these key words, which are often referred to as 'process words', and working out exactly what you are being asked to do. Sometimes rewriting the essay title in your own words, especially if the title is at all confusing, makes it become clearer. Defining the terms and considering the meaning of the question is sometimes a valuable part of the introduction to an essay.

Table 6.2 gives the most commonly used process words with a short explanation of what they require. These definitions are not necessarily definitive and if you are at all confused or unsure of the meaning of a word in an essay title you should check with your tutor.

Assessment frameworks – what tutors are looking for and how to be successful

One key reason for students not achieving the mark they are aiming for when writing essays is that they do not understand quite what their tutor wants them to do.

Table 6.1 Process list for essay writing

Task	Skills Needed	Product
1. Read the question and understand what you are required to do. Think about the subject, the purpose and the audience	Thinking academically	Essay subject
2. Think about what you know about the subject. Write it down in some way	Brainstorming	Diagrams or notes
3. Go to the library and find relevant books or articles	Library/research skills	Reading list
4. Find the books on your reading list and study them	Reading skills: skimming and scanning	List of materials studied
5. Make notes on these books and articles. Record full details of the materials you use	Reading in detail Selecting and note-taking Paraphrasing/summarising	Notes
6. Organise your essay/ assignment	Planning Organisation	Essay plan
7. Type or write your first draft	Writing from notes Synthesis Writing paragraphs Typing/word processing	First draft
8. Discuss your first draft informally with friends, other members of your group and your tutor if possible	Speaking skills Listening skills Discussion skills	List of revisions/changes
9. Revise your first draft, bearing in mind any comments that were made in your discussions. Go back to 2 if necessary. Produce your second draft	Use of dictionaries and reference books Writing introduction and conclusion Quoting/writing a list of references	Second draft
10. Proof read your draft	Checking for spelling mistakes Checking punctuation and grammar. Checking vocabulary use. Checking style. Checking organisation, references etc. Checking for plagiarism	Assignment with changes marked

(Continued)

| 11. | Produce a final typed version | Typing/word processing Writing title/contents page | Final assignment |
| 12. | Check everything | Final check | Hand in |

Source: Using English for Academic Purposes: A Guide for Students in Higher Education (Gillett, 2007)

This causes upset when receiving the mark for the assessed work as the student does not understand in what way the essay they produced was not what was required.

When marking, tutors often use a record sheet with a list of the things they want you to have done in the essay. These are called **assessment criteria**. As your tutors read your essays they will indicate against each criterion how well you have done. The assessment criteria will include both general and specific points. It is a straightforward task to consider the general points – such as, for example, 'structure and organisation', but the more subject-and title-specific criteria are more difficult to consider here. It is very common for tutors to publish the assessment criteria for particular assignments. Many module guides will include a set of general criteria, and in many cases each title will have additional specific criteria listed.

It is extremely useful, even essential if you are to do well, to be aware of, and to understand, the assessment criteria for all your assignments. Before you submit an assignment, or while you are still working on it, it can be a good idea to self-assess your work against the given criteria. This gives you an opportunity to think about your work and whether you have answered the question correctly and also whether you are happy with the piece of work you have completed. If you have had difficulties with a piece of work, it will also give you a chance to consider the advice or feedback that you would like your tutor to give.

Below is a list of nine general assessment criteria ranked in order of importance by a sample of academics:

- Relevance of material to question set.
- Evidence of understanding.
- Structure and organisation.
- Evidence of background reading.
- Relevance of background reading.
- Adequate and correct referencing.

Table 6.2 Process words commonly used in assignment and exam questions

Process word/phrase	Explanation
Account for	Explain, clarify and give reasons for
Analyse	Set out components of the subject and consider them critically and in detail
Argue	Make a case for or against a given point of view
Assess	Determine the value of, consider the importance of (cf. Evaluate)
Compare	Look for the similarities and differences between examples
Contrast	Look in particular for the differences between two ideas, systems, opinions or philosophies, and illustrate them in detail
Compare and contrast	Find points of common ground between two ideas or systems and illustrate how they differ. This combines both of the above to identify both common ground and differences
Criticise	Make a judgement supported by evidence of the relative merits of theories, opinions or facts. You will need to outline each case accurately, and in detail, as the basis for your conclusions
Define	Give the meaning of a word or phrase, in some cases you may have to examine different or commonly used definitions
Describe	Give a detailed account of. This will usually be purely factual, i.e. not analytical or critical. 'Describe' will usually be linked with another word, 'evaluate' or 'assess' for example
Discuss	Explain the background to the various viewpoints concerning a particular issue, being sure to explore both sides
Evaluate	Judge the worth, validity, effectiveness of something in the light of its truth or usefulness (cf. Assess)
Explain	Give details about how and why something is so and consider the evidence or arguments concerning the issue in question
Illustrate	Demonstrate your understanding in an explicit way; use carefully chosen and clear examples
Interpret	Give the meaning, using examples, evidence and personal comments to make it clear
Justify	Provide evidence to support a particular position, use examples and reasoned argument
Outline	Give the main features or principles of a subject, emphasise structure and avoid minute detail (cf. Summarise)
Prove	Demonstrate the truth of something by offering sound evidence leading to a valid conclusion
State	Describe the main points in clear and precise terms
Summarise	State the main features of an argument, without fine or superfluous detail or side issues (cf. Outline)
Trace	Identify, and describe in narrative form, the connection between one thing and another, either in a developmental sense over time, or in a cause and effect sense

- Style appropriate to the assignment.
- Spelling and grammar.
- Presentation.

We will look in turn at each criterion.

Relevance of material to question set   Any sources that you refer to in your assignment must be wholly relevant. Tutors will hardly be impressed by a regurgitation of factual information if it does not relate to, and help to answer, the question. You must answer the question and any material used must be included with that firmly in mind, not included simply because it is vaguely 'to do' with the topic.

Evidence of understanding   This cannot be demonstrated by presenting pages of factual information, no matter how relevant it is to the question. You must demonstrate by your appropriate use of the relevant information, and by using it to illustrate points that you make, that you have a good grasp of the subject. You might make a novel interpretation, which will show that you have understood and considered the subject well. Your conclusion is the place in your assignment where you can look back to the question and demonstrate that you understand it and that you have answered it thoroughly.

Structure and organisation   Your assignment should follow a logical, and in most cases, a standard structure consisting of an introduction, the main points and arguments, and a conclusion. At every stage it should be clear to the reader where the writing is going, and how the points relate to each other. It should be divided into paragraphs, with one theme per paragraph. Paragraphs and main points should be connected with 'signpost' words, such as 'However...' or 'In addition...' which will indicate the continuation or change of direction of the argument. The conclusion, where you draw everything together, is possibly the most important section, as it is here that you finally and clearly show that you have answered the question.

Evidence and relevance of background reading   There should be enough reference to your wider and background reading to show that you have adequately investigated the subject area. A separate bibliography, as further evidence of this, can be included for sources which are not quoted directly in your text, but which were consulted. It is not acceptable for an undergraduate assignment to rely on quotes from lecture notes, online or CD encyclopaedias, television programmes or newspapers, except perhaps as a minor illustration or introduction.

Adequate and correct referencing   References must be cited both within the text and at the end of the piece. It is very important that large chunks of text are not copied without reference as this will be considered plagiarism, which is a serious academic crime.

Style appropriate to the assignment   Different writing styles are appropriate for different types of assignment: essay, report, practical write-up, portfolio. Different stylistic constructions are acceptable in different types of assignment and in different subject areas.

Spelling and grammar   Poor spelling and incorrect grammar are not acceptable. You must check thoroughly before final submission, bearing in mind that proof reading is notoriously difficult, and that spell checkers are not wholly trustworthy. The most common mistakes are: incorrect use of commas and semi-colons; incorrect use of apostrophes; sentences that are too long; commonly misspelled words not corrected, such as their/there/they're, to/too, practice/practise, affect/effect. (There will be more about this later.)

Presentation   Ideally your work should be word processed or neatly hand-written; many departments insist on word processed submissions. Care should be taken in etting out your work. It should not be too crowded on the page, there should be sensible spaces between paragraphs. Again, in many departments there will be guidelines to follow about font and size, about spacing and other typographical considerations. You must be consistent throughout, with, for example: use of capital letters; use of headings and sub-headings; use of bullet points; numbering or lettering of sections.

In addition to all the above, you *must* be sure to have answered the question. For this reason you must pay particular note to the process words in the title, and refer back to the question constantly as you are working. In the conclusion, refer explicitly to the title and show that you have answered it.

Dissertations

It is sometimes said that the style and structure of a dissertation, and the weight given to its various sections, is a personal decision. However, particularly with your first attempt, and especially at undergraduate level, you will be best advised to stay close to the standard format which we will look at next. In many cases you will not be given a choice anyway; in some departments there will be strict guidance which you must follow. Having a clear structure to follow will be a distinct advantage, as you will know from the outset precisely what you have to do.

There are certain elements of a dissertation which are considered as standard, and will appear in all dissertations in one form or another. The most common standard elements are:

- Title page
- Acknowledgements
- Contents
- List of tables, diagrams etc.
- Abstract
- Glossary
- Introduction
- Literature review and theoretical background
- Methodology and research design
- Analysis of results
- Discussion
- Conclusions
- References/bibliography
- Appendices

Preliminary material

Title page   The requirements of the title page are that it should include the full title, the degree to which it relates and usually your name and student identity number.

Acknowledgements   This is an option some students may choose to use, perhaps to acknowledge access you were granted to a location (a school, or business for example) or if you would like to thank your supervisor or any other of your tutors for their support.

Contents   This is a fairly crucial feature if the reader is going to find your work easy to access and read.

List of tables, diagrams etc.   If your dissertation does include tables, charts, or diagrams, this is where they should be listed.

Abstract   An abstract is a brief summary of the project, including very concise details of the research question, the methodology and the findings of your work. It might be useful for you to read the abstracts of some academic articles to familiarise yourself with the style and the concise nature of an abstract. The abstract serves the purpose of letting a reader (although not your marking tutor, of course) decide whether or not to read the full article.

Glossary   Again this an optional feature. It is important to include a glossary if you use and introduce technical or unusual terms or if you make use of acronyms.

Introduction

This will set the scene for the work reported in the dissertation. It will give the general background to the situation and explain why the question you are seeking to answer is of interest and why you consider it to be important enough to be worthy of your time and effort. The reader will be in tune with the general subject area, but not necessarily fully conversant with the detail that you are considering; the introduction should correct this.

Literature review and theoretical background

This section will give the background in terms of previous work in the area that you will be investigating. It will be centred on quotations, examples, your comments, explanations and fully detailed references, including page numbers. The literature review should be written in clear and unambiguous language, as with all of your work. It should be concise, not rambling; there is usually a lot to include in what is in reality a small amount of space.

KEY PRINCIPLES

Literature review: a critical look at the existing research and other written work that is significant to the work that you are carrying out. A literature review is more than a simple summary; there is an important element of criticism and analysis.

Sometimes students gain the impression that literature reviews must be all-encompassing, and include every piece of earlier work. For an undergraduate, this is not usually possible, especially within the constraints of the word limit. However, you will need to give evidence of wide general reading as well as some more focused and specific reading which is close to the topic that you are investigating.

It is important to avoid creating a list in your literature review. If you do not group examples from the literature, and if you do not give explanations and informed comment, you will have little more than an annotated bibliography, which amounts to a list with brief notes. This is not what is required.

Methodology and research design

This is where you set out how you intend to go about your work. You will explain how you will seek to answer the research question within a framework of established research methodologies. You will present your strategy, which will be supported with reference to the research methodology literature. Often you will have been introduced to the most appropriate methodologies for your discipline and this will form the basis of what you write here. It may be that you need to consult with your supervisor, first to be sure that your chosen approach is indeed sound, and possibly for some advice about the literature relating to your chosen approach, especially if it is not something you feel has been covered in your methodology sessions.

Presentation and analysis of results

In some cases the results section may be separate to an analysis section. It is acceptable, and often advisable, to combine the two, but this is something on which you should take advice from your department guidance, or from your supervisor.

You will present your findings and engage in a process which is logical and which takes what you have found fully into account. You will draw out significant and precise conclusions; more general conclusions will be included in a later section.

The nature of the presentation will depend upon the nature of the results; quantitative data will be presented quite differently to qualitative data. Your discussion will be discursive, meaning that it will be led by reasoning or argument, by reference to your findings, not by reference to your feelings or intuition.

A note about the presentation of results   We know that the way in which results are presented will depend on the nature of the data. In general terms this will be either quantitative (largely numbers) or qualitative (largely descriptive – written notes, interview transcripts, published material). It is of course possible that you will have collected data of both types; this will depend upon the methods of collection that you chose.

Qualitative results, especially if they are in the form of interview transcripts or another narrative format, can be quite lengthy. For this reason it is important to be selective when you come to write anything in the main body of your work. It is possible that you will be encouraged to include full details in an appendix. It is important to organise the presentation of your qualitative results. One good way to do this is to extract comments or other textual detail, and group them according to certain themes or key ideas. In this way you can include all of the important data concerned with each major element of the topic under investigation. Following from this it is possible to analyse and discuss each theme in order

Quantitative results are more easily presented in a visual format – tables, charts or graphs, and qualitative results are usually presented in the form of quotations and other written comments. In a study with both types of data it can be put together much in the way that a news story might be presented. Numbers and other statistics are often reported with quotes or interviews to communicate the content of the report.

Discussion

There are different approaches to discussing and otherwise commenting on your results. Simply to present results without appropriate comment will lead to a very poor grade for your work. You need to engage in a critical consideration of what it is that you have found, and how it relates to your research intention, that is, your original research question. A good discussion section will also relate the findings to the content of the literature review.

Conclusion

This is where you will sum up what you have achieved, and where you must be sure to give an answer to your research question. A conclusion can be written in a personal style, and there is usually a place for your personal reflections, both on your findings and on the process that you have undertaken. You should highlight what you have learned, how you might have worked differently, and how you think the work might be developed. This is an important point, because almost all research generates further questions and you should show that you recognise this.

Doing research at this level, and for that matter at higher levels, is about the process of undertaking research itself as well as about the specific topic of the work. This is borne out by the fact that undertaking a PhD degree is considered to be a training process, and in many cases is thought of as the final test taken by would-be full-time academic researchers.

It is not necessary for the outcome of your work to be entirely positive. Undertaking research and writing a dissertation is a learning process and it is possible to learn a lot from research work that did not go strictly according to plan, or which failed to produce any clear findings.

References/bibliography

We cover this in detail later in this chapter. You must give full references in the form of a list of all the works referred to in the text, using the correct system. Often a bibliography is also required, or at least advisable. This will list your general background reading which you did not reference explicitly in the text. It is important not to list works just for the sake of it – you may find yourself having to talk about this list if you have an oral examination, so avoid listing material that you have not actually consulted.

Appendices

The appendix section will include any self-contained units of background information which you have referred to in the main body of your work. This could include complex diagrams or tables, technical details of tests carried out, interview or survey data, test results, copies of questionnaires and interview schedules. The appendix is not the place for anything which is original, or which is of an explanatory nature. An appendix can be a place for material which you might have included in the main body but are unable to because of word limit considerations.

Checklist for dissertations reporting research

The following checklist is amended from a framework for critically appraising research articles (Moule et al., 2003). It has been altered here so that it applies more directly to undergraduate level dissertations, and it will provide a useful yardstick to place against your work.

The introduction:

Have you included a statement about the topic being investigated?
Have you included a clear rationale for the research?
Have you included a clear statement about the limitations of the research?
Have you stated the research question clearly?

The literature review:

Have you made use of up-to-date material?
Have you made links between your work and the wider body of knowledge?

Have you made links between the literature and the formulation of your research question?

The methods section:

Have you clearly described the research design?

Have you explained why the methods selected are appropriate for the topic being investigated?

Have you highlighted any advantages or disadvantages of the design of your research?

If appropriate:

Have you included a statement about who took part in the research?

Have you included a statement about how those participating were selected?

Have you made it clear how many people took part in the research?

Data collection and analysis:

Have you included a description about how the data were collected?

Have you used a type of analysis which is appropriate for the type of data collected?

Quantitative data:

Have you explained about the choice of sample size?

Have you given detail about the statistical tests that you have used?

Have you included detail of the validity and reliability measures of your tests and data?

Are the type of statistical tests used appropriate for the sorts of data collected?

Have you made it clear how you made use of any statistical analysis software?

Qualitative data:

Have you made the approach taken to data analysis clear?

Have you described the use of any analysis software?

Have you made a statement about how you have validated your interpretations of the data?

Ethics:

Have you made a statement concerning any ethical matters?

Have you made it clear how you gained consent, and have assured anonymity and confidentiality?

The results/findings:

Have you referred back to the literature review when discussing the results?
Have you acknowledged any weaknesses in research design?

Quantitative work:

Have you ensured that the results are presented clearly and unambiguously?
Have you presented all the results?
Do the tables and charts used give a clear picture of the sample data and results?
Are the charts used appropriate for the data and for your purpose?
Are the tables easy to use?
If you are using percentages, do you also give the actual numbers?

Qualitative work:

Have you given evidence of the data collected?

Conclusions:

Have you drawn together your findings and their implications?
Have you acknowledged any implications for further research?

Academic Style and Conventions

Most academic writing is written in the third person. That is, 'I' is not used and the work takes on an impersonal tone. However, this is not an absolute rule. Over recent years the style of academic writing has slowly begun to change, possibly to the chagrin of some traditionalists. Also, different subject disciplines have different 'rules' about how this is applied. Some essay writers will take this to extremes and refer to themselves as 'the writer' in phrases such as 'The writer of this assignment considers that …', designed to avoid the use of 'I think that …'. In some cases it is acceptable to use 'I' and 'my', but usually only sparingly, and usually only in the introductory and concluding sections: 'my argument in this essay will be …'; 'based on the arguments set out above I find that …'. However, you must be guided by the advice given by your department and more especially by those who will mark your work. It is not unheard of for tutors in the same department to give conflicting advice concerning writing style and assessment, and so, even if there is a departmental norm, it sometimes makes sense to confirm particular requirements with individual tutors. If you wish to avoid the first person completely, or if you are told that you must, there are ways of expressing the same ideas which conform to the requirement: 'this essay will argue that …'; 'the arguments outlined above lead to the conclusion that …'.

Conventions for citing and quoting

Citations can be set out in a number of ways. One method is to present some information and then provide its reference immediately after it to give the source. This is referred to as 'information-prominent' citation, e.g.:

> In 1995 there were 26 days with temperatures above 20°C compared with an average of 4 days per year since 1772. (Hulme, 1999)

In some citations the author becomes a part of the sentence. This is known as an 'author-prominent' citation and is common in academic writing, e.g.

> Seymour Papert (1986) discusses a vision of schools ....

When you want to summarise the views of a particular writer, you should use reporting expressions:

> He [Bruner] uses the term ...
> According to Bruner ..., he goes on to say ...

When you want to report the views of one writer which you have read in the work of another but not from the original source, for example you read of Piaget's work in a book by Papert, you must make this clear. Whilst you should make every effort to read ideas in their original form, it is not always possible. In such cases, use the 'cited in' format:

> Piaget (cited in Papert, 1986)

The importance of accurate and consistent referencing will be considered in more detail later.

Care with use of language to express viewpoints

In academic writing care must be taken not to overemphasise or give undue importance, or credence, to particular ideas. To achieve this, language which in other contexts might seem overly circumspect is used, e.g.:

> It seems that ...
> Findings suggest that ...
> There may be a link between ...

Caution in the way that you express claims or relationships is a distinctive feature of academic writing, especially when there is contradictory evidence or there are conflicting viewpoints expressed by well-informed writers concerning a particular phenomenon.

Bullet points

It is acceptable to use bullet points in an essay but they should be used sparingly. If you use numbered (or 'lettered') points you must be sure to be consistent in your style. You should not switch from the use of the alphabet to the use of lower case roman numerals, for example. It is more acceptable to make use of bullet points in reports.

To help you in the process of coming to understand academic style, take time when you read the textbooks and journal articles to pay attention to the academic style and conventions the writers are using. Notice how the work of others is referred to; notice how the writer's own point of view is included and how, unless it is supported by clear evidence, it is put forward only tentatively; notice how links from one point to the next are made; and take note of simple things like sentence length, paragraphing and the use of lists. The more you read academic texts with a questioning attitude towards both the content and arguments involved, and the style and structure of the piece, the better you will be able to develop an acceptable academic style of your own.

The importance of accurate spelling and grammar

Being a competent writer and being able to spell and use grammar correctly and effectively are skills which are associated with being well educated and being of graduate standard. Clearly there is a good deal more to being well educated than being able spell faultlessly, but if you litter your written work with errors it will have far less impact and be given far less credit than if there were none. We mentioned the fallibility of such devices as spell checkers earlier, and it is important not to rely entirely on the spell checking facility of your word processor. The Americanisation of many words in spell checkers is one reason for caution, although these variations may be acceptable to many. Even with the English versions of spellings there are many pitfalls. A spell checker cannot check for meaning or context; a spell checker will allow a word which for your purpose is spelled incorrectly, but is actually a different word spelled as it should be: if you have typed 'late' instead of 'lace' for example, or if you have put 'practice' (the noun) when you really wanted 'practise' (the verb). The extract below, from a longer poem written in 1992 and attributed to Jerry Zar (a retired and possibly frustrated academic), illustrates this point very well:

I have a spelling checker,
It came with my PC.
It plane lee marks four my revue
Miss steaks aye can knot sea.

Eye ran this poem threw it,
Your sure reel glad two no.
Its vary polished in it's weigh.
My checker tolled me sew.
Each frays come posed up on my screen
Eye trussed too bee a joule.
The checker pours o'er every word

To cheque sum spelling rule.
(Zar, 1992)

A spell checker is most certainly not an alternative to careful proof reading, and it is good practice for you to own and have to hand a good dictionary, which you can use to clear up any doubts that you have.

More on common writing errors

It is generally agreed that clear writing should have an average sentence length of between fifteen and twenty words. Obviously every sentence does not have to conform to this, but it is a useful rule of thumb. Your sentence length will vary naturally. Good writing has a mixture of longer and shorter sentences. If you keep to the basic principle of one main idea in a sentence, perhaps with one related point, you will find that your sentences will fall into the average pattern. Long sentences can almost always be divided up in some way.

As has been mentioned before, some of the worst writing errors are caused by students trying to write long and complex sentences which they feel somehow make their writing more sophisticated and intelligent. A short sentence can often be the best way to make a point. Another crucial point is that you must not use words you only *think* that you understand. Be sure. If you are in any doubt, reach for a dictionary or use a simpler word.

Table 6.3 lists some of the common mistakes that you should try to avoid. The solutions are in many cases related to careful proof reading. Others consider that reading out loud is a better way to proof read as it invokes the use of an additional sense.

Some of these 'rules' are perhaps archaic, but they do still apply in formal written English, which is the register you will be using in your writing. There are, naturally, some who disagree with some of them, or see times when exceptions can be made. In general you should try to keep to the customary rules for writing, even in times when our language is clearly changing, as all living languages do.

If you know, or suspect that your writing is not as good as it really ought to be you must do something about it. There is no quick fix unfortunately.

There are probably two solutions. The first is to take more care, and subject what you write to detailed scrutiny. You must be prepared to make alterations to anything that you have written – one of the advantages of word processing is that this is always possible. You should look out especially for any hint of ambiguity. If you yourself are not sure of the meaning of what you have written then other readers will also have

Table 6.3   Some common errors in writing and how to avoid them

Problem	Possible solution
Missing out a word: 'The experiment was carried in complete darkness'.	Careful proof reading by you, or by a friend
Incorrect use of adjectives and adverbs: You should 'be carefully to use them correct.'	Careful proof reading by you, or by a friend
Sentence fragments presented as full sentences: 'About carbon dioxide and other gases.'	Careful proof reading by you, or by a friend
The use of double negatives: 'They soon discovered that the place where they landed did not have none of the minerals they wanted.'	Careful proof reading by you, or by a friend. When proof reading try rewording the negative as a positive statement
Pronouns not agreeing: 'Each man had their own station to guard.'	Careful proof reading by you, or by a friend
Incorrect use of commas: '…The reasons, being economic circumstances…'	Careful proof reading by you, or by a friend. Pause for each comma to check for sense
Incorrect use of apostrophes: 'Hundred's were killed on the first day of hostilities.'	Careful proof reading by you, or by a friend
Splitting infinitives: 'To finally arrive at the conclusions below…'	Careful proof reading by you, or by a friend
Incorrect capitalisation: 'the new republican Senator took his seat on Capitol Hill.'	Careful proof reading by you, or by a friend
Verbs not agreeing with their subject: 'High bacteria levels in the water causes illness.'	Careful proof reading by you, or by a friend
Change in point of view of the writer: 'A writer must not shift his point of view, nor should you be inconsistent in the style you use.'	Careful proof reading by you, or by a friend
Incorrect use of irregular verbs: 'New formats gradually creeped into use.'	Careful proof reading by you, or by a friend
Use of clichés. To give just a few examples of the many possibilities: 'in the same boat; all walks of life; calm before the storm; from time immemorial; nipped in the bud.	Careful proof reading by you, or by a friend

difficulty. As we have seen earlier, a trusted and tolerant friend is a very good person to ask for help with checking your writing.

The second possible solution is to take time in your reading to notice the style and approach taken by good writers. As well as absorbing the content of what you are reading, look at the constructions, the grammar and syntax, and the ways in which meaning is made clear. Improving your writing is a gradual process of change based on feedback, experience and practice. The adage 'practice makes perfect' applies here too.

If you are unsure about any writing conventions there are many sources of reference. A good first port of call might be a web-based resource at www.mantex.co.uk where you will find excellent freely downloadable help, as well as options to buy a range of printed guides. Another good starting point might be the support site of your own university, for example the Learner Development Unit site at www.ssdd.uce.ac.uk/learner, a site belonging to the University of Central England, offers a good range of support for academic writing and related topics.

References and Bibliography

The acknowledgement of other work that you refer to in your writing is an important aspect of academic writing, for reasons of openness and honesty, and to allow others to follow up and make use of a wide range of other academic sources. It also allows tutors to recognise the extent of your background reading and to give you due credit.

The specific requirement for bibliographies and reference lists will vary from department to department. A reference list, in most systems, is set out alphabetically according to the surnames of the authors, and must include all of all the sources that you have referred to directly in your writing. A bibliography is a list of everything that you read in your preparation, whether or not you have referred to it specifically in your writing. You must be clear about how your department defines the two terms and what your department's requirements are. For example, some will say that there is no need to list anything that is not used directly, thus making a bibliography unnecessary.

KEY PRINCIPLES

References list: a list, at the end of the main body of your work, listing all of the references you specifically referred to (cited) in your work.

Bibliography: a complete list of all sources that you have used in your preparation for the submission, including sources not referred to directly (cited) in your work.

You must use one of the conventional systems for citing sources. The two most commonly used are the Harvard (author–date) system and the Numeric (author–number) system (also known as the Vancouver system). There are others, but we will concentrate on these two here. The references for this book conform to the Harvard system, which is widely used in the humanities and social sciences. The numeric system is more commonly used in sciences.

The Harvard system

Citations   A citation is the inclusion in your writing of something from an authoritative source as a means of illustrating a point, or substantiating something that you have written. A citation is usually a quote from a reputable academic source and must be properly acknowledged. The point about reputable source is important. Any citations must be recognisable as valid, and worthy of use as substantiation of your points and arguments. A sentence from a tabloid newspaper, for obvious reasons, would not fit this definition. That is not to say that a sentence from a tabloid could not be used as an example of a style of journalism in an assignment considering the media; there will be other such examples.

KEY PRINCIPLES

Citation: a reference made in the text of your work to an external source of information. Citations in the Harvard system are made up of the name(s) of the author(s) or editor(s) and the date of publication of an item, and there are two ways of including this in your text:

Aspinall (1998) considers that ...

Some writers (Aspinall and Dickinson 1998) have written that ...

If a work has three or more authors or editors, cite the name of the first named author or editor only, followed by *et al*. (Latin *et al*, 'and others'):

A study of internet use in primary schools (Jenson *et al*. 2001) suggests ...

If you refer to two or more sources by the same author from the same year, a lower-case letter after the year is used to distinguish one from the other:

Davis (2000a), Davis (2000b), Davis (2000c)

When a quote is included directly from a work, you should also give the page number after the date:

'Learning always necessitates mental activity being undertaken by the learner.' (Howe 1999, p. 23)

Listing   The first stage of referencing is the inclusion of citations in your text, the next is the inclusion of a comprehensive list of references at the end of your work.

When using the Harvard system, the items in the references list are listed in alphabetical order by author's surname. The initials follow the surname, preceded by a comma.

If you include more than one work by an author, they should be listed in date order, oldest first. Where more than one work by the same author from a single year is referenced, they will be listed in alphabetical order according to the additional lower-case marker: 2000a, 2000b ...

The date of publication of an item immediately follows the names of the authors or editors, in brackets. If there is not a reliable date, use a question mark to show this: 2000 or 1986?

It is usual either to put the titles of books and journals in italics or to underline them. Whether you choose to italicise or to underline, you must remain consistent throughout. If a work is a second or succeeding edition, the edition number should be included after the title: 2nd edn.

The final details you are required to give are the place of publication and the publisher. You can usually find this at the bottom of the title page of the book. If there are many cities listed, it will be sufficient to list only the first named.

For a book in the Harvard format

> Author(s) surname, initials (Year) *Title of Book*. Edition. Place of publication: Publisher.

For example:

> Ager, R. (1998) *Information and Communications Technology: Children or Computers Control?* London: David Fulton.
> Ranis, G. and Mahmood, S.A. (1992) *The Political Economy of Development Policy Change* 2nd Edition . Cambridge, MA: Basil Blackwell.

For an edited book in the Harvard format:

> Editor(s) surname, initials, ed(s). (Year) *Title of Book*. Edition. Place of publication: Publisher.

For example:

> Nettl, P., ed. (1955) W.*A. Mozart*. Frankfurt: Fischer Bücherei.
> Cecil, H. and Liddle, P., eds. (1996) *Facing Armageddon*. London: Casemate.

For work in an edited book in the Harvard format:

Where a work from an edited collection is cited, you must reference both the individual work and the collection to which it belongs:

> Author(s) surname, initials (Year) Title of chapter. In: Editor(s) initials and surname, ed(s). *Title of Book.* Edition. Place of publication: Publisher, Chapter or page numbers.

For example:

> Tenshert, R. (1955) Mozart und die Kirche. In: P. Nettl, ed. W.A. *Mozart*. Frankfurt: Fischer Bücherei, p. 67.
> Derez, M. (1996) The flames of Louvain. In: H. Cecil and P. Liddle, eds. *Facing Armageddon*. London: Casemate, pp. 619–620.

Note here that following 'In:' it is usual to put the initials before the surname.

For conference proceedings in the Harvard format:

> Editor(s) surname, initials, ed(s). (Year). *Title of Conference*, location, date held. Place of publication: Publisher.

For example:

> Kinshuk, K., Sampson, D.G. and Isaias, P., eds. *Cognition and Exploratory Learning in Digital Age (CELDA 2005) Proceedings*, Porto, Portugal, December 14–16 2005. Lisbon: IADIS.

For a conference paper in the Harvard format:

When citing a paper from conference proceedings, reference to both the paper itself and the proceedings should be included:

> Author(s) surname, initials (Year) Title of Paper. In: Editor(s) initials and surname, ed(s). *Title of Conference*, location, date held. Place of publication: Publisher, Page number(s).

For example:

> Courtin, C. and Talbot, S. (2005) An Architecture to Record Traces in Learning Instrumented Collaborative Learning Environments. In: K. Kinshuk, D.G. Sampson and P. Isaias, eds. *Cognition and Exploratory Learning in Digital Age (CELDA 2005) Proceedings,* Porto, Portugal, December 14–16 2005. Lisbon: IADIS, pp. 301–306.

For a report in the Harvard format:

The organisation responsible for the research must be identified. In many cases the organisation will not have undertaken the research itself, but commissioned another party. If the report is part of a series, the series title and other details should be included:

Author(s) surname, initials (Year) *Title of report.* Edition. Place of publication: Publisher (Series and number).

For example:

Kempson, E., Collard, S. and Taylor, S. (2004) *Experiences and consequences of being refused a Community Care Grant.* Leeds: Corporate Document Services (Department for Work and Pensions (DWP) Research Report 210).

For a journal article in the Harvard format:

Author(s) surname, initials (Year). Title of Article. *Journal Title,* Volume (issue number), Page number(s).

For example:

Mitchell, V. (1996) Assessing the Readability and Validity of Questionnaires: An Empirical Example. *Journal of Applied Management Studies,* 5(2), pp. 199–207.

For an online journal article in the Harvard format:

This format is reserved for journals which are solely web-based. For online versions of print journals, reference the print version.

Author(s) surname, initials (Year) Title of Article. [Online]. URL *Title of Online Journal,* Volume(issue) (Date accessed).

For example:

Ramji, H. (2005) Exploring Intersections of Employment and Ethnicity Amongst British Pakistani Young Men. [Online] www.socresonline.org.uk/10/4/ramji.html. *Sociological Research Online,* 10(4) (Accessed 4 March 2006).

For a website (with the exception of online journals) in the Harvard format:

You should include as much detail as possible from the web page and/or home page of the piece. If a website has no identifiable author, and is not the work of an organisation, leave out the author details, beginning the reference with the title of the web page:

Author(s) surname, initials (Year, month day) *Title of Document.* [Online] URL. Place of publication: Publisher (Date accessed).

For example:

> BUBL (undated) *BUBL Information Service*. [online] http://bubl.ac.uk. University of Strathclyde (Accessed 29.05.07).

The Numeric system

There are three important differences between the Numeric system and the Harvard system, they are:

- The way material is cited in the text.
- The position of the publication date in a reference.
- The way the list of references is ordered.

Citations   Material cited in the Numeric style is identified by a number, beginning with 1 for the first citation and continuing in sequence. One of three forms of noting the number may be used:

> Aspinall[1] considers that ...
> Aspinall [1] considers that ...
> Aspinall (1) considersthat ...

Where a work has three or more authors or editors, cite the name of the first named author or editor only, followed by *et al.*:

> Wallace *et al.* [2] conclude that ...

Where quoting directly from a source, or when making reference to specific pages, the page numbers should be included after the number:

> 'The expectation from all concerned was that the prime minister would resign.' [3, p. 218]

If you refer to the same source later in your work there are two options, namely, use the same number as the first citation to the source or the appropriate number in your sequence and give an abbreviated reference to the document in the references list for the second and for any later inclusions. Below is an example of an abbreviated reference:

[1]   Papert, S. *Mindstorms: Children Computers and Powerful Ideas.* Brighton: The Harvester Press, 1982.
[2]   Kolb, D. E*xperiential Learning: Experience as the Source of Learning and Development.* Englewood Cliffs, NJ: Prentice-Hall, 1984.
[3]   Papert (ref. 1., p.621).

Listing   A references list should be provided at the end of the text. It should be in the same numerical order as the citations in the text, i.e. not alphabetical.

If there is material that you have made use of, but not cited directly, it should be listed separately in a bibliography which is placed after the reference list. In a bibliography the items should be listed alphabetically according to the surname of the authors.

In the Numeric system there are, naturally, some similarities with the Harvard system. These are the styling of authors' and editors' names, the use of italics for titles and indicating later editions. A notable difference is that in the Numeric system the date of publication follows the place of publication.

For a book in the Numeric system format:

When referring to a particular part of a book, the relevant page or chapter number(s) can be given at the end of the reference, as an alternative to recording it in the citation. This also applies to references to reports and theses:

> Author(s) surname, initials. *Title of Book*. Edition. Place of publication: Publisher, Year, Chapter or page number(s).

For example:

> [1]   Ager, R. *Information and Communications Technology: Children or Computers Control*? London: David Fulton, 1998.
> [2]   Ranis, G. and Mahmood, S.A. *The Political Economy of Development Policy Change*. Cambridge, MA: Basil Blackwell, 1992.

For an edited book in the Numeric system format:

> Editor(s) surname, initials, ed(s). *Title of Book*. Edition. Place of publication: Publisher, Year.

For example:

> [1]   Nettl, P., ed. *W. A. Mozart*. Frankfurt: Fischer Bücherei, 1955.
> [2]   Stone, D., ed. *Banking on Knowledge: the Genesis of the Global Development Network*. 2nd Edition. London: Routledge, 2000.

As with all referencing systems, both the individual work and the collection where it is found should be included:

For work in an edited book in the Numeric system format:

As with all referencing systems, both the individual work and the collection where it is found should be included:

> Author(s) surname, initials. Title of chapter. In: Editor(s) surname, initials, ed(s). *Title of Book.* Edition. Place of publication: Publisher, Year, Chapter or page number(s).

For example:

> [1] Tenshert, R. Mozart und die kerche. In: Nettl, P.W., ed. *A. Mozart*. Frankfurt: Fisher Bücherei, 1955, p. 67.
> **P., ed. *W. A. Mozart*. Frankfurt: Fischer Bücherei, p. 67.**
> [2] Derez, M. The flames of Louvain. In: Cecil, H. and Liddle, P., eds. *Facing Armageddon*. London: Casemate, 1996, pp. 619–20.

For conference proceedings in the Numeric system format:

> Editor(s) surname, initials, ed(s). *Title of Conference*, location, date held. Place of publication: Publisher, Year.

For example:

> [1] Courtin, C. and Talbot, S. An Architecture to Record Traces in Learning Instrumented Collaborative Learning Environments. In: Kinshuk, K., Sampson, D.G. and Isaias, P., eds. *Cognition and Exploratory Learning in Digital Age (CELDA 2005) Proceedings*, Porto, Portugal, December 14–16 2005. Lisbon: IADIS, 2005.

For a conference paper in the Numeric system format:

When citing a paper from conference proceedings, reference to both the paper itself and the proceedings should be included:

> Author(s) surname, initials. Title of paper. In: Editor(s) surname, initials, ed(s). *Title of Conference*, location, date held. Place of publication: Publisher, Year, Page number(s).

For example:

> [1] Courtin, C. and Talbot, S. An Architecture to Record Traces in Learning Instrumented Collaborative Learning Environments. In: Kinshuk, K., Sampson, D.G. and Isaias, P., eds. *Cognition and Exploratory Learning in Digital Age*

(CELDA 2005) Proceedings, Porto, Portugal, December 14–16 2005. Lisbon: IADIS 2005, pp. 301–306.

For a report in the Numeric system format:

The organisation responsible for the research must be identified. In many cases the organisation will not have undertaken the research itself, but commissioned another party. If the report is part of a series, the series title and other details should be included.

Author(s) surname, initials (Year). *Title of report.* Edition. Place of publication: Publisher (Series and number).

For example:

[1]   Kempson, E., Collard, S. and Taylor, S. (2004) *Experiences and consequences of being refused a Community Care Grant.* Leeds: Corporate Document Services (Department for Work and Pensions (DWP) Research Report 210).

For a journal article in the Numeric system format:

Author(s) surname, initials. Title of Article. *Journal Title*, Volume(issue number), Year, Page number(s).

For example:

[1]   Mitchell, V. Assessing the Readability and Validity of Questionnaires: An Empirical Example. *Journal of Applied Management Studies,* 5(2), 1996, pp. 199–207.

For online journal articles in the Numeric system format:

This format is reserved for journals which are solely web-based. For online versions of print journals, reference the print version:

Author(s) surname, initials. Title of Article. [Online]. URL *Title of Online Journal*, Volume (issue), Year (Date accessed).

For example:

[1]   Ramji, H. Exploring Intersections of Employment and Ethnicity Amongst British Pakistani Young Men. [Online] www.socresonline.org.uk/10/4/ramji. html. *Sociological Research Online*, 10(4), 2005 (Accessed 4 March 2006).

For a website (with the exception of online journals) in the Numeric system format:

You should include in the reference as much of the following detail as is available from the web page and related home page. If a website has no identifiable author, and is not the work of an organisation, leave out the author details, beginning the reference with the title of the web page:

> Author(s) surname, initials. *Title of Document.* [Online]. URL. Place of publication: Publisher, Year, month day (Date accessed).

For example:

> [1] World Resources Institute. *Coastal and Marine Ecosystems searchable database* [Online] htttp://earthtrends.wri.org/. 2005 (Accessed 12 February 2006).

As before, this website contains no publication details and so these are not included in the reference.

Classification

The following guide to degree classifications is designed to give a straightforward look at how an assignment might be allocated a classification. There will be other assessment criteria which are specific to any given piece of work, but as general guidance it will show how it might be possible to improve an assignment and move it to a higher classification.

First Class (1st)   To get a First your assignment must show an excellent understanding of the question. Your writing will be relevant throughout, it will be well-structured and logically argued. You will have analysed at a sophisticated level, ignoring the simplistic, and you will have included regular clear and appropriate examples and references. You will have shown that you have detailed knowledge and understanding of the material and you will have provided evidence of effective evaluation of critical sources and you will have included your own independent thoughts and ideas. You will have presented an assignment written in clear and precise language in an appropriate academic register.

Upper Second Class (2:1)   To get a 2:1 (two–one) your assignment must be well structured, with an introduction, discussion and a conclusion which relate well to one another. You will have focused on the central issues of the topic and you will have presented a logical argument. Your references will be appropriate and relevant. You will have shown a good knowledge and understanding of the material, and you will have included some critical opinion, and a convincing analysis. You have probably not included any evidence of independent thoughts and ideas, or, at least, very little.

Lower Second Class (2:2)   A 2.2 (two–two) indicates that your assignment is sound in most of the areas above. You will have provided some evidence of knowledge and understanding of the material central to the topic but there will be weaknesses in one or more of the following: structure of the argument; relevance of quotes; clear analysis; detailed understanding. Your assignment is likely to be characterised by poor planning and accuracy, and a tendency to describe rather than to analyse.

Third Class (3rd)   To get a third your assignment will show that you have some knowledge of the material studied. You will have written down most of what you know about it, whether it is strictly relevant or not, and you will not have given enough evidence of your understanding, either of the material or the question. You are likely to have strayed away from the main point of the work and you will have presented something which is badly structured. You will not have engaged in meaningful discussion of the topic. It is likely that you have written badly and left some mistakes that effective proof reading should have picked up.

Fail   A Fail means you have written down only a little of what is known about the subject and have not related any of it to the question. You will also perhaps have shown a low level of competence in your writing. You will most likely have failed to give your work an obvious structure, and you will have failed to discuss effectively, to construct a sound argument, or to use references appropriately.

SUMMARY

- Assessment takes place at different points in your course. Most often it is for final summative purposes, sometimes it has other purposes aimed at supporting your progress.
- Academic writing has certain requirements, not least of which are accuracy and clarity; there are also other conventions that you must follow, which

differ from subject to subject. Help with any problems with your writing is available from both within and from outside of your university. If in doubt get help and be sure that what you are doing is what is required.

- Some 'process words' used in assignment titles and exam questions have specific academic meanings. It is important to be aware of this and to use what you know to ensure that you fully understand and fully answer the questions that you are set.
- Writing both essays and dissertations requires adherence to academic conventions, apart from any considerations of developing arguments, presenting evidence and drawing sound conclusions.
- Clear and accurate referencing in accordance with specific conventions is more important than most newly arrived undergraduates realise. Poor referencing leads to the loss of marks.
- Tutors use assessment criteria to gauge the quality of your work. These criteria are not a secret, and you will do well to pay attention to them both before, during and after you write for assessment. If you do not provide what the assessment criteria tell you is required you will not be awarded a good mark.

Next ➡️

We have looked at the most common type of assessment, namely the essay-style submission. Many undergraduates will be assessed in ways other than the writing of an essay. The next chapter will look at report writing and exams in particular and provide other useful pointers towards approaching and being successful in your work.

Activities

Question analysis: As a way of becoming familiar with the style of questions you will be required to answer, analyse one or more of the following questions. Try to devise a structure for writing an answer and then compare it with the example given. If you would prefer to do this with a question from your own discipline, find one in a module guide or past exam paper.

- Discuss the concept of the 'selfish gene'. Why is altruism a special problem for sociobiology? Does sociobiology handle it adequately?
- Briefly describe the major legislative provisions for the protection of Intellectual Property Rights.

(Continued)

- The waterfall model (or 'classical' model) of software development was introduced to improve software development techniques. Describe the waterfall model of software development and indicate its strengths and weaknesses.

Example

This is how students who gained different degree classifications seem to have interpreted this question, which relates to the psychology of child development.

Compare and contrast the consequences of blindness and deafness for language development.

First Class
Identify the consequences of blindness and deafness for language development. Compare and contrast these consequences, drawing conclusions about the nature of language development. Comment on the adequacy of theories of language development in the light of your conclusions.

Upper Second Class
Identify the consequences of blindness and deafness for language development. Compare and contrast these consequences.

Lower Second Class
List some of the features of blindness and deafness. List some consequences for development, including a few for language development.

Third Class
Write down almost anything you can think of about blindness, deafness, child development and language development.

Sense and nonsense: Read the following sentences, which are all taken from undergraduate assignments, and consider what is wrong with them, and how they might be re-written to make sense – this may not be possible in every case. If you read them aloud their nonsensical nature becomes even more apparent.

- The reasons, of which were referred to in an earlier sentence of this paragraph, are now all quite obvious.
- Several versions of earlier versions exist in a variety of different versions.
- The precipitate was precipitated as expected.
- The jurors would later have the opportunity to discuss about the falsely fabricated evidence.
- Hence, if P is true then P is true.

Keep it short: Re-write the following over-long 'sentence' so that it makes sense and is easy for the reader to follow. Your aim should be to have a number of shorter, more manageable sentences.

'In response to an increasingly complex and diverse society and a rapidly changing, technology-based national economy, in a similar world wide context, schools are being asked to educate across a wider range of subjects than ever before, the most diverse body in history to higher academic standards than ever before and the strain is beginning to show on both the teaching workforce, which is apparently suffering from extremely low morale currently, and more importantly, perhaps, on the general health and well being of the students in our schools, which is something that we must seek to rectify as a matter of urgency.'

7 Other Forms of Assessment: Reports and Examinations

LEARNING OUTCOMES

What this chapter has in store:

- Consideration of the structure of reports and how they differ from essays
- Notes about plagiarism and ways of avoiding it
- The process of preparing for and taking exams

In Chapter 6 we looked at assessment in general and more specifically at the submission of essays and dissertations. There is a lot in Chapter 6 which applies equally to this chapter, and even if in your work you will not be expected to write essays, it would be advantageous for you to look through the chapter and learn more about assessment and some of its requirements. The sections about writing will also be very useful for you if you have any doubt about what is expected of your written style at this level.

Report writing

Certain subject disciplines rely more on reports of one kind or another rather than on essays as a means of assessment. These are mainly, though not exclusively, scientific disciplines. If your subject work requires you to participate in a practical of some sort, then you will also be required to write up your experience in the form of a report.

A report is a form of communication that will do one or more of the following:

- Describe.
- Analyse.
- Summarise.
- Criticise or praise.
- Make predictions based on an analysis of current or past events or practical experimental work that you will have witnessed or undertaken yourself.

In very many cases reports are the result of practical work or 'labs'. Practicals vary in their requirements according to subject discipline, but there are general principles which apply. You will be familiar with one way of presenting reports at least, based on your pre-university experience. It is most likely that the work in your discipline will be related to this, with the expected advances and differences associated with working at a higher level.

In general you will take part in experiments, design experiments and plan and organise experiments yourself. The term 'experiment' is used in its broadest sense here to cover a wide range of different types of work across a wide range of disciplines. Obviously you will apply what is written here cautiously and in line with guidance that you are given by your tutors. When you complete a practical you will be required to analyse your data and to write up your analysis and commentary as a practical report.

In your undergraduate study, and possibly to a greater extent in postgraduate work, you will be expected to write reports and to present findings in both written and verbal and/or audio/visual forms. You will, for example, write reports which:

- Summarise what you have learned on a particular topic.
- Present the results of individual practicals and research projects.
- Summarise the result of a group project and presentation.
- Reflect on a work experience or other placement you have undertaken.

You may also be asked to present the results of individual or group work to fellow students and tutors in verbal form, often including the use of audio/visual aids. We will look at this in detail in Chapter 8.

The differences between a report and an essay

Essays and reports are written for different audiences and for different purposes. They are therefore written in different ways. Essays are structured, as we saw in Chapter 6, but in most cases there is a limited use of headings and sub-headings, bullet points will be used sparingly and the essay as a whole will be of a discursive nature with a continuous flow and clear links from paragraph to paragraph. Reports are, in most cases, more formally structured, with greater use of headings and lists, and adhere to the structure set for the subject to which they relate. Table 7.1 sets out the main differences.

The basic format of a report

The standard report format for your discipline will be based on the format in which articles are submitted to the academic journals of your subject area. For this reason you will do well

Table 7.1 Some of the differences between a report and an essay

Report	Essay
Describes/analyses past events, e.g. experiments	Allows you to pursue hypothetical ideas and possibilities
Can be read section by section; content focused on facts and analysis	Must be read as a whole owing to its discursive nature
Presentational style makes use of, e.g, more formal language, sub-headings and bullet points	Bullet points and sub-headings not normally used, although this is not a hard and fast rule
Diagrams and charts used in the explanation of processes and the presentation of results	Use of diagrams, charts and illustrations very limited
Uses the 'passive' voice, e.g., detached, objective style of writing (see below)	Can use either the 'passive' or 'active' voice (see below)
Can arrive at clear objective findings with scope for recommendations if appropriate	Unusual to have 'recommendations', although this depends on the context of the essay and the nature of the 'question'

to spend time thinking about the format used in the articles that you read. There is another good reason for reading journal articles rather than textbooks, which we have hinted at earlier. Current journal articles are where you will find the most up-to-date work on the current issues of your subject; it is here where the accepted ideas and theories of tomorrow are first aired, and where new work associated with established truths will appear.

The basic format for reporting work in sciences, which most of us were introduced to at school, has four sections:

- Introduction
- Methods and materials
- Results
- Conclusions

This format, which is in widespread use, will take on slightly different shapes depending on the discipline. In particular, the inclusion of an abstract may be required, or, for what might be called true experiments, a separate section for the hypothesis.

The basic format derives from the 'scientific method'. Without digressing too much here, the scientific method, put simply, involves the development of a hypothesis, the

Table 7.2 Sections of a basic report related to scientific method

Section of report	Relation to scientific method
Introduction	This section will state your hypothesis. You will explain how you derived the hypothesis and how it connects to previous research. The introduction provides context for and the purpose of the experiment/work
Methods	This section describes, in detail, how you tested your hypothesis. You should make it clear why you chose to work in the way described
Results	This section provides the results of your work in an untreated way. Often statistical in nature, this section will often be in the form of tables, charts, or other clear diagrammatic formats. This section should not include any analysis or interpretation
Conclusions (Discussion)	This section is where you consider whether or not your results support your original hypothesis. It is here where you discuss the findings in detail. The limitations of your work, and possibly suggestions for improvements or future work, should also be here

testing of the hypothesis and arriving at a decision about whether your results support the hypothesis. Table 7.2 describes a report in terms of the scientific method

This basic format will be seen in reports of all types. Sometimes the sequence is altered; for example, some scientific journals require that the methods section comes at the end of the work, and sometimes other factors dictate the inclusion of other elements.

Earlier, in Chapter 6, we looked at a sequence for preparing to write an essay-style assignment. It is reproduced here with minor alterations which relate to report writing; many of the items remain unchanged, however, which emphasises the underlying similarities between any type of work submitted for assessment. The preparation sequence for a report-style assignment is:

- Select the title, question, problem or experiment.
- Divide the overall task into smaller individual tasks.
- Record your thoughts, ideas and sources, in one place and write a plan.
- Choose an appropriate method for carrying out the work to be reported upon.
- Collect source material together.

- Undertake the work to be reported upon as appropriate to your discipline and the nature of the work.
- Collect results.
- Analyse results and prepare them for presentation.
- Write up a first draft.
- Read your work and make corrections.
- Produce a final draft and proof read it one last time.

In general, a report is written in the past tense, as you will be describing an event which happened in the past, and which has been completed by the time that you start writing.

Scientific journals formerly encouraged contributors to avoid using the first person: 'I' or 'we'. This is because the researchers themselves were not considered personally important to the procedures being reported. In experimental work it is considered important that other researchers should be able to reproduce experiments exactly, based on the report; this is a way in which the results and conclusions reported might be verified. By using first person it was deemed to suggest that the experiment could not be duplicated without the help or collaboration of the original researchers. Another way in which personal references were removed from reports, and which has become a scientific convention, is the use of the passive voice in writing up research. The 'voice' of a piece of writing is an important consideration in many disciplines, not just science, and we will consider it now.

Use of the passive voice

There is often discussion about the 'voice', in grammatical terms, that should be used in academic writing. Greater interest has perhaps been triggered by the ubiquitous Microsoft grammar checking facility, which is a long way from foolproof. Precisely what the passive voice is, and how and when to make use of it, is often misunderstood. There is also some disagreement about whether the passive voice is acceptable in academic work; we have seen that as a convention it is generally used in science reporting. Acceptance, and even desirability, of the use of the passive voice differs from subject to subject, and sometimes even from tutor to tutor.

The passive voice is one of a range grammatical forms used for expressing events in language. A passive sentence comes about when the subject of an active verb is changed into the agent of the action described by the passive verb:

The ball hit the window   The ball is the subject of the verb in this active sentence.
The window was hit by the ball   The ball is the agent of the action in this passive sentence.

The use of the passive voice is often relatively straightforward to detect. There will usually be a form of the verb 'to be' (*am, is, are, was, were, have been, has been, had been, will be, will have been, being etc.*) followed by a past participle. (The past participle is a form of the verb which often ends in '-ed' and refers to events in the past: *suggested, helped, informed etc.* There are exceptions to the '-ed' rule with such irregular past participles as *hit, found, paid, kept, driven* and others.) A passive voice sentence will be in this format:

form of 'to be' + past participle

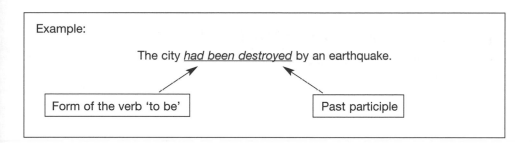

Example:

The city *had been destroyed* by an earthquake.

Form of the verb 'to be'   Past participle

Some simple illustrations of both voices might be:

We found ...	active
It was found ...	passive
The report suggests ...	active
It is suggested in the report ...	passive

This extract from an actual History Department undergraduate guide sets the scene well:

> **Passive and Active Voice:**   Where possible, avoid the passive voice, choosing instead sentence structures in which it is clear who is doing what to whom. Passive voice constructions include phrases such as: 'the cost of living was raised', 'the monarchy was abolished' and 'racist ideologies were widely disseminated'. In all of these passive constructions, it is unclear where agency and causality reside. Attempts to assess and assign agency and causality form the very heart of historical analysis, and use of the passive voice detracts from that essential task. Use active voice constructions wherever possible: they will add clarity to your writing and help you to focus on analysis rather than simple narrative. (University of Warwick, Department of History, Second Year and Third Year Undergraduate Handbook, 2006–07)

Choice of voice is in many ways a matter of personal style. It may be that you write naturally in a style that may or may not make use of passive constructions. You need to be clear for yourself whether it is acceptable to use the passive voice when writing for assessment. If in doubt, take advice from whomsoever is responsible for reading and assessing your work.

On this point, there may be other grammatical constructions or stylistic conventions that are either expected, or which are usually not allowed, according to the discipline in which you are working. An example of this might be the use of the first person 'I', which we mentioned earlier. In general the use of the first person is not considered to be indicative of good academic writing, but in some subject areas it is perfectly acceptable. You need to check, either from module or writing guides for your subject, or by speaking to your tutors.

The importance of seeking clarification and other tutorial advice

We have mentioned at a number of earlier points that in any case of uncertainty it is very important to check your understanding with those who are there to advise you and support your work. However, some university tutors are difficult to track down. For legitimate reasons they do not sit all day long in offices waiting for students to visit them, but they do provide contact details. It is important that you ensure that you know how to contact your tutors. Some will have specific times when they will be available, others will suggest you leave a phone message, or a written message in a pigeon-hole, or even under a door. One way, and probably now the most common way, to contact your tutor will be by e-mail. The ubiquity of e-mail, and the many options for accessing e-mail – at home, on the train, from abroad – mean that you will not be left waiting to have confirmation on any point that you might want to raise.

Some tutors, however, do not like to be contacted by this method, and so you should be clear about whether e-mailing your tutor is allowable for this purpose.

In some modules there is a specific time set aside for individual tutorials. Often these will be scheduled to coincide with the time when most students will be thinking in detail about the assessment for the module. Tutors will make themselves available, often on a 'sign up for an appointment' basis, to read through draft assignment plans, or to discuss your work as you prepare to complete it. Such help and advice can be invaluable, and you should think very hard if you intend not to take advantage of it. In some university departments these supervisory tutorials are mandatory. Tutors will expect you to arrive, at the very least, with ideas to discuss and questions to ask. Some will say that you should bring, or even provide in advance, a plan to discuss, or your introduction in draft. Taking advantage of an individual tutorial can help avert problems which you may not realise exist, and which, if left unattended, could lead to a poor mark.

The importance of clear, precise and accurate referencing

We have considered referencing in Chapter 6 in the context of essay writing. You are advised to look at the detail given there. Here some points are reiterated in the context of report writing.

There are several reasons why you are required to reference accurately. Namely:

- To show that you have read widely and that you are knowledgeable concerning your subject.
- To add further support to the points from the wider literature that you have made in your writing.
- To be sure that anyone reading your work can locate and refer to the material you have used.
- To be sure that accusations of plagiarism cannot be made.
- To comply with the assessment requirements of your university.

When considering references you will come across the use of a variety of terms, chief among which are 'citation', 'reference list' and 'bibliography'. You need to be clear about the meanings of these terms:

- **Citation**: a citation is a reference made in the text of your work to an external source of information. Direct quotes are citations, as are summarising or paraphrasing.
- **Reference list**: a reference list comes at the end of the main body of your work, that is before any appendices, and is an organised listing of all of the works cited by you in the text.
- **Bibliography**: a bibliography is a complete list of all sources that you have used in your preparation for the submission, including sources not cited in the text.

In any of your formal work for assessment you must be clear about exactly what the requirements are for referencing and that you meet them. For example, you must use the correct format, you must include a reference list and a separate bibliography if this is the requirement. In many departments separate bibliographies are not required.

In carrying out any piece of academic writing, the process can be viewed in two main stages:

1. Searching for, finding and reading relevant source material.
2. Using, citing and listing material in the work itself.

Note that, when reaching the second stage, it is much easier and requires far less time and effort to compile a bibliography or list of references if you have recorded details of the material you have consulted in a logical and organised way during the first stage.

The guidance in Chapter 6 provides examples showing how to apply the two most widely used referencing formats (the Harvard and Numeric systems) to the resources you are most likely to use and need to reference in your work. The examples are indicative rather than prescriptive. In referencing, slight variations from accepted styles are generally less important than consistency. In circumstances where you are told, for instance by a university department, to use a certain style and how to apply it, you should use the specified style in that way and apply it consistently.

More about plagiarism

In Chapter 5 we looked at the possibility of plagiarism creeping into assessed work and some of the consequences. Before we leave the subject of assessed written work – reports in this chapter and essays and dissertations in Chapter 6 – we will look at this area again as it is important to be fully aware of what can be seen as constituting plagiarism and how to avoid it.

Plagiarism is taking the words or ideas of another person and using them as if they were your own. It can be intentional or accidental. Plagiarism is taken very seriously in higher education. If even a small section of your work is found to have been plagiarised, it is likely that you will be assigned a mark of zero for that assignment. In more serious cases, it may be necessary for you to repeat the course completely. In some cases, plagiarism may even lead to your university registration being withdrawn.

Courter and Hamp-Lyons (1984) distinguish between four types of plagiarism:

- Outright copying – wholesale copying.
- Paraphrase plagiarism – making minimal changes to sections of text and incorporating them as your own.
- Patchwork plagiarism – interspersing sentences or phrases taken from the work of another.
- Stealing an apt term – using a way of explaining or describing something first used by another.

We can divide occurrences of plagiarism roughly into two types, deliberate and accidental, and it can happen for many reasons.

Deliberate plagiarism

For plagiarism to be deliberate you will have made a decision to take someone's work and pass it off as your own. This can be in the form of:

- Copying the work of another student
- Copying work directly from a book or article
- Copying work directly from a website
- Allowing somebody else to complete the work for you
- Using, and in some cases buying, work from the internet.

There may be a range of reasons why deliberate plagiarism is embarked upon. Perhaps you do not have the time or energy to do the work yourself, or you think your cheating will not be detected, and even if it is noticed, that the tutor will not think that it matters. It could be because you are not capable of doing the work for yourself. Whatever the reason, there is no good defence for cheating.

Apart from the fact that you do not actually learn from the process of cheating, you are very likely to be detected. Tutors will know the area of study very well and may simply recognise the work of another in your assignment. There are also increasingly sophisticated systems that tutors can turn to in order to verify plagiarism or otherwise. Detection will lead to consequences.

Accidental plagiarism

Accidental plagiarism is usually the result of ignorance or stupidity. It might be more charitable to say carelessness or lack of skill, but if you use the work of another person without acknowledgement it is still plagiarism. For some students a lack of confidence in their own abilities can lead them to seek support from the work of others, but again, there is no defence against plagiarism, whether deliberate or accidental. Some of the reasons for accidental plagiarism are set out below:

- Not knowing that you should not copy directly without acknowledgement.
- Not having the technical writing skills to present ideas in your own words.
- Not knowing how to reference the work of others in your writing.
- Taking notes from an original source and copying whole sentences or paragraphs but not making this clear to yourself. You then use the same words in your writing not realising the significance.
- Forgetting to acknowledge the words or even ideas of someone else.
- Not having time to check and complete the references properly.
- Using somebody else's notes and not being aware that some of the notes have been taken verbatim.

If we look over the list of possible reasons for accidental plagiarism we can see that this type of mistake can be avoided without too much difficulty. For most of the reasons given, a little more care and attention to detail might solve the potential problem. For others, poor technical skills in writing, for example, it is necessary actively to seek help. This help can come from three main sources: your tutor, texts designed to help in the development of academic writing skills and your university student support system. If you know that you have problems of this nature, either identified by your tutor, or because you recognise some of your own habits in the list above, you really need to address the problem. A fourth source of help, of course, could be fellow students.

Original source

From time to time this submerged or latent theatre in *Hamlet* becomes almost overt. It is close to the surface in Hamlet's pretence of madness, the 'antic disposition' he puts on to protect himself and prevent his antagonists from plucking out the heart of his mystery. It is even closer to the surface when Hamlet enters his mother's room and holds up, side by side, the pictures of the two kings, Old Hamlet and Claudius, and proceeds to describe for her the true nature of the choice she has made, presenting truth by means of a show. Similarly, when he leaps into the open grave at Ophelia's funeral, ranting in high heroic terms, he is acting out for Laertes, and perhaps for himself as well, the folly of excessive, melodramatic expressions of grief.

Kernan, A. (1979) *The Playwright as Magician.*
New Haven: Yale University Press, pp. 102–103

Word-for-word plagiarism, or unacknowledged direct quotation (plagiarised passages are in italics and underlined):

Copying seleted passages and phrases without any acknowledgement (plagiarised passages are in italics and underlined):

Paraphrasing the text while maintaining the basic paragraph and sentence struture (no plagiarism):

Almost all of Shakespeare's *Hamlet* can be understood as a play about acting and the theatre. For example, there is *Hamlet's pretence of madness, the 'antic disposition'* that *he puts on to protect himself and prevent his antagonists from plucking out the heart of his mystery. When*

Almost all of Shakespeare's *Hamlet* can be understood as a play about acting and the theatre. For example, in Act 1, Hamlet adopts a *pretence of madness* that he uses *to protect himself and prevent his antagonists from* discovering his mission to revenge his father's murder. He also presents *truth by means of a show* when he

Almost all of Shakespeare's *Hamlet* can be understood as a play about acting and the theatre. For example, in Act 1, Hamlet pretends to be insane in order to make sure his enemies do not discover his mission to revenge his father's murder. The theme is

Hamlet enters his mother's room, he *holds up, side by side, the pictures of the two kings, Old Hamlet and Claudius, and proceeds to describe for her the true nature of the choice she has made, presenting truth by means of a show. Similarly, when he leaps into the open grave at Ophelia's funeral, ranting in high heroic terms, he is acting out for Laertes, and perhaps for himself as well, the folly of excessive, melodramatic expressions of grief.*

✦✦✦

The opening sentence is loosely adapted from the original and reworded more simply. The rest of the entire passage is taken almost word for word from the source. The minor alterations of the original do not relieve the writer of the responsibility to attribute these words to their author. A passage from a source may be worth quoting at length if it makes a point precisely or elegantly. In such cases, the passage should be copied exactly, put in quotation marks, and cited accordingly.

compares the portraits of Gertrude's two husbands in order *to describe for her the true nature of the choice she has made.* And when he leaps in Ophelia's open grave *ranting in high heroic terms,* Hamlet is *acting out* the folly of *excessive, melodramatic expressions of grief.*

✦✦✦

This passage, in content and structure, is taken wholesale from the source. Although the writer has rewritten much of the paragraph, and fewer phrases are lifted word for word, this is a clear example of plagiarism. Inserting even short phrases from the source into a new sentence still requires placing quotations around the borrowed words and citing the author. If even one phrase is good enough to borrow, it must be properly set off by quotation marks. In the case above, if the writer had rewritten the entire paragraph and only used Alvin Kernan's phrase 'high heroic terms' without properly quoting and acknowledging its source, the student would still be guilty of plagiarism.

even more obivious when Hamlet compares the pictures of his mother's two husbands to show her what a bad choice she has made, using their images to reveal the truth. Also, when he jumps into Ophelia's grave, hurling his challenge to Laertes, Hamlet demonstrates the foolishness of exaggerated expressions of emotion.

✦✦✦

Almost nothing of the original language remains in this rewritten pragraph. However, the key idea, the choice and order of the examples, and even the basic structure of the original sentences are all taken from the source. Although it would no longer be necessary to use quotation marks, it would absolutely be necessary to place a citation at the end of this paragraph to acknowledge that the content is not original. Better still would be to acknowledge the author in the text by adding a second sentence such as, 'Alvin Kernan provides several examples from the play where these themes become moreobvious' and then citing the source at the end of the paragraph.

On pages 162–163 is a detailed example of plagiarism from an original text. This example is amended from a source at Princeton University (Princeton, 2003), where a section on the university's website gives some very useful background on the 'rules' which apply in academic writing.

Preparing for and taking exams

Each one of us will have different set of concerns about exams. Some unusual people say that they have no worries about exams and that they simply take them in their stride. This may or may not be true; often those who seem, and claim, to be most relaxed about exams are like swans – paddling very fast beneath the water. It is worth spending some time reflecting on your particular concerns and considering what your particular exam needs might be. Here, we will look in turn at some of the areas associated with exams which can cause concern, or even anxiety of one sort or another.

Early preparation

There are different types of examination: seen papers; open book; one question only; no choice papers; multiple choice papers. It is very important to know in advance what the structure and duration of your exam paper will be. You will of course need to know the exact time and place of the exam. If the location is not familiar to you it is a good idea to take the time to make a visit to the room so that there will be no risk of late arrival as a result of not being able to find where you should be. There are some other important things too which you really should know about some while before an exam:

- Content? What material will be covered?
- How long is the paper?
- How many questions will you have to answer?
- What choices will there be?
- Will the questions be multiple choice, essay-style, calculations etc.?
- What will I be able to take in to the exam room (books, notes, calculator, tables etc.)?
- What will be provided for me in the exam room (books, documents, tables etc.)?
- Will there be any reading material provided before the exam?
- Will the questions be available before the exam?

Your module guide, exam guide or tutor will be the source of the answers to these questions.

At this stage it is perhaps a good time to say that a high level of thinking about, and engagement with, the content of your course, and good effort made to complete course-work expectations, will put you in a strong position when it comes to the exam season. Exams are for assessing learning and if your learning has progressed well, then with a little extra work – revision – you will be in a position to be successful in exams. It is sometimes suggested that exam preparation begins at the start of the course; some incredibly systematic students who follow this line of thought will plan a scheme for revising and revisiting their work throughout their course. This, however, is not the reality for most of us.

Revision

The literal meaning of the word 'revision' is to 'look again'. This implies looking, in some way, at the material covered in a module. To be effective revision needs to be more than this. Revision needs to be a time of active engagement with the material that you have covered. It should involve organising, and possibly re-organising, material and finding ways of remembering it. In earlier chapters we have considered ways of engaging with facts and ideas, and looked at a variety of ways of recording. Many of the approaches to new material are also very useful at those times when you do need to look again at what you have done. You will do this by choosing methodical approaches, and techniques such as finding the main ideas from paragraphs and noting them, or converting written passages into charts, tables, or diagrams, or even lists. As with all learning, revision is an active process. You need to devise an approach which suits the way that you think and learn, and that will allow you to be finished and ready to perform by the time the exam arrives.

All of the same principles for carrying out academic study apply at revision times. Some students seem to think that last-minute all-night sessions are required. This is not necessarily the case. To work effectively you need to be well rested, fed and watered, and you need to plan the use of your time to match your workload and the time available, with a mind to having breaks and some contrast in your activities.

Some students like to draw up schedules and then keep to them, setting aside specific time periods for particular topics. Others draw up schedules and then ignore them. The main, and probably best, advice is that you should have a plan, and you should try to keep to it.

The process of revision Some of the material in the following section is adapted from a site for revision and exam preparation associated with the Open University. The site includes a freely available tutorial to follow which covers many of the topics in this section and parts of which would be useful to look at for specific concerns that you may have. The tutorial can be found at: http://openlearn.open.ac.uk/mod/resource/view.php?id=57346

Find out about the exam paper   It is very important that you know as much as possible about the exam paper which you are to sit. You need to know how the exam paper will be set out, the way the questions are organised and what percentage of the final mark each question carries. One way to find out this information is to look at past papers. These will usually be available in the library. Your tutor may even be able to supply copies. Exam papers almost always carry a set of very clear instructions, sometimes referred to as the **rubric**. The importance of reading these instructions and fully understanding them cannot be over emphasised.

Gather your materials together   All of your course notes, handouts, copies of articles, books and anything else relevant to the module in question need to be easily accessible, and in some sort of order: by date, by topic, by most likely to be examined, or by how complex you find the content.

Make a decision about what to revise   You may feel that you do not have a choice about what to revise, and that you have to cover every detail of the syllabus. This may well be the case, and in this situation your job is to prioritise and sequence the material. You will be able to do this in the light of any advice that has been given to you, or by looking at the emphasis given to different parts of the module – how many lectures were devoted to it for example. Past exam papers might also be useful in this respect.

Plan a schedule   Even if this is not something that you have done before, and you feel it is unnecessary, it might still be worth considering. There cannot be any rules about when revision should start. Whatever you choose to do must involve careful and systematic coverage of all of the topics of the module in question. Plan according to the time available and the volume of work to be covered. Be realistic and be flexible. A written time chart may suit you – it can be placed in a prominent position near to where you will be working, and landmark times can be highlighted in colour.

It is a good idea to review your past experiences of revising and to learn from any problems which may have arisen. Changing your approach in the light of experience is a positive move, not a sign of indecision.

Plan for understanding   Reading and re-reading your notes and handouts is not a time-efficient way of revising. Based on what you know about constructivist learning

(Chapter 1), plan to be an active, not a passive, reviser. This will always involve doing something, including, but certainly not exclusively, reading. This process should be aimed at reducing the volume of your written notes and other materials to a more manageable size. It is often useful to aim at condensing copious notes to a single side of A4 for each topic, or to a set of cue cards, or even a list of key words which will trigger access to what you know and need to include in answers and which can be referred to in the later stages of your work for the exam.

There are many active approaches, including:

- Making information sheets or cue cards – you can read through the end products on the bus or at other times.
- Condensing the content of a complex paragraph into bullet points.
- Changing a list into a table and vice versa.
- Practising writing under timed conditions – for example give yourself ten minutes to write the introduction to an essay-style answer.
- Making posters or other diagrams – these can be pinned to the wall near to where you eat or work.
- Recording audio tapes or MP3 files – the recording can be played back and listened to during travel.
- Using a computer – creating the reduced versions of your notes for example.
- Talking with fellow students – attempting to explain a complex idea or process is a very good way of getting your thoughts in order. This is often referred to as teaching to learn.

Memory and understanding   As we have hinted earlier, an exam is not really intended as a memory test; it is much more to do with the selection, presentation and interpretation of materials. Despite this, you will still be anxious about remembering all that you need. Chapter 1 considered preferred learning styles. The notions of different approaches to reading, note-taking and to study generally apply equally in situations where you are preparing for an impending exam. If, for example, you know that you are predominantly an auditory learner, you can plan to work in a way that complements this preference; you could record your notes, and replay them, or if you have recorded lectures with a digital recorder, this would be a good time to listen again.

Answering practice exam questions   Just like assignment questions, exam questions should be read carefully, because you need to demonstrate in your answers that you understand what you have been asked to do. Candidates all too often lose marks because they have failed to answer the question.

If you have access to previous questions you will be able to work through them carefully and be certain that you have made a sound interpretation of what is required. This can be an opportunity to work with others and discuss what the question is really getting at. If you do not have access to questions then you could produce your own. In an earlier section about academic reading we looked at the idea of changing statements into questions to help in the process of understanding the text. This is a technique which you could employ here too. Simply: '*The foundations of the modern scientific method are found in the writing of, amongst others, Bacon and Descartes*', can be transformed into: '*Describe and analyse the contribution of Bacon and Descartes to the development of the modern scientific method*'. From this question, based upon your knowledge, your reading and your notes, you will be able to set out a structure for answering the question which describes and analyses the contribution of the two writers to what we know as scientific method.

We considered the process words used in the framing of questions and titles for academic assessment in Chapter 6, in the section dealing with assignment titles. If you are in doubt about the meaning of particular process words you should consult the list there (see p. 124), or, again, consult your tutor.

Exam answers versus assignment answers

There will clearly be a big difference between the answer that you are able to provide in a timed exam and an answer to the same question set as an assignment. With the assignment you will have time to consider, read, plan in detail, write, draft and re-draft. In an exam you will feel rushed and possibly anxious and in all likelihood you will not be able to produce a finished product of the quality that you would achieve in a non-exam context. This is understood and expected by your tutors. Experienced markers know that there will be certain peculiarities of style, construction and spelling in written answers in exams. This is not to suggest that you should pay no attention to the structure and presentation of your work; you should aspire to write as well as you can and you should not disregard the conventions of presentation. In working quickly it is likely that you will not have time to spend considering the precise structure of your sentences, or the subtle distinctions between different words and phrases. In exams you will have to write everything as a first draft, and in most cases this will be the final draft as well.

If you do have the luxury of time left at the end of an exam you should re-read everything. At this stage it is quite likely that you will come across certain oddities or mistakes which you should correct. At this stage you must be sure that any crossings out, or alterations, are clear and obvious, and not in any way ambiguous or confusing.

Sometimes advice is given about how to deal with an unfinished answer when time is about to run out. Different advice is given by different tutors. Some might suggest that you write the remaining sections of your answer in very brief note form. This will at least show the examiner that you have more to offer and will give a picture of your thoughts and plans. Other tutors will not accept this, and will suggest that you keep writing until the last minute. If you have written a brief outline of your answer, as a planning tool for yourself, and crossed it out before you start the answer proper some tutors will tell you that they will look at it if the answer is signalled as being unfinished. You need to know the expectation of the marker and the best way to find out about this is to ask. It may be that you are given advice for exams, either in a taught session, or in written guidance. You must pay attention to anything relating to exams and if in any doubt you must ask beforehand. You will recognise this advice to ask if you are uncertain, because it relates to a good deal of what you will be concerned with in your academic work.

Dealing with exam nerves

Not everyone suffers from pre-exam nerves, but most of us will recognise the feelings of anxiety that accompany such occasions as exams or job interviews. The anxiety that is generated by the prospect of an exam may be only slight, but it can in some cases escalate to the point where it is debilitating. The importance of most exams, coupled with the unusual conditions – time limit, silence, for example – serve to heighten anxiety. This in turn can lead to your producing work of a lower quality than you are really capable of.

One way to help to subdue and minimise exam nerves is to practise relaxation techniques, sometimes referred to as techniques for managing anxiety. If you choose to follow this route, it is important to begin early, that is, several weeks before the exam. This is for two reasons: first, you will need to become practised with the techniques if they are to be of any benefit, and secondly the benefit may well be that you are better able to concentrate and apply yourself to your revision if you have reduced your feelings of nervousness.

We will look at two approaches here (relaxation and visualisation), but there are others. If you would like to find out more about anxiety management you could seek out some of the self-help material available in book format or through the internet. You could seek professional advice, possibly through the university counselling service, or by asking your doctor.

A breathing exercise
1. Breathe in slowly through your nose as you slowly count to ten. Imagine that you can feel your stomach, followed by your chest, gently filling with air.
2. Hold your breath for another count of five, or for less time if this becomes uncomfortable.

3. Breathe out slowly through your mouth, again counting slowly to ten.
4. Hold your breath again, for a count of five, this time with virtually empty lungs.
5. Repeat this at least three times, but no more than five.

A relaxation exercise

Sit or lie comfortably, breathe slowly and evenly while working through the following

1. Tighten your stomach muscles, hold for a count of five, then relax.
2. Clench both fists tightly, hold for a count of five, then relax.
3. Stretch you fingers apart, hold for a count of five, then relax.
4. Push your elbows tightly into the sides of your body, hold for a count of five, then relax.
5. Tighten the muscles in your legs, hold for a count of five, then relax.
6. Push both feet downwards against the floor, hold for a count of five, then relax.
7. Repeat two or three times.

This is an exercise that can be done during an exam without drawing attention to yourself, or disturbing others.

The stop technique

This technique can be useful in a situation where you suddenly feel a surge of anxiety.

1. Say the word 'Stop' to yourself in as abrupt a fashion as you can manage; it is good if you can say this out loud, but circumstances might prevent this.
2. Breathe in slowly and hold your breath for a count of five then slowly breathe out through your mouth. As you breathe out let your shoulders drop and relax.
3. Breathe normally for a count of five and then breathe in slowly again and hold. As you breathe out slowly through your mouth let the whole of your upper body relax.
4. Repeat step 3 two or three times before waiting quietly for a short time and then returning to what you were doing.

Visualisation   Visualising scenes of calm is a technique used in many different contexts and for some people it is an effective way of relaxing and creating a feeling of well-being.

Before beginning a visualisation exercise it is a good idea to sit, or even lie down and work through something like one of the breathing or relaxation exercises above.

Method one:

1. Imagine yourself in a calm relaxed state actually taking the exam.
2. Imagine yourself as calm, purposeful and confident.
3. Imagine yourself at your desk in the exam room.
4. Imagine yourself feeling content and completely at one with your surroundings.
5. Imagine yourself getting on with the work effectively and concentrating well.
6. Visualise this setting, and your state of mind, repeatedly for two or three minutes.

Method two:

For this method you need gradually to build a picture of a scene, which can be real or wholly imagined. The important part of the imagining is that the scene that you build must be a safe and welcoming place. There should be nothing which could cause feelings of concern or uneasiness. Work at making the scene as real as possible, include the warmth of the sun, the breeze in the air; think about the sounds and colours. When the scene in your mind is complete, allow yourself to look around and take in all of the detail. The scene could be of a holiday location, or the security of a room from your childhood home. It could be a real, partly real or wholly fictitious setting. When you have practised this visualisation several times you will find it easier to slip into the imagined scene and draw from it a sense of calm before returning to reality.

These simple techniques can be used almost anywhere at almost any time, including both inside and outside of the exam room itself. If you do not find them particularly helpful you might decide to modify and personalise them in some way – there are no rules about this. If you find that your anxiety becomes extreme and debilitating you should speak to your personal tutor, or perhaps a university counsellor or your doctor. There will be a range of options available, including special arrangements for taking the exam itself if this is considered appropriate.

On this point, you should always be sure that your tutors know, well in advance, of any particular difficulty that you may have in an exam as the result of, for example, a back injury which means that you cannot sit comfortably for long periods, or perhaps some form of dyslexia, formally diagnosed, which might entitle you to additional time, or the use of a computer.

Finally

It may not seem wholly appropriate to give advice here about such things as knowing where your exam is to be held, and knowing that you need to take official university identification with you, but sometimes small details can become important beyond belief. All university tutors who have been involved with exam arrangements or invigilation will be able to tell a story of what seems like exam season stupidity which came about for the simple lack of a snippet of information. There are many small details that may need your attention. Those below may or may not apply in every case, but it is certainly worth reading through the list:

- Do you need to know your exam number/seat number in advance?
- Do you need a formal means of identification?
- Will you need to sign in, or fill in an attendance slip?
- Are you allowed any 'luggage' (bags, folders etc.) with you?
- Are you allowed any food or drink in the exam room?
- What are the regulations about using the toilet?
- What are the arrangements for late arrival?
- What are the regulations about leaving the exam before the end?

You will probably be able to think of questions to add to this list without too much difficulty.

SUMMARY

- There are many overlaps between writing essays and other types of writing – the need for clearly presented, grammatical writing for example. However, different types of written submissions have different specific requirements and reports, as we have seen here, are written in a different style and certainly in a different format to essays.
- Plagiarism, even if it is accidental, can be disastrous for your work, and in extreme cases, even for your university career.
- Exams need to be prepared for carefully and taken seriously. It would be a crime for three years' hard work to be lost for the sake of the extra effort to pass an exam. There is a great deal that can be done to be as sure as possible that you will be successful.

Next

Another academic activity which is sometimes the focus of assessment is the giving of presentations. This can be a harrowing experience, but it is one of the essential graduate skills to be able to communicate effectively in a range of different ways. In the next chapter the art, if it is indeed an art, of giving presentations is looked at in detail and many sound approaches to giving a successful presentation are included.

Activity

Past papers:

Look up a past paper and go through the questions below. Pay particular attention to the rubric, which explains what you have to do. Write down your answers to each of these questions:

- Is the paper arranged in sections?
- Are there compulsory sections or questions?
- Are there any multiple-choice questions?
- How many questions are there, and how many must be answered?
- Are long or short answers expected?
- How are the different questions weighted?
- How long is the exam, and how much time should each question be allocated?
- Are particular questions or sections related to particular topics or units of the module?
- Are there any 'seen' questions which will be available before the exam?
- Are you allowed to take in any notes, books etc.?

See also the activities for Chapter 6 relating to assessment and writing.

8 Giving Presentations

LEARNING OUTCOMES

What this chapter has in store:

- Thoughts about the purpose of oral presentations.
- The importance of thorough preparation.
- Approaches taken to assessing student presentations.
- The use of electronic and other visual aids, including notes, cue cards and handouts.
- Keeping calm and appearing confident.
- Ways of learning more about what makes an effective presentation.

We noted earlier that in many situations for a number of reasons you may be expected to give an oral and/or visual presentation. This could be to share some of your work with a group; this is a way of covering more content in group sessions than would be possible in other situations and is favoured by some tutors; it could be to feed back your experiences on a placement, or to report on a practical. Sometimes, as we will see, presentations might be assessed. The notion of assessing presentations might seem alien to you if you are studying a subject which does not involve any sort of teaching or dramatic input, but as we have seen, the ability to communicate effectively in a range of ways, including presenting to a group, is an essential graduate skill. (See 'Transferable graduate skills' in Appendix.1)

'The first time I gave a speech I was so nervous that I kept my eyes closed through most of the monologue. I kept hoping that if I didn't look at them they would quietly go away. When I had finished, I opened my eyes and, unfortunately, my wish had been granted. There was only one person left in the audience. He was a bookish-looking fellow wearing a sour expression. Hoping to find some solace in this catastrophe, I asked him why he stayed. Still frowning, he replied, "I'm the next speaker."'

Victor Kiam

What is a presentation?

In answer to this question, we get a fairly broad and vague definition from the nearest dictionary to hand:

1. Something, such as a lecture or speech, that is set forth for an audience.
2. A performance, as of a drama.

(www.dictionary.com)

What might it mean when you are asked to give a presentation as an element of your work for a particular module? You might well find yourself in a position where you have to give a seminar presentation on your own, or you might be one of a pair, or part of a group which must organise a presentation. The presentation might be a simple talk without any aids, or with simple devices such as an overhead projector (OHP) and slides, or a pre-prepared flip chart. Or you might be expected to make use of slightly more sophisticated tools, such as Microsoft PowerPoint, which could include pictures, diagrams and video clips. You might have a strict time limit, as little as ten minutes, or you could be asked to take responsibility for the whole seminar, of one or two hours, which could include providing activities and leading a discussion.

Giving a presentation of any kind is likely to be a difficult task for many, but it is a necessary element of most undergraduate programmes. The whole process is a learning experience in itself and can lead to an increase in your knowledge and understanding, and in your confidence.

What is the purpose of presentations at university?

Giving a presentation is becoming a more common form of assessment in degree programmes, but the purpose of asking students to prepare and deliver a short talk or presentation, which can for some be a thoroughly gruelling and draining experience, is more than simply to provide an opportunity for you to be assessed.

We have considered, briefly, the notion of 'graduateness'; that is, those qualities that are generally expected of someone who has succeeded in completing a course of study at an institute of higher education, or similar, leading to the award of a degree. High amongst those features expected of a graduate are skills of communication. Clearly not all graduates will need the skills associated with high level communication at high powered business meetings, the media, or even in the political sphere. But graduates should have the ability to communicate clearly and precisely in a range of different contexts. These contexts will include job interviews, business settings, case conferences, training and teaching situations, and many more. They will involve one-to-one communication and also one-to-many. This is not to say that graduates should be trained as public speakers, or entertainers ready to join the after-dinner circuit, but they should be able to communicate effectively to interested audiences in the context of their knowledge and expertise. The ability to give presentations is one skill amongst many that graduates should possess. If you choose to pursue your studies beyond your first degree, and especially if you choose to follow an academic career, you will have to make presentations of many different types. Giving a presentation to a group is an important way in which academics share knowledge with each other. Preparing and giving a presentation is a vital part of your learning experience, which can often be fulfilling – usually when it is over.

Preparing and delivering a presentation

Giving presentations is one of the experiences that many undergraduates become very anxious about. Needless to say there are some who do not experience fear as the prospect of speaking to a large group looms; but there are many who do. There are ways of preparing for and of delivering presentations that can minimise this fear and lead to effective and satisfying communication.

Beginning the process

As with most tasks that you will have to complete during your university course, it is a good idea to begin the process of preparation as early as possible. This might mean thinking about it as soon as you first know that it is planned for the module you will be following, or at least starting to think about topics and ideas as soon as the tutor has informed you of the need. This will usually be in the first session when an overview of the module will be given.

There are no real 'truths' when it comes to the topic or content of a presentation which tutors might ask you to undertake. It is obviously unrealistic to ask you to cover an enormous amount of content in a short presentation, but one of the skills that you might be assessed on is your ability to select and condense.

Different subjects will, naturally, have different types of presentations which are considered to be of benefit. Literature-based subjects might well ask for a presentation concerning the works, or a specific work, of an author in relation to the wider themes of the work. Subjects with a more practical bias might well ask for a presentation of the results of lab work, a demonstration, or other practical elements of the course. There is a very wide range of possibilities. One presentation topic which can be asked for across a range of subjects is the précis of a piece of academic work. With this type of presentation it can be that you are given a journal article to work on, or you might be asked to select a suitable chapter from a book. With all presentation tasks there is a possibility that you might be asked to work in pairs or small groups. We will consider group work later.

In some ways preparing for a presentation can be more difficult than preparing a written assignment. The difficulty is likely to arise when you have gathered together a lot of material that is relevant to your topic, and you need to pare it down to something that will fit into the time that is allocated. However, you should approach your presentation in much the same way as you would approach other pieces of work. The more you have read, and the more that you know about the topic, the better prepared you are for the presentation and the better equipped you will be if there any questions at the end.

When planning a presentation you need to make sure of certain points:

- Is there a specific title or are you expected to talk on a general topic, or choose for yourself?
- How long should the presentation last?
- What is the date of the presentation?
- Is the presentation to be **assessed**; if so, what are the assessment criteria?

Once you have these things clear in your mind you can move on to the main tasks involved. First you must take time to understand the task. Unfortunately for some students, they receive poor marks for their work for one main reason: that is, they fail to understand the task and as a result fail to complete what is actually expected of them. We have already seen the importance of answering the question when writing an assignment for assessment, and we have stressed the importance of constantly referring back to the title of the work that you are undertaking. The same is true with presentations. You must understand the task, and then do your best to complete it. If you are in any doubt about what you should be doing, ask for help; your module guide or your tutor should be your first port of call.

To help in coming to understand the task you might find it helpful to write down the aims of your presentation. In particular, decide what it is that you want the audience to have gained when you have finished. In a sense you are in the position of teacher, and good teachers have clear aims in mind, which are referred to as 'learning outcomes' – what will the audience, or class, know, understand, or be able to do by the end of the session that they did not know, or understand or were not able to do before? Here we are talking about knowledge, concepts, skills and perhaps attitudes (see Chapter 1). In some cases, especially in the case of student presentations, the learning outcomes should perhaps be in terms of knowing more about, understanding better and being better at, that is to say, adding to what the audience know, understand or can do.

The next stage is the actual preparation. The first part of your preparation will involve seeking out appropriate resources. You will probably have some basic references from your tutor, and you should approach these first. This will mean a visit to the library, where you will be able to follow up the references and look across the breadth of the topic in the library catalogues, shelves, or through a search of the electronic resources.

In parallel to this you should think about the style of your presentation, about the resources that you will use. It could be that the presentation is to be informal and you have been told that it is not necessary to use PowerPoint, or to produce visual aids. Alternatively, it could be that you are required to use presentation tools, and required to produce visual aids and handout materials. Either way, it is likely that you will have some choices to make.

Planning

The stage of more detailed planning comes next. When you have become immersed in your topic and you are as familiar with the area as you can be in the time that you have, you need to think about how to build your presentation by dividing the material into sections, each one dealing with one important point. The structure of your presentation will depend in some ways on the topic that you are dealing with, but in general there should be an introduction, a set of main points and a concluding summary.

Some people like to approach the planning of a presentation by planning and writing a fairly lengthy piece which can then be reduced to main points. The benefit of this is that you will have prepared detailed information which you will be able to refer to during the presentation and you will also be in a position of strength if questions are asked. For some presentations you may be required to submit an accompanying paper, or set of notes which may be assessed alongside the presentation itself. Alternatively, some people like to compile a set of headings, and based on these headings to write a short paragraph which will form the core of what they will say at each point in the presentation. As we know from what has gone before, the precise approach that you take is a matter of personal choice, but it is probably wise to prepare in detail and then reduce rather than constructing a bare skeleton and trying to add flesh. Whichever approach you choose, you will end up with a set of notes which you will most likely want to use as a guide during the presentation.

Once you have the content more or less finalised, you should think more about style. This is the right order in which to consider your presentation because you do not want to produce something which is high on style and weak on content.

For the sake of this section we will assume that you have a short presentation to make and you are expected to make use of aids of one sort or another. We will go on to look in detail at the options for presentation tools, such as PowerPoint, in a later section, and so we will consider these tools only in passing here. If you are to use overhead projector slides (also known as acetates), which is still a possibility even in this age of computer technology, the notional 'rules' to bear in mind are very similar.

For example:

- In a presentation lasting between ten and fifteen minutes you should aim to have no more than ten slides.
- Eight slides for ten minutes is probably about right.
- Each slide should have no more than six lines of text.
- The text MUST be easily read by everyone in the room. Simply copying standard size text onto an acetate, or into PowerPoint, is unacceptable.

Obviously these rules are notional, and should not be seen as 'hard and fast' (except the last one), but experience has taught that they are deserving of attention.

We will consider some of the technical aspects of software such as transitions and other effects, for example, later.

Briefly on the point of the use of an overhead projector, many academics will produce a PowerPoint presentation and then, as a backup in case of technical difficulties, copy their slides on to acetates and have them ready in case of a presentation emergency. It is a good idea to have this or some other contingency plan in place.

Slides

You need to have a clear idea of the purpose of your slides. Certainly they are not to pass on everything that you want to communicate concerning your topic. This would amount to producing all of your notes on slides and this would not be a good idea. The slides are more a way of focusing the attention of the audience and to give them help in understanding what you are talking about. The information on the slide is really a pointer to what it is that they are about to hear. There are different views about how to expose the different points on your slides.

Some feel that the whole slide should be shown immediately, others that each point should be exposed as you come to it in what you are saying. A good rule to consider here is that you should not have so much going on that you actually distract the audience away from the points that you are making when you move to the next sentence or phrase by sliding a piece of paper down the screen (and possibly making a mess of it), or clicking from one transition to the next. Keep it simple. The acronym KISS is often referred to on this point – Keep It Simple, Stupid – and this is good advice. Sometimes you may want to hold on to the next item for the sake of effect; for example, a surprising counter-example, or something else unexpected, can have more impact if it is exposed at the point when you talk about it rather than its having been on the screen for some time.

If you have too much information on display at any one time it is likely to distract your audience. They are likely to become engrossed in reading rather than in listening. You may well feel that this diverts attention away from you, which you might like, but it does not make for a good presentation. Some presenters feel that text on slides is distracting *per se*, and avoid its use as far as possible; they will use diagrams, graphs and charts perhaps which illustrate their points and, as we will see later, are possibly more effective in many ways than slides made up simply of text.

Some presenters use their slides as notes. The headings on the screen act as prompts for them to know which points to make next. This is probably an advanced technique, but some beginners might find it useful. The danger of this is that you may be tempted simply to read what is on the screen, which gives the impression that you do not know your material well, or that you think the audience cannot read for themselves.

To read or to paraphrase?

When it comes to the actual presentation you need to decide whether you will read from what amounts to a script, or whether, based on your notes, you will speak without reading directly. Certainly when a presentation is delivered in one of these two ways there is a noticeable difference, and it has to be said that in most cases the reading of a script comes across less well. It depends to a certain extent on the way that you have written the script. If you have written it in a formal academic tone then it will sound stilted. If you are able to write it in a more conversational style, then you will have a better chance of making it sound relaxed and natural. (More about this will come later.) Some presenters know that they need every word written down and without the security of their detailed notes to read from they would be unable to perform.

There is a halfway house solution to this problem. It is possible to read certain short passages and intersperse them with more spontaneous-seeming comments based on short key word style notes. However, whichever you choose, you should take time to practise, especially if you are not used to this sort of task.

Form of language

It is important to recognise and respond to the difference between formal written language and spoken language. There are certain words and constructions that are common, acceptable and even expected in written forms of language, which do not sound good when spoken. In fact, they can sound nothing short of silly. If you attempt to speak in the way that is usually reserved for writing you will not come across well.

The English language has the luxury of having a choice of different words with the same, or virtually the same meaning. This is because of the rich heritage of Latin, Greek and Anglo-Saxon influences on our language. Some words are used more formally, and others in less formal and spoken language. Sometimes police officers (probably mostly in comedy contexts) when giving court evidence say that they were 'proceeding' along a certain road, instead of simply walking, driving or even 'going'. Here are some other examples:

articulate	say
commence	begin
endeavour	try
forthwith	immediately
purchaser	buyer
sufficient	enough
thus/hence	and so
utilise	use

There are many more.

A famous example of over-formal spoken English comes from the former Prime Minister John Major. He easily managed to make himself sound both pompous and silly at a stroke when he said, in answer to a question in a radio interview:

'I have been known on occasion to call in at a local hostelry with whomsoever I happen to be.'

While being sound from a grammatical point of view, it is far from suitable for almost all forms of spoken language; irony, or at attempt at humour might be two exceptions.

When giving a presentation it is not obligatory to use complicated language constructions, to use long words, or to speak in nested and convoluted sentences. Many would argue that quite the opposite is true. The purpose of speaking to an audience of any kind is communication. If you choose to speak in a way that does not necessarily come naturally to you, or is in some way made more complicated than it needs to be, you will in all probability not communicate effectively. The same principle applies here as we considered earlier. You must keep it simple (KISS). There is a strong case for speaking in shorter sentences and using simpler vocabulary when giving a presentation. This does not mean that you should not use correct vocabulary, especially when dealing with technical terms, which clearly form an important element of the content. There is a case for giving an explanation, or simple definition, of technical terms as they arise for the first time, particularly if you are dealing with an area of your subject which is new to the audience.

The following quote from George Orwell's essay 'Politics and the English Language' gives his view of the unnecessary use of over-complicated language:

> Never use a metaphor, simile, or other figure of speech which you are used to seeing in print. Never use a long word where a short one will do … Never use a foreign phrase, a scientific word, or a jargon word if you can think of an everyday English equivalent. (Orwell, 1946)

Orwell certainly had political and journalistic writing in mind, but it is not unreasonable to extend these thoughts to academic contexts. When students comment on this quote from Orwell they suggest some rules of their own, the most popular of which is 'Keep your sentences short.'

Having said all of this about informality, and keeping it simple, it is also important not to slip into the use of slang or colloquialism. This is as true for the spoken word as it is for written work. Both can detract from effective communication.

Intonation

Some people seem to forget how to speak as soon as they stand up to address a large group. They use words which they would not normally use, they pronounce words in new and unusual ways and they also choose to use intonation and stress differently. In extreme cases they begin to sound like the robots made famous in 1960s science fiction films.

The example below of the sentence 'I didn't say you painted my tortoise', illustrates the effect of stressing different words. The meaning can, in some cases, be quite different according to a simple difference in emphasis.

I didn't say you painted my tortoise.	Somebody else may have said it.
I *didn't* say you painted my tortoise.	I deny saying it.
I didn't *say* you painted my tortoise.	I may have written it.
I didn't say *you* painted my tortoise.	It may have been somebody else.
I didn't say you *painted* my tortoise.	I may have said that you did something else to it.
I didn't say you painted *my* tortoise.	I may have said that you painted somebody else's tortoise.
I didn't say you painted my *tortoise*.	I may have said that you painted something else of mine.

The secret, if it is a secret, of being sure that what you intend to say is what you actually do say, is to speak as closely to your normal style of speaking as possible.

Another concern for those giving presentations is that of speaking too quickly. When speaking to an audience of any size it is advisable to speak more slowly than your normal speed, and to leave pauses occasionally. Speaking more slowly and pausing is even more important if you want the audience to pay attention to words, diagrams or pictures on a screen at the same time. Speaking slowly is not the same as speaking hesitantly, and although being nervous might lead to hesitance, it is a good idea to work towards eliminating this. A series of hesitant "ums" or "ers" can be distracting and potentially embarrassing, while purposeful and well-judged pauses for the audience to take in what you have just said, or to reflect on an idea on the screen, are an essential element of an effective presentation.

The solution, or perhaps partial solution, to these potential problems is preparation and practice. Preparation and adequate practice are crucial at every level, and their importance should not be underestimated.

Cue cards

Many presenters use a cue card system. For each point they are to make, they write a heading, a short phrase or two, or a set of key words, on a post card, or similar, and arrange the numbered cards in the correct order to follow through the presentation. These cards might also have other reminders: 'Refer to diagram'; or 'Mention references on the handout'. PowerPoint allows for notes to be attached to each slide, which will not be displayed to the audience, but which can be printed out alongside the slides and used by the presenter.

Visual aids

Audiences in general like something to look at, especially if that something is clear and obvious in what it is, or in what it is illustrating. The best type of visual aid is usually something which is wholly pictorial, rather than being a table of figures or a chart of some type. The use of a diagram to represent a process, or the interactions between various aspects of a system, for example, can be a great help to some members of an audience, but if you bear in mind the learning preferences that we considered earlier you will realise that even if a good proportion of your audience may benefit from a picture or diagram there are others who may well find it less useful. For this reason you should take time to describe the diagram, simply, but effectively.

We are told that in presentations 55% of the way that we take in information is visual compared with only 7% for text (Presentation Helper, undated). If you use more pictures and diagrams than text, you will possibly help the audience to take in what you are saying. This is because we are also told that after three days an audience will have retained 7% of what they read (bullet points, or other notes on the screen), but 55% of

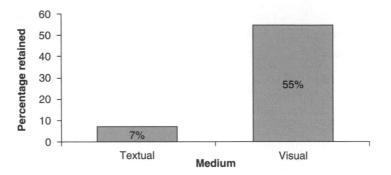

Figure 8.1   Retention after three days from textual or visual displays (Presentation Helper, undated)

what they saw pictorially (charts, pictures, diagrams) (Figure 8.1). However, it is not possible to use images for everything that you will want to put across. Up to 38% of what is taken in by those present is through the spoken word, which highlights the clear need for what you say to be audible and very much to the point.

Often it is possible to illustrate a point with an object or artefact that may be only representative, that is, it may be something which in reality is not directly related to the idea that you are explaining, but will serve as a good analogy. This can be useful, but it is important not to take things too far: peeling off the layers of an onion to represent the process of delving deeper into aspects of sociological research may be a good analogy, it may be fun, but it could also be messy and detract from the point that you are making; it could fix the idea firmly in the minds of the audience, but it could lead to them remembering the onion and not the point in question.

Handout material

Sometimes you will be expected to produce a handout of some kind. It could be that the assessment criteria, if your presentation is to be assessed, refer to the usefulness and quality of whatever you choose to distribute. Again you need to consider the style and content, as well as the purpose of anything of this nature. Some options are:

- Main points/headings.
- Notes generated by the presentation software that you have used. Possibly an edited version of a long presentation would be a good idea.
- Headings/main points, with space to write notes.
- Diagrams.
- Charts.

- Statistics.
- References.

Final preparations

Once you have finished the preparation you need to think about a rehearsal. It is possible to practise alone, and for many this will be fine, but practising with a small audience, even an audience of one, will probably be more valuable. You will probably want to time your presentation when practising, but you must be aware that on the day of the presentation you may well speak more quickly. Some people like to record their practice run and listen back to how they sounded.

You should also practise with any visual aids or equipment that you plan to use. There is nothing more frustrating or embarrassing than not knowing where the switch on the overhead projector is because you are not familiar with the particular model, or not being able to get the digital projector to work. You should practise in the room where you will be presenting if possible. If this has not been possible, arrive early and find plugs and switches in advance.

You could anticipate some of the questions that might be posed, or ask friends of colleagues to attempt this for you. When anticipating the questions, you should also consider what your responses will be.

It is sometimes difficult to know how to pitch your voice. Obviously you need to be heard. When you practise, speak clearly and ask if you can be heard at the back of the room. If the suggestion is that you cannot be heard well, do something about it. Practise the speed at which you will make your delivery. Do your best not to rush. On the day your nerves will almost certainly make you speak faster.

Use your practice 'audience' to check that your visual aids, such as pictures, posters, charts and diagrams, are big enough to be seen and that you have not presented too much information at a time. Information overload comes about when there is too much to take in at one time. A complicated diagram and an equally complex simultaneous explanation can lead to the audience closing down.

The presentation

Advice given on topics like this can only be general and some of it will not be good advice for some presenters. However, read through the next section and for each point consider its validity in your circumstances, and consider putting into practice those pieces of advice which you find potentially most useful. None of the points below should be discarded as obvious or common sense. It is quite common for a nervous presenters to rush into a talk without having made any introduction of themselves or the topic.

- Introduce yourself.
- If you are new to presenting you might like to tell the audience, and even mention that you are nervous. This can elicit support.
- Explain what you are talking about and why.
- Give a brief outline of your presentation.
- Give a brief preview of the conclusions that you have reached.
- Give an interpretation of the facts you are presenting.
- Present your points in a logical order.
- Re-state the main points.
- Stress your conclusions.
- Express your own feelings on the subject.
- Leave a couple of minutes at the end for questions.
- Thank the audience when all is finished.

You need to have confidence, which is very easy advice to give, but harder to follow. Remember that you do know what you are talking about because you are very well prepared. You probably know more about the topic of your presentation than the audience, even, in some cases, more than the tutor.

It is very easy to be apologetic when you are new to presenting, and certainly there are times when an apology is needed – if you realise that you have made a factual error perhaps. An overly apologetic presenter does not inspire confidence, and if those in the audience have no confidence in you, there is a tendency for them not to listen attentively. An audience not listening is not a good omen for any presentation. This is why you need to remain confident, at least on the outside, and why you need to present in an interesting and lively way. On this point, it is important to keep the attention of the audience throughout. Body language has a part to play here. If your body language and voice indicate tedium then you may well lose them. There are certain approaches which can sometimes help to keep an audience with you.

If you begin positively and catch the audience's attention by establishing a rapport, you are more likely to keep it. You should stand up straight and speak directly to your audience, making eye contact and smiling, though not inanely. If you can do this, you will let them know that you are confident and you have something to say that is worth listening to. You may have heard advice about making a joke, and the use of humour in general, and this can work very much to a presenter's advantage in some situations. In general, you need to know the audience very well, and in the context of a seminar group who have worked together for some time you may well feel that this is such a situation. A planned amusing remark can go a long way to generating interest and enjoyment in a presentation, but often rehearsed jokes seem not to have the expected impact. Spontaneous comments can also be valuable, but by definition this is not something that you can plan for. Good advice is to avoid too many attempts at making the audience laugh. You may be skilled in this area of social interaction, but we have to remember that we are dealing with what are usually serious academic concerns (not to say that certain topics are not amusing) and to turn a presentation into a stand-up routine is probably not the most sound approach to take. Your jokes may well fall flat and that will leave you feeling unsettled and will affect the way that you carry out the rest of your job. You need to judge the situation very well and to have the personal wherewithal to make a success of comedy in formal situations; for many, especially beginners, this is too difficult.

Dealing with nerves

If you feel your nerves trying to get the better of you, and you feel a rush of anxiety, try breathing deeply, slowly and smoothly. Calm breathing will also have a good effect on your voice and give you more volume than you might ordinarily be able to manage. In Chapter 7 we looked at some techniques designed to calm excessive exam nerves; these could be equally useful here.

Most public speakers say that they feel most nervous just before they begin to talk and during the first few minutes, and then things get much easier. During your preparation it is worth considering how you will handle your own anxieties and nerves. If you are aware of the symptoms of your anxiety you may be able to act to limit their effects. For example, if your hands shake, avoid holding notes in your hand; if your mouth dries up, have a bottle of water to hand; if having a roomful of people looking at you directly makes you feel uncomfortable, begin with an interesting visual aid which will attract the focus of the audience; if you fear that your mind may go 'blank' have your notes available and be sure that they are easy to navigate – in a large, easy to read font, or highlighted in a bright colour, for example. Finding what are often quite simple ways of controlling the symptoms of nervousness is likely to help you to feel less nervous.

Individual or group presentations

It is quite possible that at some stage you will be involved in a group presentation. The principles are the same when working with others, but the process and implementation will necessarily be different. The initial research needs to be just as detailed, the planning and preparation are equally important, some might say more so, because if you miss something out or move away from the plan in a group presentation you may throw everyone else off course. The presentation itself requires the same level of attention to detail for each presenter, no matter what their role is on the day.

Meeting to plan the work can sometimes be a problem, especially if you are not together in other modules, or if you do not know each other particularly well. You need to work hard to get round this difficulty, with diaries and determination. Meeting and planning together is crucial if a joint presentation is to be effective.

A fair division of labour is essential too. Apart from the notion of fair play and justice, you do not want to be a part of a group where you have done the lion's share of the work and the credit goes to others. Relying on one or two from the group to do all the research, with the others being given the job of presenting, is not really acceptable either. If you are put in a position of presenting work prepared by others you could find yourself in a difficult position if you are not fully familiar with the background and a question is asked which you cannot answer. Teamwork and shared responsibility are important, but are not always a given with some groups.

As a group you need to set agreed deadlines, which might not always be easy. If you are working in a group with other members who are of a different nature (in terms of general temperament, learning style, or sense of urgency) you will probably have to work harder to keep the group on target. The make-up of the group might not always be under your control, or it could be the case that you are free to choose whom you work with. There are advantages and disadvantages whichever is the case.

The nature and style of your presentation need to be decided, and again the division of labour has to be agreed. If, as may well be the case, not every member of the group is to take part in the actual presentation, it is important to be sure that they are acknowledged formally as they will have contributed. It is important that all group members are present for the event, for obvious reasons.

Follow up discussion

As we have already considered, making presentations and even leading discussions may well be an integral part of your future work. If this is to be the case then a supportive environment with opportunities for constructive feedback is no bad place to begin the process of becoming a competent presenter, and leader of discussion. We have also considered that one of the aims of a degree course is to equip you with certain transferable skills which will serve you well in a range of future contexts. Facilitating and leading discussion is one of these skills.

Unfortunately discussions cannot be relied upon to happen just when and as you want them to. Obviously in some cases, with some groups, on some occasions, things may go well, but sometimes it can seem like an uphill struggle for the person in the hot seat. Discussions need to be planned and orchestrated. There are some steps which can be taken to help the progress of a planned discussion.

It is usually better for the participants in a general discussion to sit in a way that allows them to have eye contact with each other; that is, in a rough circle or semi-circle, rather than rows. This might be out of your control, but if possible pay attention to it.

Your attitude towards the discussion, and, more subtly, your body language can have a distinct bearing on the atmosphere, and the discussion, or lack of it, which is generated. You need to be enthusiastic and to assume that the group are enthusiastic too.

As the 'leader' you take on the role of teacher for the duration, and as such it is your responsibility to generate an atmosphere where each contribution is welcomed and where there is no fear of embarrassment or even ridicule – which has been known in these situations. Without contributions there is no discussion, you need to be sure that the members of the group feel that their voice will be welcomed and taken seriously. As the leader of the discussion you will need to have considered your desired outcomes. This was considered earlier as an element of planning for a presentation. It might be that your aim is to 'Broaden understanding of …', but you might consider something more focused: 'Explore in detail the arguments for and against … '. Your aims for the session are likely to have an impact on the way that the discussion goes, and the way that you choose to direct it.

Some measure of guidance is usually needed in order for a discussion to begin. The group need to know the point, or aim, of the discussion, and you can make this clear in a number of ways. If the discussion follows on from a presentation, and you have used slides of one sort or another, you could display the notional aim of the discussion along with one or two starting points in the form of questions. You could read out the same information, and repeat it at appropriate intervals.

You should have a set of general questions or points for discussion ready to share with the group. It is best to make these clear, concise and made known from the outset. It could be that you do not use all of them, but they will be there in case they are needed. If you leave a summarising-style discussion point until last you could skip ahead to it if time begins to run out.

If you do not intend to display the points for discussion you might consider giving out copies to each member of the group. This will allow them to focus and to plan ahead a little. As a way of helping a discussion to start, and to allow for simple contributions, you could begin with simple questions which need only simple answers. In general, closed 'yes/no' questions should be avoided, however, because they can lead to a very swift completion of what never became a discussion.

The questions, after the initial simple variety, should aim to take the topic forward. As the leader, it is important that you wait for reponses. There is a strong temptation to move quickly on, especially if you feel nervous, but time is needed for potential contributors to the discussion to process and understand the question and then to formulate a response.

Listen carefully to responses and think about how you can develop new questions from the response. This is known as active listening and can be a very useful skill in many situations apart from leading discussions.

As the leader it is important that you keep a rapport, and eye contact, with the group. When responding to a point talk to the whole group, not just the person who made the point. This will make it more likely that others will join in.

It can be useful to take a flexible approach to your list of points for discussion. It could be that the discussion begins to work well even though it seems to have gone at a tangent to your plan. As long as the discussion is relevant and does not wander right away from your topic you should let it ride. Some of your points may well not have been covered by the end, but you can perhaps move to your last point to bring the discussion back on track to finish the session. The rule of thumb should perhaps be: 'If it is going well, leave it.'. If the discussion strays too far away from your theme, however, rein it back in.

You need to show respect of course, but you should allow yourself to disagree. Some of the best discussions can be born out of a healthy, respectful disagreement. You should avoid being drawn into a one-on-one argument, and be quick to ask for the support of the rest of the group if need be. This can be done by opening up with a question like: 'What do the rest of you think?'

It might be a good idea to use whatever resources are available. A flip chart can be used to set out the main points arising from the discussion. An interactive whiteboard could be used for the same purpose with the added advantage that the notes can be converted to text, saved, printed and distributed as a record of the discussion. This can also help you if you intend to summarise at the end, which you should if at all possible.

Leading discussion can be hard work and quite draining. It can also be very rewarding. The more experience you gain, the more confident and competent you will become. When it is someone else's turn to lead discussion, be ready and prepared to participate.

Presentation tools

In many presentations there is no call for any tools or aids. The tutor will perhaps have made it clear that there is only a short time and a simple oral report is all that is called for. Even with these clear instructions some members of the group will produce a hand-out or a poster, or write a list of points on a flip chart. On this point, the use of a well-presented poster can be a very effective means of focusing attention during a presentation. If prepared in advance and produced in a clear and precise style, without overcrowding, and with perhaps places where additional points might be added during the talk, a poster can be a valuable aid. Some posters can be as simple as a handwritten list of headings on a flip chart, others can be noticeably more sophisticated – produced by desktop publishing, enlarged and even laminated. (Laminating involves heat-sealing the poster in a high grade plastic covering with a specially designed machine.) Poster presentations are not uncommon in the academic world, and in many high profile conferences there are poster sessions where researchers present their work, most often work in progress, as a poster which is displayed with the owner on hand to answer questions.

In other, more involved presentations, there will be an expectation, even a requirement, to make use of one or other of the range of tools or technologies available. The list of tools will include older technologies, such as a slide projector, or an overhead projector, but will also include technological, computer-based tools.

Electronic presentation tools

Computer software is now widely used to present text, graphics and other material, sound and video for example, to an audience. Two common versions of what is sometimes referred to as 'slide show' software are PowerPoint, a Microsoft product, and Sun Microsystems' StarOffice Impress. Other IT tools, such as web browsers or word processors, can also be used to present information, but are less flexible. The use of an electronic whiteboard, or interactive whiteboard (IWB) as these devices are commonly known, is also an option. An interactive whiteboard allows you to make changes on the screen by using either your finger or a specialised stylus, on the display screen itself. This means that from a position standing before the board at the front of the room you can do something as simple as move to the next slide, or something less straightforward such as add an annotation to the screen, move to an internet site, or play a video clip.

Points to bear in mind when preparing an electronic presentation   If you want to include screen shots in your presentation be sure that they will be easy to read. You can make changes to the text size of web pages via the browser's menu, and you can also crop and then expand the actual image once it has been taken and inserted into one of your slides.

There are certain mistakes with the use of visual aids in presentations that you will do well to avoid. The common ones are:

- Slides too crowded.
- Text too small.
- Unnecessary, or overuse, of pictures, animations, text entry devices or sound effects.
- Use of colour that detracts from the main content of the slide, or that makes reading the text difficult.

- Spelling and/or grammar mistakes.
- Diagrams that are too small or over-complicated.

Of these, the two to be most wary of are probably having the slides overcrowded with too much text and using too small a font.

How will the presentation be assessed?

As we have said, some presentations will be assessed and the resulting mark will go forward, usually, as a part of the overall mark for the module. Alternatively, some presentations do not carry any assessment weighting towards a mark of any kind, but you may well receive feedback on what you have done.

Figures 8.2–8.5 are examples of different presentation assessment criteria from different university sources. They give an indication of the variation in detail that is provided, and also indicate the elements of the presentation that are of importance. Content is, naturally, crucial, and in some of the sets of criteria this is all that is mentioned. Some of the more practical skills – maintaining eye contact, appropriate use of visual aids, responding to questions – are also assessable and highlighted as important in others. It is important that you are fully aware of the specific criteria for the assessment of your presentation, and that you plan towards meeting them at the highest possible level.

Sometimes tutors encourage peer assessment of presentations and this is something that should be taken seriously. As a peer assessor, you should be aware of the criteria for success that are in place and try hard to evaluate against them. Tutors will usually retain the right to moderate the grades of peer assessment. Sometimes this form of assessment is restricted to peer feedback, which can be helpful, if perhaps a little demoralising if your peers are perhaps a little insensitive in their comments. Peer assessment is not a popularity competition.

The role of the audience in student presentations

It is interesting to see in Figure 8.4 that the part taken by the student in the presentations of others is graded. A presentation can fall flat if it does not have an attentive and responsive audience. Some tutors will insist on your presence, and your participation. A well-focused and well-intended question to a presenter can be helpful in a number of ways, and as a responsible member of the group you can contribute a lot simply by paying attention, and joining in if need be. As a member of the audience it is a good idea to exhibit empathy; if you are supportive of others you are likely to be supported later.

Adjudication marks are entered onto a form which is provided for each student. Marks and comments are provided in sections for:

- Introduction
- Delivery
- Content
- Visual aids
- Timing

Possible marks range from 0 to 6 for each of the Contents and Visual Aids sections; fewer marks for the other sections. The total possible marks, 21, are distributed along a spectrum from G —+ to A+, demonstrating the final grade. Most of the form allows comments to be made, either by marking around the printed comments (e.g. too little depth/about right/too much detail) or by writing specific comments at the bottom of the form. The overall grade is returned to the course organiser. The adjudication sheet is given to the students.

Figure 8.2   Presentation assessment criteria (1):

www.heacademy.ac.uk/asshe/topics/asshe251.pdf

The presentation should fulfil the following criteria:

- Length 10–15 minutes
- Introduction of group members
- Explanation of aims and objectives of the presentation
- Inclusion of a clear discussion which gives different viewpoints
- Equal use of all members of the group
- Ability to respond to prepared and unprepared questions which arise from a discussion within the class.

Figure 8.3   Presentation assessment criteria (2):

www.heacademy.ac.uk/asshe/topics/topic.asp

Assessment Criteria for Student Presentations

Each of the following criteria will gain credit in the assessment:

Brief plan for the presentation completed and e-mailed to the module lecturer by the deadline (0, 1 or 2 marks)

Talk includes: relevant material; in adequate depth; adequate quantity; acceptable accuracy; and with an evaluative analysis (what is good or bad about the representations/techniques/ theories/approaches you discuss) (0, 1, 2, 3, 4 or 5 marks)

Clarity of exposition (0 or 1 mark)

Contributions to other talks, by attending other talks and making other contributions (0, 1 or 2 marks)

Figure 8.4   Presentation assessment criteria (3):

www.cs.bham.ac.uk/~ddp/AIP/Presentation_mark_scheme.html

PRESENTATION REVIEW ASSESSMENT

DELIVERY

High Quality:

- Student was clear and confident.
- Student's delivery holds the audience's attention from beginning to end.
- Student makes direct eye contact.

Acceptable:

- Frequent eye contact but refers to notes occasionally.
- Student makes a few distracting movements and expressions.

Unacceptable:

- Student does not appear sufficiently prepared.
- Student rarely makes eye contact and reads from notes the majority of the time.
- Student has extensive distracting movements and expressions.
- Student does not speak for 8 to 10 minutes.

ORGANISATION

High Quality:

- Organization of presentation significantly enhances understanding.

Acceptable:

- The presentation is organised.
- Introduction gives an overview of the content.
- There is a clear beginning, middle and end of the speech.
- The conclusion summarises the main points.

Unacceptable:

- Introduction does not give an overview of the presentation.
- Order and progression of ideas creates confusion.
- Transition from one part of the speech to the next is unclear.
- There is not an obvious conclusion and the presentation ends abruptly.

CONTENT

High Quality:

- Student makes insightful connections to personal experience, observation and reading.
- Student chooses exceptional details in supporting main points.
- The use of visual aids or demonstrations significantly enhances the presentation.

Acceptable:

- Main points are supported with appropriate information and details.
- Student makes relevant connections to personal experience, observation and reading.
- Incorporation of visual aids supports presentation.

Unacceptable:

- Student does not develop or support his or her ideas with sufficient information and details.
- Student fails to make relevant connections to personal experience, observation and reading.
- Quality of or reliance on visual aids sufficiently detracts from the quality of the speech.
- No tangible product is used.

Figure 8.5   Presentation assessment criteria (4): University of California

www.nccte.org/publications/ncrve/mds-11xx/mds-1198.asp#Heading29

Final thoughts on presentations

It is often the extroverts amongst us who are able to enjoy presenting whilst others see it as an ordeal. Those with self-confidence usually do well, but they still need to pay attention to clear and accurate content. For most of the others, presenting is an ordeal at first, but it gets easier. It is not at all unusual to be self-conscious, self-critical and sometimes almost fatally embarrassed. Being good at presentations is not a skill which we either have or do not have at birth. It is a skill like many other skills that we can master. Practice is one of the ways that all skills can be improved, and giving presentations is not an exception. One of the best ways to help a presentation to be a success is to be thoroughly prepared, and to practise.

Advice comes in many forms and from many sources, and sometimes it is difficult to sort out the sound from the less sound. When I was thinking about writing this section, and looking up a range of different suggestions and advice, it became clear that a good deal of the advice, and many of the 'golden rules' were totally contradictory. Such suggestions as 'Always animate your text in PowerPoint' and 'Do not use the text animation features in PowerPoint' can be hard to reconcile. The reasons for these blatant contradictions are to do with personal preferences and subjectivity. As a student in an assessment situation you often have to do your best to pick your way through this tangle of good advice. Again, if you are in doubt about how certain aspects of a presentation might be received, especially by your tutor, you must ask.

Having considered the potential dangers of taking 'good advice', one last piece will be offered. If you want to know what works well in presentations pay attention in seminars, lectures and other situations where someone is addressing an audience, and think about what the presenter is doing to make the presentation go well. Think about the opposite too. What is the presenter doing that makes the presentation go badly? It is highly likely that in your experience, at university and elsewhere, you will sit through some very well managed presentations and also through some which leave a lot to be desired. You can learn from the skills and experience of your tutors and perhaps some of your peers, in the way of how, and how not, to give a presentation. Naturally, you should not focus too narrowly on presentation techniques because you will miss the point of the presentation.

SUMMARY

- Presentations are likely to be a feature of your work at university; some may be assessed.
- The key to a successful presentation seems to be thorough preparation.
- The principle of keeping things simple (KISS) applies with presentations as much as in other aspects of your work.

- Presentation tools, such as PowerPoint, can be a very good vehicle for presentations, but should be used with care, especially the 'whistles and bells' features.
- If you appear confident, despite how you may feel inside, you will engage and keep the attention of your audience. Stand up straight, speak clearly and slowly and give as much eye contact as possible.
- Be aware of how others undertake presentations; learn from those whom you come across who seem to do a good job.

Activities

Good and bad presentations: Think about presentations you have seen or heard in the past. What were the features of both the good and bad? Write a list under two headings (Good, and Not so good). Consider your lists and choose five features from each list as: (i) Important to foster and (ii) Important to avoid.

Learn from your own experience: Presentations are rarely perfect, even for those who give them on a regular basis. There are, therefore, always things that you can learn. One of the best ways to learn is from your own mistakes. If you know that you often have a crisis of self-confidence, it is not a good idea to go in for this reflective learning immediately following your presentation. If you have a friend whose judgement you trust, get them to listen critically to your presentation, so that they can give you useful feedback, say, twenty-four hours later.

To complete this activity effectively it would be very useful to have either a video, or perhaps more realistically, an audio recording of your presentation. With the smaller than pocket-sized digital recorders which are available it is quite easy to record what you say, and the response of the audience. If this is not possible it is still worth reviewing your presentation based on your memory of the event.

When you have time, but not too long after the event, re-live your presentation, and consider the following questions:

- Which aspects seemed to work well?
- Were there any times that you floundered or sounded less than confident?
- Were your audience attentive all the way through? If not, why not?
- Did you manage the time well?
- Were you speaking too fast or too quietly?
- Did you put enough expression into your voice?
- If you were to do the presentation again, what would you change?

Treat the experience as a rehearsal for the next one. One important aspect of the human condition is that we learn from experience. The development of the skills associated with giving effective presentations are not an exception to this.

Appendix 1
Transferable Graduate Skills

As we saw in the Introduction, and elsewhere in the book, it is widely held that there is a set of skills which it is possible to acquire, or develop further, during a course of study leading to the award of a degree. These skills, which can be practised and honed during your time at university, have become a recognised expectation for groups such as employers. If you are aware of these skills it is possible that you can recognise in yourself their development, and you will be aware of those which might seem less well developed. You can then work towards improving them through your study and participation in the process of study during your course. Some universities offer short courses in some skills – computer use for example, as well as many others.

A good definition of what are also referred to as core transferable skills comes from the website of the Anglia Ruskin Careers Service in Cambridge, a part of the Anglia Ruskin University:

> Core transferable graduate skills are generic attributes that are acquired and developed through study, work and other extra-curricular activities, including societies, sport and hobbies. (ARU, 2004)

At a simple level, The Association of Graduate Careers Advisory Services (AGCAS et al. 1999) suggest that employers are interested in recruits who can communicate effectively, work both independently and in teams, and apply a logical and analytical approach to the solution of problems.

The list below has been compiled from a range of different sources, including the websites of the Anglia Ruskin University Careers Service (ARU, 2004) and Griffiths University, Queensland, Australia (Griffiths University, 2005), and various sources included in the Department for Education and Skills 'Using Graduate Skills' project (DfES, 1998).

Oral communication skills

Graduates are able to communicate confidently and effectively with a range of audiences, in a variety of modes or registers and settings, including persuasion, argument and exposition, and they are able to make use of different support tools, including visual, audio-visual and technological.

Written communication skills

Graduates are skilled in using the conventions of their disciplinary style to communicate effectively in writing with a range of audiences, in a variety of writing modes, including persuasion, argument and exposition. Graduates can write effectively in standard English, using a good range of appropriate vocabulary.

Information literacy skills

Graduates recognise when information is needed and are able to use a range of tools and systems, including computer technologies, to find, evaluate and manage information effectively.

Numeracy skills

Graduates are able to work effectively with numbers and other numerical data. They can collect and process numerical and other data and are able to interpret and present information based on numbers.

Teaching skills

Graduates are able to pass on their knowledge to an interested audience or individual in a clear and logical manner.

Organisational skills

Graduates are able to set priorities, and anticipate potential problems or needs. They are able to set and achieve targets in relation to both study and workplace tasks. Graduates are able to manage their time effectively.

Interpersonal skills

Graduates have the skills to be able to work effectively with a range of people in a range of different contexts, including teams, where they can be effective members and, if required, leaders, including organising team roles and activities. Graduates are open to the ideas of others. Graduates are capable of listening and understanding in a range of contexts.

Problem-solving skills

Graduates are able to identify and define problems and through the use of skills of analysis and critical evaluation plan an appropriate course of action and devise solutions. Graduates are able to make judgements concerning different possible solutions. They will be able to make use of creative and lateral thinking.

Computer skills

Graduates are comfortable with the basic skills of editing and organising information on screen. They are able to present information in a clear and logical way. They are able to make use of common applications such as word processors, spreadsheets, databases and web browsers.

We need to bear in mind that it would be a very unusual graduate who possessed all of these skills at a high level. According to the area of study it is likely that different strengths will be present in different graduates, in terms of the skills listed above. Good graduates will have acquired many of these skills. The skills of communication are of particular importance.

Hyland (1994), in considering the skills identified as being worthy aims for graduates to master, says that 'these aims are basic minimum, lowest common denominator ones' (p 99). He is making the point that there is a good deal more to being a graduate than a set of skills to be acquired and that to have acquired skills is not the same as having the knowledge, values and experience which are needed if they are to be applied effectively in new, and possibly challenging, contexts.

Appendix 2
Concept/Mind-mapping Resources

From the web page referenced below you can download FreeMind software. This freeware mind-mapping tool can be used for tracking, brainstorming, note-taking, recording, organising information and more. This page includes screen-shot examples of maps created using this software, and further information about its features and system requirements.

The other references below are to the sites of commercial software dealers where you can buy software. It is worth exploring also the possibilities of using software paid for and provided by your university.

FreeMind	http://freemind.sourceforge.net
Inspiration	www.inspiration.com
Spark Space	www.spark-space.com
Mind Genius	www.mindgenius.com
Smart Draw	www.smartdraw.com

Glossary

Academic year   The university year. The academic year at most universities runs from September or October to June. It is divided into either terms or semesters. *See*: Semester; Term

Accommodation [learning theory]   The process of amending a schema in order to accord with new or contradictory data. *See*: Schema

Admissions Office   The office within any university or college which handles the applications and enrolments.

Admissions Tutor   The person in a department or faculty who is responsible for applications and other enquiries about the admissions process.

Alumni   Former students (singular: alumnus).

Assessment   The way you are examined in your academic work. An assessment could be an essay, a presentation or an examination.

Assimilation [learning theory]   The process of adding new data to a schema. *See*: Schema

Athletics Union/Sports Union   The organisation that runs student sports clubs and sometimes sports facilities.

Behaviourism   A school of learning theory based upon reward and punishment. Considered good for the memorisation of factual knowledge but not for deep understanding.

BUSA   The British Universities Sports Association.

Bursary   A scholarship of some kind. This contributes towards your fees and/or living costs whilst you are studying.

Campus   The area of land on which the university buildings are built. Not all universities are built on a campus, while some have multiple campuses at scattered sites.

CATS (Credit Accumulation Transfer Scheme)   A scheme which allows students to gather credits for individual modules and is a more flexible way to get formal qualifications. Students usually take 120 CATS points a year. CATS points are also sometimes just called 'credits'. *See*: Module

Chaplain   University chaplains are on hand to offer religious guidance and support to those who want it.

Cheating   Any form of unfair help to try to get high marks in an assessment. *See*: Assessment; Plagiarism

College   A vague word that could mean (a) a sixth form college or college of further education where students do A levels and other more vocational qualifications; (b) a semi-self-contained unit in a collegiate university; (c) an institution of higher education that is not allowed to use the title university; or (d) any university, college of higher education, its buildings and/or its administrative authorities. *See*: University college

Combined Honours   A degree in which you study three or more subjects. *See*: Joint Honours

Constructivism [learning theory]   A school of learning theory concerned with individuals actively constructing their own understanding through experience gained in a wide range of different ways. *See*: Social constructivism

Course   A programme of study leading to a degree or other qualification. Courses may be referred to as 'programmes', and are usually made up of a series of modules. *See*: Module

Coursework   Work that you do during your studies which counts towards your final mark for that module (e.g. an essay). *See*: Module

Database   A collection of data arranged for ease and speed of search and retrieval; in modern usage this refers exclusively to information which is stored in a computer.

Deadline   The last date you can submit coursework. *See*: Coursework

Degree   A higher education qualification of a certain level. Degrees are split into undergraduate degrees (or first degrees), which are usually bachelor degrees

(BA, BSc etc.), and various postgraduate degrees (masters, doctorates). A university is not a university if it does not teach and award degrees, although some do other higher education qualifications too, such as Higher National Diplomas (HNDs). BA (Bachelor of Arts) for a first degree in Arts and BSc (Bachelor of Science) for a first degree in Science are the two most common undergraduate degrees. Degrees can be in a single subject (Single Honours), two subjects (Joint Honours) or three or more subjects (Combined Honours).

Department   Most universities break down different subject areas into departments and students 'belong' to whatever department teaches their course. It gets more complicated if they study more than one subject, because they may be associated with more than one department. Some universities are not organised in departments; they have schools, which may cover several subject areas. *See:* School

DfES   The Department for Education and Skills, Government department formerly responsible for higher education. *See:* DIUS

DIUS   The Department for Innovation, Universities and Skills. New government department established in June 2007, with responsibility for higher education.

Dissertation   An essay or report usually of several thousand words on a specific subject. Usually completed during a course of study, often in the final year.

Distance learning   Allows you to learn through self-study, using printed materials, CD-ROM and, increasingly, web-based resources.

ECTS   The 'European Credit Transfer System' helps students across Europe to understand different academic credit systems. *See:* CATS

Ents   Short for entertainments, which are usually run by the Students' Union and include concerts, club nights, comedy gigs etc.

Exam Board   A formal meeting which is convened to note the marks and grades of all students following specific modules of courses. Exam boards are usually very thorough, with each student being considered individually, and any extenuating circumstances may be taken into account. The exam board is the formal arbiter of all marks and results.

Faculty   Universities are usually divided into departments or schools, which are grouped together into faculties, e.g. Faculty of Science; Faculty of Arts.

Finals/Finalists   Finals are the exams taken in the final year of study that decide the outcome of your three or four years of study. In awarding the final degree classification, some degrees also take into account the results from your previous years' study.

First   A degree awarded with first class Honours – the highest grade attainable.

Formals   Some universities have formal dinners where students dress up – sometimes in black tie, sometimes in suits or sometimes in gowns.

Foundation year   If your qualifications are not in the right subjects or at the right grades to meet the entry requirements for your chosen course (usually a science or engineering course, or fine arts), you may be able to do a one year foundation course. If you complete this to the required standard you will be guaranteed a place on the first year of your chosen course.

Freshers   First year students in their first few weeks at university.

Freshers' Week   This is the first week of the first term of the first year of a student's university career. The week is filled with introductory events and entertainments designed to help students settle in, make friends and to tell them everything they need to know about how the university and the Students' Union work.

Further Education (FE)   Further education comes after primary and secondary education, i.e. it is usually for 16-to18-year-olds who do not choose to stay at school. FE colleges often concentrate on vocational courses, but not exclusively.

Gap year   Many students decide to take a year off – or a gap year – after school or college and before going to university. The time is usually spent gaining work experience, earning money, travelling or doing something exciting. Some just take it easy.

Graduand   A student in the period between finishing their course and attending graduation.

Graduate   Someone who has successfully completed a degree course and been awarded their degree.

Graduation   The ceremony where you are officially awarded your degree.

Grants   Students used to get grants which paid for their tuition and grants which went towards their living costs. They still exist in Scotland for Scottish students only. Nowadays the usual source of funding is the student loan. *See*: Student loan

GTTR (Graduate Teacher Training Registry)   The GTTR processes applications for PGCE courses. *See*: PGCE

Halls   At most universities, 'halls' means halls of residence, the accommodation blocks which traditionally provide catered meals (but increasingly are becoming self-catered), cleaners, heat, light and electricity and a variety of amenities such as launderettes, common rooms and TV lounges.

Higher Education (HE)   The stage of education after primary school, secondary school and possibly further education (A-levels, Highers etc.). Higher education takes place at universities and colleges of higher education. HE includes under-graduate and postgraduate degrees, Higher National Diplomas (HNDs) and certain other vocational qualifications (such as LCPs for lawyers, for instance).

Higher National Diploma (HND)   The HND is based on vocational studies, generally aimed at preparing students for a particular career or industry. It can lead on to, or count towards, a degree course.

Highers   In Scotland, students take Highers as the equivalent of A levels.

Hons   A degree with Honours.

Honours degree   Most degrees are Honours degrees and, depending on how you do in your exams or coursework, are split into: first class (a first); upper second class or 2.i or 2:1 (said as 'two–one'); lower second class or 2.ii or 2:2 (said as 'two–two', sometimes referred to as a 'Desmond' (after Archbishop Desmond Tutu)); and third class (a third). If a student does badly, but not quite badly enough to fail, they might be awarded an ordinary degree instead.

Jobshop   A student employment agency usually run by the Students' Union. Apart from advertising vacancies, jobshops are sometimes more proactive and actually look for appropriate paid work for students.

Joint Honours   A degree in which you study two subjects. *See*: Combined Honours

Journal   A periodical published for a special group such as a learned society, or profession.

Junior Common Room (JCR)   A common room for undergraduate students.

Learning Resources Centre (LRC)   Basically, a library, but with more emphasis on non-book facilities such as e-journals, PC access and multimedia archives.

Lecture   One of the main teaching mechanisms of universities. Numbers attending tend to be larger than a regular school class and there is less interaction. *See*: Seminar; Tutorial

Lecturer   Lecturers are academics at a certain level in the hierarchy, well above postgraduates but below readers, professors and deans.

Level (of study)   There are usually three 'Levels' of study. Level 1 is the easiest and Level 3 the most advanced.

Literature review   A critical look at the existing research and other written work that is significant to the work that you are carrying out. A literature review is more than a simple summary; there is an important element of criticism and analysis.

Local Education Authority (LEA)   Body with responsibility for allocation of student loans, carrying out means testing etc. Students apply for funding to the LEA for the area in which they live full time (i.e. normally their home not their university addresss). *See*: Means testing

Mark   The numerical rating given to a piece of work. This is not always disclosed; you may be given a classification which covers a range of marks.

Mature student   A mature student is anyone aged 21 or over when they start a university course.

MA – Master of Arts   A type of degree that leads to a postgraduate qualification (i.e. a higher degree than a BA).

Means testing   Used by Local Education Authorities to assess how much money students (or their family households) have at their disposal before handing out any money in the form of loans or grants for maintenance.

Metacognition   Strictly this is cognition about cognition, or even thinking about thinking. Metacognitive knowledge is the knowledge that an individual has about their own cognition, which can be used to consider and to control their cognitive processes.

MSc – Master of Science   A type of degree that leads to a postgraduate qualification (i.e. a higher degree than a BSc).

Modular courses   A sort of pick 'n' mix course comprising a number of components (modules), either within just one department or across a range of subjects.

Module   A module is the term used for an individual, usually self-contained, section of study. Each module is examined separately. A degree course is made up of a number of modules studied during each year. Some universities refer to modules as course units.

Module code   Each module has an identification code. The letters in the module code usually show the department, and the first number usually shows the level of study (e.g. MUS 314 would be a Level 3 Music module).

National Union of Students (NUS)   The National Union of Students provides research, welfare information and services to individual Students' Unions which are affiliated to it. NUS is also the national body that represents and campaigns on behalf of students.

National Vocational Qualification (NVQ)   The National Vocational Qualification is usually taken when you already have a job (or work experience). NVQs are taught at an industry-agreed standard, so employers in those industries can be keen if you have one on your CV.

Nightline   A telephone counselling service, similar to the Samaritans, but usually run by students for students.

Non-completion/non-progression rate   A polite term for the 'drop out' rate.

NUS Card   You will get your NUS Card from your university Students' Union. It can be very useful; it can get you into nightclubs and other places for free, or money off very useful things like train tickets or books.

Open days   An opportunity for prospective students to be shown around the university.

Ordinary degree   Most students are awarded an Honours degree. You will be awarded an Ordinary degree if either you decide to aim lower for some reason or you fail an Honours degree, but not so badly as to receive nothing.

Oxbridge   The collective name for the two oldest universities in England, Oxford and Cambridge. Both are collegiate, both are traditional and both are highly respected around the world.

Personal tutor   At many, if not all, universities, students are assigned to a personal tutor who is charged with responsibilities beyond the purely academic. The extent of their remit and of their usefulness varies enormously. Some have regular meetings with their students to discuss everything from exams to debt; others have little involvement.

Plagiarism   Using other people's ideas and words in academic work without clearly acknowledging the source of that information. Plagiarism can be deliberate or accidental but either will be considered cheating and will attract severe penalties.

Polytechnic (Poly)   There used to be a divide distinguishing between universities and polytechnics. Polytechnics tended to have a slant towards vocational courses and an often unfair reputation for lower academic standards than universities. Now they have become universities themselves.

Postgraduate/postgrad (student)   A student studying for a second degree, i.e. they already have one degree and now they are following a course or programme working towards another, higher degree, such as a masters, a doctorate (PhD), a Postgraduate Certificate in Education (PGCE) or something similar.

Postgraduate Certificate in Education (PGCE)   A one-year postgraduate course which qualifies a graduate to become a teacher. A PGCE is not the only way to become a teacher; you can also do a four-year Bachelor of Education (BEd.) undergraduate degree.

Practical   A form of learning, usually used in science subjects, which involves you doing an experiment or something similar.

Professor   Often the head of a department/school/faculty. Always well respected in their field of study. In some university hierarchies there are also assistant professors and associate professors, which equate to lecturers and senior lecturers.

Rag   Rag (from 'Raise and Give') is an excuse to dress up in silly clothing and get up to antics in the name of charity. Collectively, student charity Rags raise millions of pounds each year.

Redbrick   Refers to a style of building – or a period from around the turn of the twentieth century through to the Second World War. Used to describe a university whose main buildings are in that style, and is shorthand for 'not Oxbridge but well established'.

References [academic writing]   Notes in a written document (essay, dissertation, thesis) that refer the reader to another book or other source of information that has been used.

Sabbatical (sabb)   Every year at most universities, a few students take a year off from their studies to be employed by the Student Union. Sabbatical positions usually include roles such as SU president, welfare officer, communications officer etc. Not just anyone can take up these positions though – they almost always have to be elected by the other students. Academic staff are sometimes entitled to sabbatical leave for the purpose of further study or research; this is often known as study leave.

Sandwich course   A course that involves vocational experience. Usually it takes a year to gain commercial or industrial experience and, as a result, most sandwich courses last for four years.

Schema [learning theory]   A notional mental framework for storing, remembering and understanding information.

School   An alternate name for a university department.

Semester   A semester is the American word for a term and is used in the UK to describe American-style college terms that are longer (usually about 15 weeks) than British terms (between 8 and 11 weeks). Generally speaking, universities have either two semesters or three terms. *See*: Term

Seminar   A teaching class, overseen by a lecturer, attended by anything from 6 to over 30 students. Seminars are teaching situations which can involve direct teaching, discussion, other activies and exercises. Similar to tutorials, but involve more students. *See*: Lecture; Tutorial

Single Honours   An undergraduate degree involving one main subject. *See*: Combined Honours; Joint Honours

Social constructivism [learning theory]   A branch of constructivist learning which emphasises interaction with others and stresses the importance of language and dialogue. *See*: Constructivism

Socs   Short for 'societies', these are the student clubs, which range from serious political battlegrounds to sporting teams, from cultural groups to seriously silly socs.

Student loan   Low interest loan from the government to help pay student living costs and tuition fees. *See*: LEA; Student Loans Company

Student Loans Company (SLC)   This organisation was established to administer the system of student loans and repayments. See www.slc.co.uk

Students' Union (SU)   Almost all universities have a Students' Union and students are usually automatically members, though they can opt out if they wish. As a rule, an SU is usually a services and representative organisation run by students for students. It offers a range of activities (e.g. sports clubs, leisure clubs) and represents the views of students to the university authorities. Also the name given to the building where the SU offices are based and where many social activities take place. (Occasionally known as Guild of Students.)

Students' Representative Council/Committee (SRC)   Yet another name for a students' union or part of one, especially the part that focuses on representation.

Term   The academic year is split into three terms (autumn, spring and summer) with vacations in between. *See*: Semester

Transcript   A Transcript is a record of your learning achievements. Also the written content of a recorded interview, often used in research.

Tuition fees   Tuition fees (sometimes also called 'top-up fees') are set by the government and paid to the university directly by you or by the Student Loans Company.

Tutor   An academic who oversees or supervises the work of individual students. *See*: Personal tutor

Tutorial   A small group of students who meet with a tutor and discuss their studies. Sometimes students have one-to-one tutorials, which are a great opportunity to discuss individual ideas, thoughts and problems with work. *See*: Seminar

UCAS   The Universities & Colleges Admissions Service is the organisation that handles most university applications. Prospective students fill out a UCAS form online (or on paper) and submit it to UCAS who send it to the universities the student wants to apply to. The student then gets offers (or not) and can accept one and an insurance (usually lower) offer. UCAS oversees the process to check that no one finds themself with more than one place and tries to match students with vacancies as efficiently as possible.

Undergraduate (student)   A student who is studying for their first degree, i.e. they are studying on an undergraduate degree course/program, such as BA or BSc. *See*: Postgraduate

University   Not nearly as easy to define as you might have thought, although officially a UK university has to be founded by Parliamentary Statute. There are plenty of places like certain university colleges that deserve the name as much as many of the places that have it. In essence, a university is a place to get a higher education.

University college   Officially, a college that has the power to award its own degrees, but is not a fully fledged university, or administered by a full university. HE colleges which are independent, but whose degrees are rubber-stamped by a university, are not allowed to use the title 'university'. *See*: College; University

Vice-Chancellor   Basically this is the person who runs the university, but students rarely get to meet them. Where there are vice-chancellors, there are also chancellors, who are the heads of the institutions and are usually a famous person. They are not usually present except for special occasions.

Vocational course   Any course that is intended at least to train students for a particular profession, career or job. These courses often involve practical experience in a work environment, such as placements, or doing projects similar to what goes on in real-world jobs.

References

Alexander, G. (1999) *Clear Thinking Activity.* [Online]: http://sustainability.open.ac.uk/gary/papers/clearth.htm (Accessed 1.12.06).

AGCAS et al. (1999) *Association of Graduate Careers Advisory Services.* www.agcas.org.uk/ (accessed 12.8.07).

ARU (2004) Anglia Ruskin University. http://www.anglia.ac.uk/ (accessed 12.8.07).

Biggs, J.B. and Moore, P.J. (1993) *The Process of Learning.* New York: Prentice Hall.

Brown, A. (1987) Metacognition, executive control, self-regulation, and other more mysterious mechanisms. In: F.E. Weinert and R.H. Kluwe, eds., *Metacognition, Motivation, and Understanding.* Hillsdale, NJ: Lawrence Erlbaum, pp. 65–116.

BUBL (undated) *BUBL Information Service.* University of Strathclyde http://bubl.ac.uk/ (Accessed 29.5.07).

Buzan, T. (2002) *How to Mind Map: The Ultimate Thinking Tool That Will Change Your Life.* London: Harper Collins.

Chipongian, L. (2004) *What is 'Brain-Based Learning'?* The Brain Connection

http://www.brainconnection.com/ (Accessed 17.1.05).

Courter, K. and Hamp-Lyons, L. (1984) *Research Matters.* Newbury: Newbury House.

CSUSB (undated) California State University St. Bernardino library www.lib.csusb.edu (accessed 12.8.07).

DES (1985) *Curriculum Matters 2: The Curriculum from 5–16.* London: HMSO.

DfES (1998) *Using Graduate Skills Final Evaluation Report.* London: DfES.

Dunn, R. Dunn, K. and Price, G.E. (1989) *The Learning Style Inventory.* Lawrence, KS: Price Systems.

Gillett, A. (2007) *Using English for Academic Purposes (UEfAP): A Guide for Students in Higher Education.* University of Hertfordshire. www.uefap.com/ (Accessed 30.1.07).

Greenfield, S. (2005) Answer rich, question poor. Teaching and Learning Supplement, *The Times Educational Supplement*, 28 January.

Howe, M.J.A. (1999) *Psychology of Learning.* London: Blackwell.

Hughes, K. (1993) *Entering the World-Wide Web: A Guide to Cyberspace.* www.cib.unibo.it/intro/www-guide/www.guide.html (Accessed 27.5.06).

Hyland, T. (1994) *Competence, Education and NVQs: Dissenting Perspective.* London: Cassell.

Medawar, C. (1978) *The Social Audit Consumer Handbook.* Basingstoke: Palgrave-Macmillan.

Moule, P., Pontin, D., Gilchrist, M. and Ingram, R. (2003) *Critical Appraisal Framework.* Available at: http://hsc.uwe.ac.uk/dataanalysis/critFrame.asp (Accessed 17.5.07).

Novak, J. and Gowin, D. (1984) *Learning How to Learn.* Cambridge: Cambridge University Press.

OCLC (2003) About Dewey and OCLC. http://www.oclc.org/dewey/about (Accessed 24.3.05).

Orwell, G. (1946) *'Politics and the English Language'* (Essay). London: Horizon (Great Britain).

Presentation Helper (Undated) www.presentationhelper.co.uk/ (Accessed 8.2.07).

Princeton (2003) *Academic Integrity.* www.princeton.edu/pr/pub/integrity/index.html. Princeton University. (Accessed 10.5.07).

Pritchard, A. (2005) *Ways of Learning.* London: David Fulton.

QAA (2000) Code of practice for the assurance of academic quality and standards in higher education. Section 6: Assessment of students. www.qaa.ac.uk/academicinfrastructure/codeOfPractice/section6/default.asp (Accessed 24.6.06).

Reid, J., Forrestal, P., and Cook, J. (1989) *Small Group Learning in the Classroom.* Scarborough (Australia): Chalkface Press. London: English and Media Centre.

Saur Verlag, K.G. (Undated) *The Making of the Modern Economy.* www.biblio.unisg.ch/org/biblio/web.nsf/SysWebResources/MOME-Guide/$FILE/MOME-Guide.pdf (Accessed 28.5.07).

Wray, D. and Lewis, M. (1997) *Extending Literacy.* London: Routledge Falmer.

Zar, J. (1992) *Candidate for a Pullet Surprise.* www.bios.niu.edu.zar/poem.pdf (Accessed 12.8.07).

Index